W9-AZL-404

What they're saying about Ted...

* * *

"Some are attracted to Ted Nugent for his lifestyle of conservation management, others for his political courage, and many more for his rock 'n' roll. For me, it's all three. Nuge has had me in a 'Stranglehold' for years, and his musings in Ted, White, and Blue will keep me on his tour bus for many more."

—Michael Smerconish
Philadelphia's number one radio talk show host

"Ted Nugent is the closest thing to a human tornado I've ever met. He lives life at mach speeds, boldly pouring himself into matters deeply personal to him. His efforts to support U.S. troops wounded in the defense of freedom and his selfless devotion to children with life-threatening illnesses are just two indications of the gentle heart that beats beneath the surface of this wild-eyed warrior. His story is as American as rock 'n' roll and as inspirational as Horatio Alger. I hope Ted, White, and Blue opens your eyes to the challenges of our times and the limitless opportunity in our country. I pray it encourages you to live life boldly and in the spirit of the wild!"

—Rick Perry
governor of Texas

"Ted is a great American. He is a rock 'n' roll god, a true patriot, a tireless worker and somebody who lives his life his way."

—Dennis Arfa
president/CEO of Artist Group International

"I am proud to have the good fortune to call Ted Nugent my friend and I am glad that we have him in the corner of the liberty-loving, self-respecting Americans who will accept no less than absolute freedom for ourselves and our future generations."

—Jeff W. Zimba
production manager, Small Arms Review *magazine*

"Never in my life have I met a more fervent and impassioned person. The man gives 1,000,000 percent to all he believes in. His family, his politics, his hunting, and his guitar playing! I see the gooseflesh he gets while playing Stranglehold 33 years after it came out. THAT is DEDICATION!"

—Greg Smith
bass guitar, Ted Nugent Band

TED, WHITE, AND BLUE

TED, WHITE, AND BLUE

THE NUGENT MANIFESTO

★ **TED NUGENT** ★

Since 1947
**REGNERY
PUBLISHING, INC.**
An Eagle Publishing Company • Washington, DC

Copyright © 2010 by Ted Nugent

All rights reserved. No part of this publication may be reproduced or transmitted in any form or by any means electronic or mechanical, including photocopy, recording, or any information storage and retrieval system now known or to be invented, without permission in writing from the publisher, except by a reviewer who wishes to quote brief passages in connection with a review written for inclusion in a magazine, newspaper, or broadcast.

Cataloging-in-Publication Data on file with the Library of Congress
ISBN 978-1-59698-605-3

Published in the United States by
Regnery Publishing, Inc.
One Massachusetts Avenue, NW
Washington, DC 20001
www.regnery.com

Manufactured in the United States of America

10 9 8 7 6 5 4 3 2 1

Books are available in quantity for promotional or premium use. Write to Director of Special Sales, Regnery Publishing, Inc., One Massachusetts Avenue NW, Washington, DC 20001, for information on discounts and terms or call (202) 216-0600.

DEDICATED TO
MY WONDERFUL FAMILY, FRIENDS,
THE U.S. MILITARY WARRIORS,
AND MY BLOODBROTHERS
EVERYWHERE.

"I am a black Jew at a Nazi Klan rally.
Let's get it on."

★ ★ ★

Ted Nugent

THOSE WHO KNOW TED BEST...

✶ ✶ ✶

"As with all crusaders, you can not head him off or make him quit. Trying to do so only adds fuel to his already blazing internal inferno of self motivation, determination and persistence. Where the dust and sweat is swirling in the arena is where you will find Ted Nugent. Oh, and one more thing: he parks where he wants."

—WARD PARKER

"I've been riding shotgun with this human fireball of intensity & passion for the better part of two decades. And here's what I know for sure. Ted's boundless energy is exceeded only by his talent. And his talent is exceeded only by his heart. Any questions?"

—LINDA PETERSON
assistant to Mr. Nugent

"For the last 30 years, I've been running alongside a runaway freight train. His name is Ted Nugent. Look out, hop on, or get run over."

—DOUG BANKER
long time manager

✶ ✶ ✶

WWW.TEDNUGENT.COM

Ted Nugent Management:
Doug Banker
McGhee Entertainment
Suite #200
8730 Sunset Blvd.
Los Angeles, CA 90069
www.mcgheela.com

A NOTE ON STYLE

Some folks might remember that George Bernard Shaw—a sandal-wearing socialist vegetarian—tried to reform the spelling of the English language. Big deal. Big musty flop. This book—by the hard-drivin', hard-lovin', full-throbbin', high-octane, deerslayin', allthings-scarin', ballistic guitarboy—Nugetizes it. Get ready to rock, doc.

CONTENTS

THE ONGOING SAGA OF LOGIC AND THE AMERICAN WAY

Old school still rules. Thanks to Ted Nugent for keeping it real at Shrine Catholic Academy in Royal Oak, Michigan. Ted related to the students in a way that only he can—with humor, honesty, and his unique brand of talent. I believe that my students learned more about life in the time spent with Ted than they would have in weeks of pouring through books, doing research, and taking tests. He taught, he motivated, and he inspired. Best of all—he led by example.

★ ★ ★

—Elaine Hewitt, English Teacher at Shrine Catholic Academy, March 10, 2010

Since the celebratory opening volley of *Ted, White, and Blue: The Nugent Manifesto* first scorched upon an unsuspecting civilian public many months ago, much in the same way *God, Guns, & Rock 'n' Roll* did a few years previous, my crowbar of truth and logic has never been busier.

The tsunami of *Amens!* thrust upon me in all my nonstop travels and activities across the land continues to be very gratifying, uplifting, and rewarding, particularly in the context of today's America filled with a growing army painfully and embarrassingly caught up in the curses of apathy and denial. Many have made it perfectly clear that my sharing and celebrating my own simple, self-evident truth and logic driven life is indeed applicable and miraculously transforming in their own. Can I hear a hearty "No shit, Uncle Ted!"

Of course I can, and believe me, I do constantly, as it should be.

Know that it is in no way a Nuge thing. Rather, all evidence points clearly to a throbbing "We the People" thing that is once again rising from those disconnected ashes of apathy and building steam most notably in the Tea Party movement. It's about damn time.

I hate to be the one to say, "I told you so," but the runaway freight train of self-imposed, comfortably numb ignorance that has for so long yanked the carpet out from beneath so many Americans is slowly but surely coming to light. And though I am not yet convinced that a real and meaningful wake-up call has taken place, it is nonetheless apparent that this new Tea Party movement is a step in the right direction. Truth is a beautiful thang.

More and more hard working, sacrificing Americans from the asset column are beginning to admit that the majority of those in the liability column are there because they like it there. They are, after all, rewarded for it.

Sadly, America has the perfect president and commie-infested administration for the soulless sheeping of a once great nation. The parasites may very well outnumber the producers, and Obama's Mao fans make it abundantly clear that they hate America, do indeed wish to fundamentally transform her into a Euro wannabe, and look to Lenin, Marx, Mao, Castro and Che, Reid, Pilosi, Van Jones, and other anti-American monsters for direction and inspiration. Phenomenally stupid and suicidal.

Why do you think they call it dope?

Much of the world looks upon us as spoiled brats who got fat and lazy and don't appreciate what we have. Watching rude, arrogant, out-of-control bureaucrats spend like maniacs with impunity and a blatant Big Brother, oversized government meddling-where-no-American-government-has-gone-before in direct and obvious violation of the U.S. Constitution and all things common sense has created a long overdue backlash of good, old, down-to-earth "We the people" activism. The worm has turned.

I want to personally salute Rush Limbaugh, Sean Hannity, Mark Davis, Mark Levin, Michael Savage, Laura Ingram, Neal Boortz, Mark Stein, Walter Williams, Thomas Sowell, David Limbaugh, Jed Babbin, Michael Smerconish, Michael Reagan, Newt Gingrich, Michelle Maulkin, Ann Coulter, Neal Cavuto, Roger Hedgecock, and most of all, the amazing Glenn Beck for sounding the most important alarm in the history of the free world. These brave souls and many more like them are spotlighting cockroaches like never before, and the people are responding. I am proud to be a part of this growing wave of activism, even though I started around 1966. Surely, such a glorious experiment in self-government should include all Americans. Self-government is not an abstract, it is a job description, and it is good to see so many Americans punching the clock for a change.

HealthCare hell indeed, TARP, stimulus packages, cap and trade, amnesty for invaders, releasing September 11 conspirators, shutting down Gitmo, trying terrorists in civil court, blatant redistribution of wealth, government-run banks, government-run car companies, government-run insurance companies, government-run schools, government-corrupted mortgage firms, government-run social engineering, the Marxist battle cry of "social justice," ad nauseum—it is all way too obvious what needs to change, and I pray to God every day that it is not too late.

Social justice in the vulgarity of the progressive's language is anti-social and unjust. Know it.

I cannot take credit for the following little ditty, but when I got it from a friend, I immediately posted it on my Tednugent.com TalkBack, and it pinned the logic meter on DefCom Uno. This would certainly be a good first step back to The Founders vision:

HERE'S WHAT WE ALL CAN UNITE ON & MAKE HAPPEN!!

Congressional Reform Act of 2010
by Allen L. Roland

1. **Term Limits:** 12 years only, one of the possible options below.

    A. Two six-year Senate terms

    B. Six two-year House terms

    C. One six-year Senate term and three two-year House terms

    Serving in Congress is an honor, not a career. The Founding Fathers envisioned citizen legislators; serve your term(s), then go home and back to work.

2. **No Tenure/No Pension:**

    Congressmen collect a salary while in office and receive no pay when they are out of office.

    Serving in Congress is an honor, not a career. The Founding Fathers envisioned citizen legislators; serve your term(s), then go home and back to work.

3. **Congress (past, present, & future) participates
in Social Security:**

All funds in the Congressional retirement fund moves to the Social Security system immediately. All future funds flow into the Social Security system, Congress participates with the American people.

Serving in Congress is an honor, not a career. The Founding Fathers envisioned citizen legislators; serve your term(s), then go home and back to work.

4. **Congress can purchase their own retirement plan
just like all Americans.**

Serving in Congress is an honor, not a career. The Founding Fathers envisioned citizen legislators; serve your term(s), then go home and back to work.

5. **Congress will no longer vote themselves a pay raise.**

Congressional pay will rise by the lower of CPI or 3%.

Serving in Congress is an honor, not a career. The Founding Fathers envisioned citizen legislators; serve your term(s), then go home and back to work.

6. **Congress loses their current health care system and
participates in the same health care system as the
American people.**

Serving in Congress is an honor, not a career. The Founding Fathers envisioned citizen legislators; serve your term(s), then go home and back to work.

7. **Congress must equally abide by all laws they impose
on the American people.**

Serving in Congress is an honor, not a career. The Founding Fathers envisioned citizen legislators; serve your term(s), then go home and back to work.

8. All contracts with past and present congressmen are void effective 1/1/11.

The American people did not make this contract with congressmen; congressmen made all these contracts for themselves.

Serving in Congress is an honor, not a career. The Founding Fathers envisioned citizen legislators; serve your term(s), then go home and back to work.

If America is truly alert to the communist/Marxist hit parade that is the current White House, then that is what we should all fight for. And the Tea Party cannot do it alone at its current size and voice. It is going to take an increased fiery, passionate activism by millions more Americans who still believe. I still believe, I believe in America.

I just watched a public television special on the poor abused middle class of America here at my home in Texas this very day, March 23, 2010. It showed a parade of losers, some at the hair salon having their hair and nails done, whining about the horrors of credit card debt, and feebly expressing how they cannot imagine how it caught up with them like it did. Hey asshole, if you're in debt, YOU CANNOT AFFORD TO GET YOUR HAIR AND NAILS DONE! Then they went out to dinner. Dear God in heaven, if that doesn't say it all.

It's like the denial-riddled clown we all saw at the soup kitchen, getting his daily handout, but this time from Michelle Obama. Amazingly, this guy supposedly couldn't afford a meal, but he was able to take a photo of the president's wife with his state-of-the-art cell phone. Not being able to make ends meet must suck. The average "poor" American hasn't the faintest idea. Have another smoke, fire up the bass boat, microwave, flat screen satellite TV, feed the pit bull, and think about it. Make ends meet, my ass.

Spread the good word my fellow Americans. I, for one, know it is not too late. The American Dream of excellence, independence, and individualism throttles on for all willing to work hard and sacrifice.

Study history. Study the U. S. Constitution, the Bill of Rights, the Declaration of Independence, the Ten Commandments, and the Golden Rule. Prod your family, friends, coworkers, neighbors at church and school—everybody you can—to wake up, to get involved, to raise hell. Put pressure on your elected officials and your regional media. Let the voice of real Americans drown out the new Maoists.

Meanwhile, your dear Ol' Uncle Ted will just keep on doing what I've been doing nonstop since the roaring '60's:' raising hell. Spotlighting cockroaches. Swinging the crowbar of truth-logic upside the heads of the deserving. And believe you me, there has never been a more target-rich environment.

Courageous American military warriors continue to make the ultimate sacrifice, time and time again, to protect and secure freedom and our American Dream. How dare we fail them by not utilizing and putting to work these unique American liberties, for which they gave so much. Do it for them. The stakes have never been higher, and the future of America never so threatened. We can do it. We must.

Trample the weak, hurdle the dead. Sometimes we give the world the best we got, and we get kicked in the teeth. Give the world the best we got anyway.

Ted Nugent
March 2010

Friend, you cannot legislate the poor into freedom by legislating the wealthy out of freedom. And what one person receives without working for, another person must work for without receiving. The government can't give to anybody anything that the government does not first take from somebody. And when half of the people get the idea they don't have to work because the other half's going to take care of them, and when the other half get the idea it does no good to work because somebody's going to get what I work for. That, dear friend, is about the end of any nation.

Dr. Adrian Rogers,
Love Worth Finding Ministries

TED NUGENT THROUGH THE EYES OF BOB COBURN

★ ★ ★

Let me begin this treatise by acknowledging that I have known Ted Nugent for over thirty years. That means that I have known The Nuge just as long as I have not known him. That alone is a pretty scary thought. I've been playing his music even longer than that. In fact, The Amboy Dukes' classic song "Journey to the Center of Your Mind" became a national hit in the summer of 1968. I started my radio career in fall of 1968, so we have been on the rock 'n' roll train together the whole time. We were just riding in different cars for awhile. We met face to face for the first time in 1975 when his legendary, eponymous solo album TED NUGENT hit radio like an RPG. With the killer song "Stranglehold" augmented by "Hey Baby," "Just What the Doctor Ordered," and more, Ted cemented his spot in the rock pantheon with his greasy, sexy, R&B injected brand of rock reminiscent of the Detroit sound that held sway nationwide. Nugent put some stink on his music coming out of the gate. He was a young white punk influenced by the African-American rhythms he grew up with in the Motor City. But this was anything but assembly line rock. Those tribal sounds have stayed with him for a lifetime and helped define the man as well as his music. I asked him once if he liked Pantera's cover of "Cat Scratch Fever" and he said he respected the band, but disliked that they took the grind, the bump, and the undulating rhythm out of it. They made it Wonder Bread in his view.

I was working at the legendary KMET in Los Angeles in '75 when program director Sam Bellamy was wondering why the music director was adding the Ohio Players and the O'Jays, The Stones and The Eagles, but not Ted. This was back when radio personalities on the fledgling FM dial were allowed to play what they wanted. How I miss those days. But you can't play an album that's not in the studio. She wanted to know if I would have added the *Ted Nugent* album into the "available for airplay" box. Well, hell yeah! One thing led to another and soon I was helping Sam pick the music the staff could choose from and anchoring afternoon drive. Theodore inadvertently helped my career take off.

KMET was a juggernaut back then, actually becoming the #1 station in LA for quite some time. Adding Ted's album to KMET's selection of music helped his career take off too. I call that a fair trade. Inevitably Nuge came rolling into town to do some damage at a local venue and he stopped by the radio station for a little on air chat. The energy level in the studio was suddenly enough to power the transmitter and half of Hollywood; the man crackled with exuberance and enthusiasm. I figured he was high as a kite, but pretty soon learned a lesson about the Motor City Madman. This was au natural. This was default mode. This was amazing, because in that era Peru was the most popular country in the world. Frank Zappa's classic line applied to Nugent too, "Can you imagine me on drugs?" No, and I really don't want to ponder the possibility. This will become a salient point as this story progresses. As an aside, Nuge was on Zappa's DiscReet Records for 1973's *Call of the Wild* album. Hardly two peas in a pod, but both were sober, controlled, and bright talents.

I was sent to Chicago by Metromedia to begin a Windy City version of "The Mighty Met" called WMET in 1979. If you really know "Theadocious Atrocious," you are aware he has Chicago roots as well as those in Detroit. We would often have Ted's mom, Marion, (everybody just called her "Ma Nuge") call in or drop by the studio because everybody loved her, and she could actually outtalk Ted. The only person I've met with that capability. This was an early lesson in genetics. At WMET we even had a "Mother's Day with Ted's Ma" one year. It's a good thing Nuge wasn't there because she busted out some pictures that, for once, I guarantee would have left him speechless. "You must have been a beautiful baby…." Hey Baby, indeed! It was one of the most fun and successful promotions we did at The MET in Chicago. Ma was a charmer and a wonderful person. The proverbial apple didn't even fall from the tree in their case.

One morning I went to the Chicago ABC TV station on State Street to pick The Nuge up from an interview on "Good Morning Chicago," or whatever it was. This is 1979, remember, and Ted was way past larger than life at this point, past the hugely successful "Cat Scratch Fever" and was one of the most recognizable faces in America. I sent out a memo to the entire station staff telling, no, make that "warning" them that he was coming in and that there were to be no tours, no gawking, and no pressuring him for autographs and such. Well, as the cliché goes, not everyone got the memo. I came strolling in with Ted and immediately walked into a station tour of girl scouts. You know, you can't make this stuff up. He was immediately mobbed, grabbed, poked, prodded, and what then ensued was akin to a swarm of bees with 'roid rage. I waded through the young ladies and grabbed him by the arm and told him not to worry, that I'd get him out of there. He shoved my hand away and screamed, "Are you crazy? I've been waiting my whole life for this!"

Of course, Ted remained a gentleman, signed everything pushed his way, charmed everyone around him, and gave some young ladies a moment I guarantee they still remember. I think my morning drive guy got ten minutes tops with him. Priorities, gotta get them straight.

Naturally, I have had many, many more encounters with The Nuge over the years. He's been a frequent guest on Rockline, my nationally syndicated radio show, and he has never been late for a show or even close to it. He's never had a rider, or an "I want this or I won't do the show" list. He's never been rude to a caller, cajoling maybe. He trusts my instinct in choosing the music and never tells me what I "have" to play. He is the only guest on the show that has never forgotten a caller's name, never needed to have a question restated, assuming he heard it in the first place. You play that loud for forty years! He's just as energetic as that first encounter way back in 1975. He's always lucid, cogent, opinionated as hell, and as entertaining as anyone I've ever encountered. This is where that no drug policy comes in. Say what you want about Ted Nugent, and most everyone does, he is still firing on all cylinders, has all of his brain cells left, and is as sharp as a tack. He also possesses a wickedly acerbic sense of humor and often uses it to make a point, or just rattle your cage.

Still, through all the years and all the interviews and all the shared moments, he still bugs the crap out of me sometimes. It's really difficult to debate Ted, because he has all of his arguments in place, and all of his points of view are well thought out. He has an incredible, and sometimes irrefutable, sense of logic that somehow prevails even though I disagree with it. His politics are vastly different than mine, a huge understatement, yet I always manage to at least see his point of view. As you know, Nugent can be very persuasive. He makes me feel like a hypocrite sometimes, without knowing it, because he does hunt and fish and loves guns and bows and arrows and kills animals. I eat meat too, but I get mine from places far more cruel to animals than anything Ted would ever do, or even consider. Nugent is far more humane than most of us who buy flesh at Albertsons or Kroger, knowing full well it came from animals living in horrendous, overcrowded conditions.

Guns are just not my world. I don't own any and don't plan to. Personally, I don't really have a problem with those that value firearms; it is protected by law last time I checked. But I didn't appreciate taking the disc out of his *Craveman* CD only to have a picture of him drawing a bead on me with a pistol. A Glock 10mm, I believe. That creeped me out. I guess I failed to appreciate the humor. (I can hear Ted cackling in my head right now).

He shot a beautiful buck earlier this year, twenty points or something, an absolutely beautiful creature. I think he called him "Big Wide" because of his stunning, powerful girth. I asked him if it didn't bother him, even a little bit, and he emphatically said no. He shot it fair and square; he either eats it himself and with his family, or passes it on to the homeless and needy that have no resources for food at all. But geez, Ted, couldn't you have spared just this one? No, he lived a long life, the herd needs to be culled or they fall out of balance, their lives become diminished because there are too many of them and he stood a chance of inadvertently becoming someone's hood ornament anyway. And you know what? He's correct. There are tens of thousands of deer vs. automobile crashes every year.

It pisses me off because I like to think I love animals, but deep down in my heart I know his logic is irrefutable. I know that if we quit killing deer and culling the herd that they'd be all over the place and would pose a danger to thousands of humans, which are creatures I like even more. I also know that if you go to his house, he'd be happy to grill you a tofu burger. Just don't tell him what he and his family can eat, and he will respond in kind.

As I write this, there is a huge news story about millions of pounds of beef being recalled. Sick cattle raised in deplorable conditions and mixed in with the healthy and served to non-hunting carnivores everywhere. So who is more out of tune with nature? Ted with his bow and arrow, by far the most sporting way to hunt, or one of us pulling up to the McDonald's to order a sick cow on a bun? You're a vegan? I couldn't respect you more and admire your stance regarding animals. Perhaps that's evolution, I don't know. But don't order my dinner for me either, please.

Back to the politics for a moment. Sometimes I feel Nugent's stance is ludicrous and laughable. Sometimes he is as accurate as the flight of the arrows he shoots so well. But regardless of whether any of us agree on any particular issue or not, he is a tremendous catalyst for starting conversation, for looking deeply at the issues, the reasons and the resolutions of the myriad problems we face. When it comes down to stepping into the voting booth his vote counts exactly the same as yours or mine, but what have you done to generate interest, to be a participant in democracy, a concept that requires us to be involved?

I've never discussed this with Ted before, but quite often after his appearances on Rockline, I get hammered with email and letters from angry people who disagree with his perspective. This used to bother me, it made me consider if I am doing the proper thing by allowing someone on the show whom many consider to be an extremist of profound proportions. Well, guess what? All those challenges have caused me to be more adamant than ever regarding his appearances. When he is on the show the phones blaze, the discussion begins, the ideas fly and I see the true spirit of democracy working full speed ahead right in front of me. I'll fight for the right to allow him to espouse his point of view, just as I would for you to verbalize yours. This is what America is all about. This is the essence of why hundreds of thousands of our brothers and sisters are half a world away, so that we remain free and are allowed to choose our own point of view and to shout it out loud if we choose. I opposed that war from the beginning. I felt that we were invading a country when it was an ideology that attacked us on 9-11. But we are there, and I am beyond proud of those who have answered the call and are fighting for our freedom. There is no greater champion of the Constitution than Nuge, and he has shown his overwhelming support for our troops on multiple occasions with concerts and direct involvement, right down to individual soldiers.

Ted sometimes sends me graphic descriptions of what our law enforcement officers go through to keep us safe. I read every word and look at every picture, even though some are beyond gruesome. I am stunned at the courage and resolve of some of my fellow Americans who put their lives on the line daily to keep us safe. Nugent provides me with a constant reminder of the real world in which we live. And it's not always bunnies frolicking in a field of wildflowers under sunny skies. Did you watch *Planet Earth*? This is a tough chunk of rock we live on. I am thankful for these missives from Ted as they remind me of the wonderful life I get to live, in part, because of many people whom I do not know and will never meet.

So, yeah. Sometimes he ticks me off. Sometimes he makes me proud. Sometimes he makes me take a long hard look at myself. Sometimes he makes me laugh. Sometimes he makes me forget what a great entertainer, guitarist, and performer he is. But he is always on top of his game; he always has a well thought-out point of view; he always is a man of huge heart and tremendous passion, no matter what the endeavor. He is the eternal American patriot and conservationist. Thank God we have him. I cannot imagine our country (or rock 'n' roll music) without my friend of thirty years, Ted Nugent.

BloodBrothers, forever.
Bob Coburn, RockLine radioshow, USA

"Sometimes you give the world the best you got
and get kicked in the teeth.
Give the world the best you got anyway."

✸ ✸ ✸

Ted Nugent

This is my manifesto. According to my dictionary, a manifesto is a written statement of beliefs. What you have here in your workin' hard, playin' hard hands is a collection of some of my basic beliefs. The topics I chose for this manifesto are rooted in principles that I believe are critical to our quality of life. I tried to address the timely, very important issues that could literally change the course of America.

If my manifesto achieves anything, I hope it makes you think and pisses you off—heavy on the piss-you-off part. I then hope it spurs you to join me in throttling the pathetic sheep so soullessly locked in the widespread slumber of apathy across this otherwise great land and lights the fuse of your internal powder keg of activism.

There is nothing in here about my sacred hunting life. You may find that surprising, but if you don't know where I stand on this issue, you haven't been paying attention. Hunting, fishing, and trapping are the last, pure, perfect, hands-on conservation, real-world, positive environmentalism, and resource stewardship roles available to mankind. If you don't hunt, fish, or trap, you are not doing your fair share in managing our quality wildlife, air, soil, and water. Fortunately, many of us have you covered.

Read my manifesto and then read it again. Get everybody you know who grasps the concept of upgrade to read it. Formulate your own ideas and then kick yourself and everyone you know in the ass and get busy. I adamantly believe that one determined man or woman cannot be stopped. Let's get it on. America needs us now more than ever.

Trust me, I will never be stopped or deterred. I won't go away. Write that down.

Ted Nugent

July 2008

"I don't really know and I don't give a damn,
but I know where I'm goin'
and I know who I am."

★ ★ ★

"Still Raising Hell,"
Love Grenade, 2007

I'm just a guitar player, but my amazing American Dream remains so damn cool, full of adventure, and appreciated more intensely each and every day that I cannot simply keep it to myself. I am one lucky bastard, and I am willing to share. My Spirit cup runneth over. Giving is better than receiving, so I give you my manifesto, loaded with and celebrating what so many Americans embrace as abundant truth, common sense, and inescapable logic. The sheer, immeasurable joy of what and how I live is not a mystery or a trick. No smoke and mirrors—and the joke that is being a celebrity is irrelevant. The secret to living like me—living every day to the fullest—is paying attention, taking intelligent, calculated, yet instinctual risks in pursuit of excellence, making smart choices to the best of your ability, and working your ass off. It means living clean, sober, lawful, defiant, and of course making some mistakes, but admitting to them and putting your heart and soul into adjusting your conduct in order to avoid making the same mistakes over and over again. And it's about a whole lot of luck and gung-ho perseverance. Human beings can be such numbnuts. Look at me. I hope you're smiling. I am.

And I'm "Still Raising Hell"—my ferocious Hi-energy Motor City bombastadon rock song from my LOVE GRENADE CD 2007 says it all:

Downtown Johnny lookin' for a catfight,
I do my best work just a little after midnight.
I don't really know and I don't give a damn,
but I know where I'm goin' and I know who I am.
I might fall down, but I'll jump back up, I might fall back down,
but I will never never ever ever give up.
'Cuz I'm alive & well, still raising hell, still alive & well, still raising
hell.
G.I. Joe lookin' for a firefight,
everywhere I go I try to make things right.

I don't really know but I sure give a damn,
and I know where I'm goin' and I know who I am.
I might fall down, but I will jump back up, I might fall back down,
but I will never never ever ever give up.
'Cuz I'm still alive and well, still raising hell, still alive and well,
still raising hell!

So be it.

SPIRITUAL ERUPTION

I was born in Detroit, Michigan, on December 13, 1948. Rumors abound that I danced out middle finger first, in blackface, doing a little James Brown two-step ditty with splits, wailing "Boogie Chillen,'" swinging from my own umbilical chord, gargling my placenta, and snarling. Simply not true. It was a relatively quiet, peaceful, Michigan winter wonderland event that brought much joy to my mother and father.

My parents—God rest their souls—Warren Henry Nugent and Marion Dorothy Johnson-Nugent were post-war America personified. Hard-working, loving, and frugal disciplinarians, they were ready to surf the industrial revolution wave into the modern world. In a country buoyed by the hard-won victory over the evil Japanese and demonic Nazis, a more positive social environment for the American Dream could not have been created. Clearly, the experiment in self-government and the joys of freedom, independence, and individual rights had crushed tyranny and oppression for all the world to see. The roaring fifties were about to erupt. Ed Sullivan was on TV. Long live rock 'n' roll. I was addicted at an early age.

We lived in a little cookie-cutter house at 23251 Florence Street, one door east of Hazelton Parkway, above the stinky Rouge River in Redford just west of Detroit proper. Our mailing address was simply Detroit, 28,

MI. I seem to recall Dad mentioning that the house cost us somewhere around $18,000. And yes, we had a white picket fence. I painted it.

Electrified guitars, amplifiers, radios, televisions, refrigerators, washers and dryers, telephones, fast cars, paved highways, cheap transportation by rail, air, and automobile and—dear God—gas at nineteen cents a gallon, unleashed a whole new quality of life in a brave new world of adventure and exploration. America's middle finger was on fire. Not a mean-spirited middle finger, mind you, but one of jubilant, positive *"don't tread on me"* defiance that was a threat to wannabe führers, emperors, kings, tyrants, slave drivers, despots, and dictators. At the same time, it celebrated a nation of goodwill, decency, generosity, unprecedented productivity, and deep, soulful compassion the likes of which the world had never seen before. Hell, we saved Europe, didn't we? Time to party.

My dad had served bravely in the U.S. Army Cavalry and fought in World War II and Korea. Tragically, yet typical of the Greatest Generation, he never discussed the wars with us nor did I ever hear him talk about it with anyone else. Amazing really, considering the clear-cut case of good over evil in what should have been great cause for celebration. The only mistake made by these amazing warriors was keeping it all inside and failing to share the good, the bad, and the ugly with everyone about "the War" from their first-person, eye-witness, hand-to-hand-combat perspective. At the least, it would have educated us all of the necessity of war being the answer when corrupt, evil governments slaughter innocent citizens by the tens of millions.

Surely good must always wage war against evil. When good fails to do so, evil thrives, freedom dies, and innocents are slaughtered. Period. This should be written on the cover of every schoolbook read by every school kid in the free world. The absence of this truism has allowed a cult of denial to flourish, where the "give peace a chance" fantasy encourages tyrants and dictators to run amok over the unsuspecting, while good people get killed like so many clueless sheep. Imagine that, John Lennon.

Little do Gandhi and Mr. Lennon suspect that in order to give peace a chance, all the Hitlers, Idi Amins, Pol Pots, Stalins, Lenins, Maos, Vincente Foxes, Charles Taylors, Husseins, Kadafis, Mugabes, and other nefarious gang-bangers, tyrants, dictators, and soulless punks of the world would have to be killed and wiped out before they implemented their evil control over their unarmed, helpless victims. The shattered skulls of tyrants should be used

> ★
>
> **The shattered skulls of tyrants should be used for traction under the boots of justice.**

for traction under the boots of justice. I prefer steel-toed, deep-cleated Vibram lugs, size 12 with bloodproof Gortex, thank you very much.

We all know that World War I was "the war to end all wars" and that World War II was "the good war," but evil never sleeps. Failing to learn from history's painful lessons will guarantee a repeat of history's most tragic mistakes—and that is where we went horribly wrong during Vietnam, and where, to a great degree, we are going wrong in the War on Terror today. There is only one way to face wars—they're inevitable, and you fight them to win with overwhelming force. I wish to hell that my dad would have sat us down and told us all the gory details of his pain and suffering in the European and South Pacific Theaters—and why it was worth it. I know it is the tendency for parents to shield their children from traumatic events and discomforting information, but that can be a terrible mistake.

Hiding from disturbing information that is a part of reality makes us extremely vulnerable to the dark side of life which will, unfortunately— yet inevitably—affect every person's life at some point. Denying that bad things happen leaves us clueless in how to prepare or react.

Conduct determines outcome. Ignorance is vulnerability. Denial is stupid. I would rather be fortified by tales of terror and inspired to prepare and train for such events than find myself surprised and overcome by the attack of miscreants. I would rather hear the whimpering of children upset by the inescapable truth that wildlife is not cuddly, cute, and existing for their entertainment—but actually dangerous and deserving of their fear and respect—than hear the cries of a family at the gravesite of loved ones killed by wanting to pet one of California's "protected" cougars. And surely we can agree that it is far better to educate your child about the reality regarding wild animals than deal with the inevitable distress of a willfully ill-prepared person going through the agony of rabies treatment because the Disney generation wants to be friends with a raccoon.

Cute can get you killed. Truth saves lives. Deal with it.

REAL WORLD PRIORITIES

My brain is a tsunami of incredible memories—sixty years of amazing, nonstop stimuli. It is pretty much all good, too. Even my early memories are positive. My brothers and sister would be quick to point out the heavy, oftentimes inexplicably brutal hand of my father, but for me, the grins surely far outweigh the tears. For the most part, our loving Ma Nuge was such a constant source of laughter and fun, and the good times spent with dad and the dogs, shooting guns and bows, and exploring the mystical "Up North" forests, overwhelmingly obliterate the moments of fury and torment when Dad got all pissed off, for what was surely—more often than not—no good, logical reason at all.

And what good dad doesn't get pissed off? I was a pretty decent kid most of the time for the simple fact that I was scared to death of Dad's thunderous voice of authority and that leather-wrapped, steel-stripped, horse-training riding crop that he had brought home from the war. It hung somewhere up in his bedroom, and though I had seen him wield it occasionally, I don't recall his ever actually hitting any of us with it. But the threat was there. Threats will do in the learning years. Fear is a beautiful thing. Until our young, developing brains are up to the task of deciphering cause and effect, good old-fashioned fear will suffice, thank you. God bless my father. Tougher love is always the answer.

By the time I was seven or eight years old, I had discovered the mystical flight of the arrow and the ultimate, animal, soundtrack weapon of mass destruction: the electric guitar. But neither of these forces had completely taken over my heart just yet. I would play around with my guitar and shoot my bow everyday, but I was still in discovery mode, as a young boy should be. My dear mother has described on more than one occasion how I was a handful, and that I needed more monitoring than my older brother Jeff. My lifelong fascination with knives, tools, saws, sickles, machetes, and other sharp-edged weapons and projectiles began early. I clearly remember being hauled on numerous occasions up to the emergency entrance of the Redford Hospital at Grand River and Six Mile Road to stitch up a succession of gashes, cuts, slices, and wounds of various descriptions and degrees of limb-threatening severity. To this day I have many handsome, manly scars all over my arms, hands, and legs as a painful reminder of how close I constantly came to dismembering the future guitar player. I was the GashMaster long before I qualified as the WhackMaster.

A good, tough, rough and ready boy plays like a boy, pushes and challenges himself, and goes for the cliffhanger, literally. When we played war games as kids, we would really get it on. We dug tunnels and foxholes in the forests, ran wild through the neighborhood and woods while climbing and leaping from garages, fences, rocks, and cliffs. We climbed trees incessantly—the higher the better. Long ropes were hung up over towering oak limbs on which we swung out over streams, rivers, and precarious ravines. We all had pocketknives, BB guns, pellet rifles, slingshots, and bows and arrows, and we shot them in each others' backyards throughout our neighborhoods. It is critical to note that nobody shot anybody and nobody put out anybody's eye. And school shootings and stabbings were unheard of. The age of discipline and consequences was alive and well. Dear God, we must return to that modus operandi, ASAP!

My childhood and the man it produced stand in stark contrast to today's "average" male. I am saddened by the blatant decay of rugged individualism resulting in a pathetic lack of real boys and real men across America today. Considering that I am extremely blessed to share SpiritWild campfires with the absolute, most manly, last of the Mohican, real mountainmen in the world gives me pause and hope when I otherwise see a preponderance of mealy mouthed, milquetoast, fat, slow, hunched over, starry-eyed zombies everywhere I go. Soulless slouchers. Softies. Wimps, clueless in their pathetic, dependent little whiney girlyman lives. Hell, just the way many young men carry themselves—sagging, flopping shoulders...shuffling, stumbling feet... hanging heads...blank stares—combined with barely audible mumbling and a total incapacity for any meaningful dialogue makes me crazier than a bear in a nest of hornets.

I am convinced that most kids today have never heard the word "posture." Combine that with abandoned table manners and the result is too many kids resembling the chimps they supposedly evolved from. We can't forget that parents produced these failures and didn't teach or discipline their children to greet people properly, shake hands, or at the very least say a caring, kind "hell-o." And with

> ⭐
> **We are seeing reverse evolution at its worst.**

nobody at home or at school telling them any differently, we are seeing reverse evolution at its worst which of course affects our society. This neglect is rather depressing and terribly indicative of these kids' resulting state of mind. It ain't right. That Ozzy Osbourne's drug-addled, retarded behavior is considered entertaining is both sad and pathetic. At least Koko the gorilla could occasionally push a blue button and get food. These losers can't open a can of soup.

OLD YELLER:
ULTIMATE CAUSE AND EFFECT

Though my intense passion and cravings for the great outdoors were overwhelming from my earliest years, I was never alone in my venturings. My first dog was the family dog named Duke. Legend has it that he was a dog pound refugee, Labrador/Weimeraner mix. Regardless of pedigree, he was a big, black, lovable mutt who taught me about loving and caring for animals. Duke would pull us around in our red American Flyer wagon in the summer and our snow sleds each winter. I would construct forts of cardboard and scraps, and Duke and I would hunker down in our makeshift shelters from brutally cold rain and snow till Mom wouldn't take it anymore and called us in. We would wander and explore my beloved Skunk Hollow marshland down by the Rouge River forests, stalking the elusive river rats and vermin of my Natty Bumppo dreams. Duke was my constant companion.

All children should own a dog. It teaches companionship, teamwork, and ultimately, the responsibility of caring for an animal. Spiritual stuff.

After Duke was gone, we got another black dog named Kippy, a medium-size spaniel-looking hound that was my best buddy, too. We were inseparable. My true love for my dogs to this very day is a grand source of joy and heart-glowing experiences and memories, but the most important animal relationship reference guide that I, or anyone could have, is the movie *Old Yeller*.

Old Yeller was indeed man's best friend. Everybody loved Old Yeller. Every American should watch the movie *Old Yeller* every year from kindergarten through high school to remind them constantly of the inescapable but necessary unpleasantries in life, and how we must always do the right thing even when the right thing is gut-wrenchingly painful.

Our loving companion Old Yeller saved the chickens from the fox. This courageous mutt saved the little boy from the cougar and performed all sorts of beneficial family chores in the romantic wilderness setting of pioneer America. He brought us our slippers. We hugged and kissed him.

But then the good is crushed by the inevitable bad and ugly when one fine morning we awake to the horror of our dearly beloved "man's best friend" foaming at the mouth. Damn. I hate it when that happens. Well, the heartbreaking reality is that our good, lovable buddy has come down with rabies, probably from fighting all those mangy, wild critters. Regardless of all the good he accomplished, he contracted the deadly disease and the snuggling, hugging, petting, loving, slobbering days of Old Yeller are over, rover.

Yes, dear, a bullet to the head is the only decent, responsible thing to do. I know the loving dog was adorable, precious, cute, sweet, and cuddly, but rabies has no cure and will bring much prolonged, painful suffering for our old dog. Plus it can get us all killed or at the very least, deadly sick. So move aside my dear, and let a man do the right thing and put a .22 slug twixt his cute eyeballs. Animals have no rights.

> **Move aside my dear, and let a man do the right thing and put a .22 slug twixt his cute eyeballs.**

Along with the manly, macho, studly act of blowing out Old Yeller's brains to save the lives of my family, it is equally manly to bawl my eyes out, sobbing uncontrollably over the heartbreak and trauma of such an act. I know, for I have had the painful and mind-wrenchingly difficult duty of putting down many of my beloved dogs, cats, and horses over the years. As a land owner and steward, I have also had the responsibility of shooting many injured wildlife critters as well, and though clearly the only decent thing to do, it is nonetheless always difficult and emotional as all hell. I don't consider a life more valuable just because it comes in a cute package. Whether it is an ugly-ass wild hog too sick to walk away, or the most adorable little spotted fawn lying helpless in the swampgrass, it is the job of a reasoning predator and a responsible man to put them out of their misery while the city folks sleep comfortably in their neighborhoods. Old Yeller, I love ya, dog. BANG! Godspeed, my friend. Godspeed. Next.

CHAPTER TWO

DEFY GRAVITY

"Dare I repeat—yet again—that the jury
has returned a verdict: drooling, stumbling, puking,
and dying do not a party make."

★ ★ ★

From Tednugent.com TalkBack,
a typical daily post by Nuge

Longevity is IT! God has granted me yet another glowing day of life. I shall live it to the fullest. I will scorch the earth and all its inhabitants with a firestorm of positive energy and goodwill. I will be ultra-productive and force myself into the asset column for my self, family, neighborhood, America, and earth. It's so simple, it's stupid. LIV IT UP!! Itsa decision. Go wild.

As I gather firebrand spirit, steam, and yet another year of ultra piss and vinegar overflow for Nugent Rolling Thunder RockTour '08, guaranteed to be the very best rockout of my life, I am forced to remind myself every few minutes to take a deep breath, try my best to calm the hell down, pay attention, organize my thoughts and plans, and fall to bended knees thanking God Almighty for the roaring beast of indescribable hi-energy that pulsates throughout my very being to this day.

☆

I will scorch the earth and all its inhabitants with a firestorm of positive energy and goodwill.

Nearing my sixtieth birthday, I am more amazed than ever at the never-ending smile blazoned across my face from sheer joy of life. I just cannot get over the lust for life that I still have, every day, especially for the same inspiring activities that turned me on and drove me wild from my earliest memories. Gung-ho rockin', screaming guitar soulmusic, bows and arrows, BB guns and slingshots, wrenches, crowbars, sharp-edged instruments, skinny women, campfires, dogs, wildlife, sex, great food, and of course, right here, right now, the magnification of it all in communicating these joys to whomever will listen. And based on the glowing positive energy that I share nonstop at tednugent.com, in my travels, and far-reaching communications daily with the greatest people from every imaginable walk of life across America, around the world, and beyond, goodwill and decency is alive and well. Life is an orgy of adventure maximized when shared. It's not so much the road less traveled as the thrilling roads known and enjoyed from past explorations. But most important are those fascinating, alluring trails not yet attempted. Can you say runaway freight train into uncharted spiritual wilderness? Say it. Know it.

MY DAY

I awoke again one fine Texas spring day recently to hug and say good morning to my wonderful son Rocco Winchester and dangerous wife Shemane (dangerous, as in, gorgeous and compelling). After brewing up a fresh cup of Nuge Java with a squirt of Hazelnut cream and grabbing a quick bacon treat for the three Labradors, I bid Rocco a hearty "Carpe Diem" as he headed out to the final days of his all A-honor student Waco High School senior year. What an amazing kid.

Shemane prepared for her ritualistic gungho morning workout, and since it wasn't hunting season, I fired up my inescapable laptop computer. While it warmed up, I slid out the back door with the hounds and performed my daily walk-run around the large backyard and tennis court just to get the old bones and plumbing a-pumping for another grand day of American Dream fun.

Before heading out the door, I made sure to insert my Walker's Game Ear amplifiers so I wouldn't miss the beautiful songbird symphony that so inspires me each morning. I turn up my sensual radar so as to maximize and absorb all that nature has to offer, surrounded by brilliant creatures, fowl of every description flying overhead, and the concrete and metal sounds of productive, hard-working Americans doing the industrial "be the best you can be" boogie in the distance. Godbless the American workforce—it's still a powerful force to reckon with.

The distant sound of a pounding jackhammer and magnum truck back-up alarms harmonized with the rolling thunder of early morning

> ★
> **Yes, I have my own brandname coffee, thank you. Have some!**
> **www.tednugent.com**

traffic nearby. A school class was being held outdoors to our south a ways, and a teacher's voice chimed in over a loud speaker system with instruction for the youngsters. A lawnmower growled. I grinned.

As I strolled briskly and pumped on, my main hunting dog, Gonzo the Wonder Lab, began some intense barking, joined soon by Thunder and BlackJack as they lit up at the sight of a pesky fox squirrel in one of our pecan trees. I double-timed it to the house and retrieved my silent but deadly Crossman pellet rifle, loaded a .22 caliber lead projectile, pumped her hard four times, and raced to the tree surrounded by excited dogs. Based on all the intense commotion, you would think I had a pack of bloodthirsty Black and Tans, Walkers, and Redbones cornering a livestock-killing cougar up that tree.

> ━━━━ ☆ ━━━━
> **I really, REALLY love anything with the name "Jack" or "Hammer" in it. Combine the two, and it is music to my ears.**
> ━━━━━━━━━━━

Me and my pups don't mess around. We are extremists and damn proud of it.

After much difficult straining, my eyeballs finally picked up a thin sliver of russet hide hugging tightly to a high branch, and like Crackshot Nuge of the pumpgun sniper brigade, I took careful aim, took a deep breath, let it out halfway, and gently squeezed the trigger as the front sight settled into the rear groove, squarecenter on the top of the limb-rat's head. Phoomp! Down came the rapscallion rodent, and the dogs went wild, chomping, and shaking their furry prize. Pure Nature at her best in a tooth, fang, and claw ballet.

A neighbor once lamented that they have a squirrel problem—the overpopulated little rodents keep destroying their eves and attic space. I mentioned to them that we don't allow squirrel or rodent problems at the Nugent house. The rodents have a Ted problem, as it should be. What fun.

With a bit of a physical workout under my belt, and the joy of reducing vermin numbers while making three dogs very happy as further inspiration, I returned to my laptop and began my daily tsunami of key-punching directions, delegations, and productivity, working closely with ace personal assistant, She-Thor extraordinaire, Linda Peterson, as we go wild organizing my fiftieth year's insane Rolling Thunder RockTour with manager par excellence Doug Banker and commando tour manager Ted Emporellis.

Believe it or not—and I have witnesses—this is an average morning at my house. Typically, I then grill up some magic venison burger doused in olive oil, garlic salt, garlic pepper, and Montreal Steak seasoning (with some onion and pepper shrapnel thrown in) to fortify my belly and spirit for the daily assault that I lovingly refer to as my life. In between bites, I take care of things—like putting a new license plate on Shemane's hotrod or taking out the trash. Oh, yeah, and give the dogs some biscuits and shoot a few arrows into my 3-D targets.

It's now around 10:00 a.m. I'll brush the dogs and cat, and do another four laps or so around the yard. I am about to get. it. on. I still have my trapline to check, more vermin to kill, feeders to fill, fence to check and fix, guitars to abuse, food plots to disc and plant, barns to sweep, trash to burn, cedars to cut, chainsaws to adjust, and a flat tire on an

ARROW-FLINGING

Arrow-flinging is a daily ritual for me, and often for Shemane. Being one with the path of the arrow is soul cleansing to say the least, and fine-tuning one's mystical flight-of-the-arrow skills does more than hone our venison procurement capabilities, but such deeply soulful discipline goes straight to all other endeavors in life. Focus, attentiveness, and that higher level of awareness is critical for anything and everything worth pursuing. As goes the arrow, so goes the soul. Believe me.

A DAY IN THE LIFE

Team Nuge and I work on perfecting the intensely demanding Normandy Invasion-like logistics of dates...times...places...sound...lights...trucks...busses...hotels...private jets...military, law enforcement, and youth charity activities...band rehearsals...setlists...photographers...videographers...new songs, amps, guitars, strings, wha-wha's, microphones, and gadgets...guest lists...radio, TV, print, and Internet media interviews...Indian reservation bear hunts...Alaska bear hunts...the NRA convention...university, corporate, military, and sporting event speaking engagements...more flights...hotels...the testing of new bows, arrows, broadheads, and camo...new bug dope, boots, sox, knives, bait, rope, backpacks, energy bars, thermoses, mosquito zappers, energy drinks, headnets, optics, rangefinders, ammo, holsters, fire starters, and gutting gloves...wrapping up the Toby Keith movie, *Beer For My Horses*...setting up a recording session for the Guitar Hero videogame...arranging to shoot Criss Angel through the chest with a hunting arrow for his A&E TV show...coordinating the arrival of the Wounded Warrior Project heroes from Brooks Army Medical Hospital to band rehearsals...signing guitars and stuff for the U.S. Marine Corps Law Enforcement Foundation...making arrangements for Jim Brown of Bremen Castings (my machinegun and ammo guru) to bring a truckload of machineguns and ammo for the rehearsal festivities...discussing the final tune-up of my own MP5K 10mm machinegun with Jeff Zimba of Small Arms Review magazine...ordering pallets of 10mm ammo...emailing my completed Guitar World interview coordinating the arrival of the ATV

continued

★ ★ ★

magazine folks...sending off my cover story for *Bronco Driver* magazine...nailing down the arrival of Anthony Bourdain's *No Reservations* Travel Channel TV show...scheduling the ongoing and upcoming interviews in Europe, Britain, and North America on an endless list of news, talk, rock, and sports radio shows as well as various TV shows...finalizing the schedule for recording my killer new song "I AM THE NRA" *(see lyrics on page 224)* with Christian rocker David Crowder at his Waco studio...nailing down the artwork, lyrics, and credits for the CD with daughter Sasha in time for my speaking engagement at the NRA annual meetings...speaking with the governor of Alaska's office and Alaska Fish & Game about bear hunting regulations...putting out antigun fires in about five states...reviewing the de-listing of the grey wolf with Don Peay of Sportsmen For Fish and Wildlife...reviewing the wolf and bear hunts to save Alaska's dwindling moose populations with Jack Frost, director of the National Bowhunting Education Foundation...reviewing artwork with Regnery Publishing for this book...writing this book...sending chapters out for proofreading...proofing Jim Brown photos for this book...emailing my latest writings and photos to my magazine editors...ordering chocolate-covered strawberries from Shari's Berries and other Mother's Day goodies for all the mothers in my life...reviewing new stage production with team...ordering new fallow deer breeding stock for SpiritWild Ranch (SWR)...ordering new Heartland Wildlife supplemental feed for SWR & Sunrize Acres...having Joe Bob fix the steel plate targets...asking Charlie Moore the Mad Fisherman to send us some fishing gear for the wounded warriors...getting Derek Dieringer from Woodbury Taxidermy in Ingram, Texas to ship out a few boxes of my custom venison for the rehearsal BBQ...finalizing the

continued

⋆ ⋆ ⋆

arrangements to hunt turkeys in New Mexico at the Diamond A Ranch with State Representative Dan Foley...setting up our fall New Mexico elk, deer, and pronghorn hunts with Harry Wood and Jerry Dollins... arranging our Glenn Beck Clark family hunt at the Knowlton's Laguna Vista Ranch...designing a special wheelchair bracket with Pete Odland for the kids...making sure some Ol' Man treestands and Double Bull blinds are sent to the Washington State Quinault Indian reservation for my upcoming bear hunt...shipping out goodies for grandkids...arranging for an auction company to auction off a ton of stuff while I'm on tour...arranging to move everything from our Waco home to our China Springs home during tour...double-checking Rocco's graduation ceremony and party arrangements...getting my brothers Jeff and Johnny to join me in Alaska on the El Dorado trawler for the bear hunt...Emailing the final design for my new experimental custom PRS hollow-body guitar...directing attorneys to get rid of a forty-one-year-old arrest in Michigan that was supposed to be expunged from my record...filling out my Texas Concealed Handgun License paperwork...signing and sending a bunch of stuff to the military heroes in Iraq, Afghanistan, and various veterans hospitals...finding boxes, envelopes, tape, and stuff for shipping some autographed guitars, arrows, guns, bows, knives, photos, flags, and assorted items for military, law enforcement, and children's charities...I could go on, but I've got too much stuff to do to waste my time writing more down.

ATV to get unstuck and fixed. Then I will shoot a few hundred arrows and a few hundred rounds of 10mm and .223 ammo just to calm myself down a bit. I might even put a new Trijicon or Bushnell scope on a rifle or two and sight them in.

And I ain't even warmed up yet. Shemane and I may hit a favorite dining establishment, or just slap a scrumptious venison backstrap over orange mesquite coals for a perfect brunch. Of course, we will film this sacred protein preparation as a SpiritWild pure, free-range, flesh-cooking celebration segment for our award-winning *Ted Nugent Spirit of the Wild* TV show on Outdoor Channel. And believe you me, if you have never savored such a meal as our standard daily fare, your taste-buds are on standby, and dare I say, in cruel denial of the most delicious, healthiest food God has ever provided. Delightful.

> ★
>
> **There are no "quickie" meals at the Nugent campfire. To us, fast food is a running shot.**

I can't even imagine a Plan B. Sleeping in? That's weird. And somewhere, some chimp is whining that it can't make ends meet. Push the blue button, Koko. Get food. I'm sure that the Hillarys and Obamas of the world will get their Mao commie mitts on enough of my hard-earned cash to cover your hopelessly, soulless, pathetic, good-for-nothing, "Darwinism stopped here," enslaved, and inbred primate ass. Go ahead and wait for the evolution train to arrive. I'm sure Mike Tyson and Ted Kennedy are as confused and angry as anybody else to be left out. Punks.

HOW DOES THIS PARLAY INTO A GRAVITY-DEFYING MUSICAL CAREER?

Me? I'm into intelligent design. I do my best to intelligently design my life and daily activities for optimal enjoyment and productivity. Those opposed to intelligent design can be easily identified by their hyper-scramble to avoid anything intelligent. Take my wonderful, glowing, defiant musical career for example. After witnessing Billy Lee and The Rivieras's ace guitar commando Jimmy McCarty scorch the unsuspecting, terminally Caucasian, American Bandstand pop fans at the infamous Walled Lake Casino near Milford, Michigan, back around 1960, with his fiery Gibson Byrdland histrionics, I knew that I needed to practice my guitar-playing a whole lot more. Ultimately, I had to get my greasy, Motown-wannabe, cracker hands on one of those incredible Gibson hollow-bodies and a Fender Twin amp, ASAP. The defining impact that the sound of this band (soon to become Mitch Ryder and the Detroit Wheels) had on me at the tender age of twelve and (most demonstrably) the ferocious tone and guitar wizardry of the tall, lanky, cranking Jimmy McCarty conclusively determined the unstoppable, cosmic path of young Ted. Hi-energy soulmusic and feedback guitarnoize: my calling had been defined and my fate sealed. Somewhere in my belly, "Stranglehold" rumbled to pre-life.

> ★
>
> **Those opposed to intelligent design can be easily identified by their hyper-scramble to avoid anything intelligent.**

But at the time—1961 or '62—all I had was a cheap little Fender Duo-Sonic guitar and a small Maestro amp. Not even close. But thank God, dear old dad had helped me out with the purchase of this first electric guitar setup from another guitar wizard hero, Joe Podorsek at Capitol School of music. However, the most important factor at play in determining my guitarwizardry destiny was the pivotal lessons Dad forced on me. He taught me simple cause and effect and that rewards are only obtained from hard work and genuine effort. No shit.

All my fellow young musician friends in those rock 'n' roll baptismal days seemed to get whatever they wanted from their parents. Guitars, bass, drums, amplifiers, PA systems—anything. And I do not recall any of them having jobs by which they could pay for such equipment. Meanwhile, I delivered the *Detroit News* seven days a week to ninety-six customers, one hundred issues of the *Shopping News* every Saturday, caught night crawlers most evenings to sell to Mr. Briggs next door, washed cars, raked leaves, painted fences, shoveled snow, mowed lawns, and did every odds-and-ends job I could find in order to pay off my Fender and Maestro. The dream of a big, loud Fender Twin amp and the beyond-belief possibility of an $1,100 hand-carved, arched top, top-of-the-line Gibson Byrdland was unimaginable. I improvised and adapted with gungho dreams of overcoming one way or another. The arsenal of dream-inspired work ethic and sweat equity would eventually save the day. I just knew it.

Enter Lyle Gilman at the Roselle School of Music in Roselle, IL, 1965. I thought my eyes would blow out of my face, when, on a fine Saturday that summer, I strolled into this little suburban music store to buy a couple of guitar strings and maybe a pick or five. There, on the wall behind the counter, literally glowing a firehole into my soul, ablazing like the burning bush, was the most gorgeous, stunning, natural blonde Gibson Byrdland guitar. It was more than I had ever imagined in my life. The beautiful graphic grain of the hand-carved spruce top was more mind boggling than any short-skirted cheerleader I had ever drooled over. A totally unprecedented dynamic took a hold on me, a *stranglehold* if you will, and for the first time in my life, I clearly understood a definitive, essential need to possess something. I was in a trance. Spellbound. GaGa. Mesmerized. Stunned. Stoned. Ripped. Bleary. Zombied. Speechless. Gonzo in love. Owned. Helpless. Sold.

The kind, jolly gentleman behind the counter could see my infatuation and generously offered me the chance to touch the beast. It was all over the very second my hands came into contact with the neck and body—as if God had designed it to match my body and touch. My eyes closed and my head went back, my knees began to buckle and Chuck Berry licks erupted into a ballet of grinding soulmusic to cleanse my innards. Good God Almighty, somebody help me out here!

Well, if ever it was appropriate to say *"the rest was history,"* it would be right about here. Nobody is getting outta here alive. Mr. Gillman,

God bless his trusting soul, allowed me to trade in my Epiphone Casino hollow body—the same guitar George Harrison & Keith Richards played. And with a $100 down payment, I took home the consummate, soon-to-be trademark Ted Nugent guitar from hell.

It is important to note that, other than Jimmy McCarty, (and rare moments with Gene Cornish of The Young Rascals, Roy Clark, and Eric Clapton many years later), I would be the only really hard rocker to ever attempt to milk extreme, screaming, aggressive, outrageously loud sounds from this rather rare jazz guitar.

> ☆
>
> **With a $100 down payment, I took home the consummate, soon-to-be trademark Ted Nugent guitar from hell.**

My uncharted journey on and with the mighty Byrdland would drive me to discover not only my own, unique signature sound, tone, and playing style, but feedback sounds and licks that I would become known for. To this day, they remain nearly unprecedented, and for the purpose of this chapter on sheer, animal tenacity and perseverance, are thoroughly demonstrative of a career and dream that cannot be stopped or messed with in any way. This is my favorite part.

Sometimes you give the world the best you got, and you get kicked in the teeth. Give the world the best you got anyway. Success and happiness drive the assholes berserk. That is simply a bonus.

I had mentioned above that all my musician buddies seemed to get any gear that they wanted, mostly from mom and dad. Coupled with the transparent misdirection of wanting to be a "rockstar," the music and professional pursuit thereof became secondary, and their passion dwindled accordingly. Well, it is very noteworthy that not a single one of them amounted to jackshit as musicians, though they would tell you that there was nothing more important to them. Remember, these were better musicians than I was, but they lost sight of The Beast. The Beast of *excellence.*

And for some of the more pathetic amongst them, with the guaranteed ball and chain of dope smoking and the soulless punk fantasy of the hippie lifestyle joke, they got nothing. A big, fat, sad, unhappy *nothing*. Such a waste.

I have always maintained hardcore focus on the music. When you look in astonishment at the worldclass musical virtuosos I have been privileged to collaborate with, you can clearly see the quality control modus operandi of not only myself, but my amazing bandmates. The very concept of *rockstar* has always been meaningless to me. My genuine love of the music and musicians who put their heart and soul into their craft has forever been my driving force.

MUSICAL GODS

Tom Noel, Pete Prim, Jon Finly, John Brake, Jim Butler, Gary Hicks, Bob Lehnert, Gale Uptadale, Dick Treat, Dave Hawk Walinski, Dave Palmer, Bill White, Greg Arama, Andy Solomon, K.J. Knight, Vic Mastrianni, Joe Vitale, Gabe Magno, Rob De La Grange, Derek St. Holmes, Cliff Davies, Dave Kiswiney, John Sauter, Charlie Huhn, Carmine Appice, Michael Lutz, the Wagner brothers, Gunnar Ross, Bobby Columby, Dave Amato, Tommy Shaw, Jack Blades, Michael Cartellone, Denny Carmassi, Tommy Clufetos, Tommy Aldridge, Marco Mendoza, Barry Sparks, Mick Brown, and Greg Smith—these are the dynamo musical gods that have propelled my American rock 'n' roll Dream beyond any dimension I would have dared to expect, and I thank them all for their professionalism, dedication, incredible talents, and sheer gentlemanly heart and soul camaraderie, where applicable.

I am truly a blessed man. My days are filled with much adrenalin dumpage. With calendars jam-packed with fascinating adventures of both the urban and wilderness extremes, the primal scream is most resonate wherever we may go. Tackling my quests keeps me bright-eyed and bushytailed to the max. I have perfected the flatline, relaxation lay-back as well as the firestorm of passionate adrenalin overcharge that fuels my wonderful life. It is all about priorities and well-thought choices. That we humans are inclined to blow it on occasion inspires me to be cognizant of this shortcoming and diligently watch out for the danger signs of pending screwups. I've damn near cut 'em off at the pass to a dazzling degree. Quality control is always much easier and immeasurably less painful than damage control. And the mighty MotorCity Madman rock 'n' roll freight train throttles on, relentlessly. It cannot be stopped. God help us all. Being both a loner when need be and a bug-eyed, gregarious people animal, I feed on the communication and positive energy of the great people I associate with in varying degrees—and, of course, on the incredible, constant love of my family.

>
>
> ### *Stranglehold*
>
> "Some people want to get high, some people got to start low. Some people think they gonna die someday, I got news, ya never gotsta go."
>
> —Ted Nugent

UPON REFLECTION

It has never been easy, and in honest overview analysis, I wouldn't want it to be. Whether struggling to create the ultimate soulful guitar lick, organizing band rehearsals, getting to fulldraw on a wary beast, or conquering intimacy with the sexiest woman in the world, nothing deeply gratifying in life ever transpires without a good, challenging effort and usually a frustrating, repetitious struggle. Easy shit just don't get it done for me. And my rock 'n' roll epitomizes this craving for rewards through determined excellence. Easy stuff is abandoned while the more difficult things in life keep drawing us back. The path of least resistance is not compelling.

That is the most powerful reasoning behind my conscious choice to remain clean and sober for sixty years. I need all the help I can get, and to intentionally partake in activities that guarantee the reduction of one's sensuality and overall level of awareness is for chimps, losers, and dead hippies. No thank you.

Virtuosos much more gifted than I perished at the hands of the pathetic *we the sheeple* lie of peer pressure, more interested in impressing the petty Ozzy-like stoners amongst us than focusing on their music. To this day, I am dazzled at such a soulless condition of dependency and anti-human herd mentality. Choices are made, prices are paid.

I Just Wanna Go Huntin'

"Punks used to laugh at me, said how can you rock and not get high? Well I just stood my ground, and I watched those assholes fall and die. Cuz I just wanna go huntin, it makes me feel so good. I just gotta go huntin, try to find me in the woods."

—*Ted Nugent Hunt Music*, 1989

Please excuse me, won't you? I've got the world's greatest rock band and crew waiting for me as we hit the American Rock 'n' Roll Dream Hiway for my 50th rocktour and 6000th rockout. Excuse me whilst I kiss the sky. When in doubt, I whip it out, I got me a rock 'n' roll band. It's free for all. Boogie chillin.

I'M THE FRIENDLY, TOLERANT GUY

I like sizzling meat on the grill. Wild, huh. Anybody? Now we all know ol' Nuge isn't by any stretch of the imagination a weirdo when it comes to the choice of an omnivorous diet. Especially here in the great Republic of Texas, where a smiling, drooling preference for succulent, protein-rich, nutritious backstrap over aromatic mesquite coals is as American and natural and right as mom, apple pie, and the Flag. It's beautiful really.

But as many watched on my two TV shows, *Wanted Ted or Alive* and *Surviving Nugent*, the culture war raging against such universal self-evident truths would be laughable if it were not so deranged. There are people who not only choose a vegetarian lifestyle which itself is harmless in its rare implementation. However, many of these genuine weirdos are actually on a crusade to outlaw the consumption of flesh. I have musical touring associates who have been fired from their jobs with ex-Beatle Paul McCartney for sneaking a hamburger. You heard that right—fired for eating meat by the animal-rights maniac, hardcore vegan bass player. The entire agenda of the gazillion dollar financed joke known as PETA is outlawing meat. We all know how insane they are, but they are out there and there are a lot of them. Pam Anderson, Bill Maher, Bob Barker, Mary Tyler Moore, Alicia Silverstone, and many other high profile "celebrities" live for it.

I know for a fact that neither I, nor any hunter or meat-eater on the planet have any desire whatsoever to influence any vegetarian's choice of diet or to force them to eat meat. We are the friendly, tolerant Americans.

This is but one of many issues that represent the line drawn in the sand between liberals and conservatives. Our own intrepid editor at the

continued

Waco Trib, my friend John Young, doesn't want to simply make the choice to be unarmed and helpless for himself, he has again recently insisted that you and I must also comply with his soulless condition of unarmed helplessness. That's the difference right there. Nobody from our side wants to force anybody to have a gun or defend themselves. It is we, the conservatives, who are for individual choice.

And one only has to hear the treacherous words of Mao Tse Tung come roiling out of the mouths of the Left's heroes to know it is true, when without hesitancy, Ted Kennedy, Hillary Clinton, et al unflinchingly quote the Founding Fathers of Communism while politicking for a redistribution of wealth. The death tax is one result—the government gets to tax American families on after-tax life savings following the death of a loved one. This unfair, un-American, unconstitutional death tax literally destroys mom and pop businesses across the land. Think about it. Communism has ruined every life it has touched and entire civilizations. The wall is down, yet some (mostly Democrat) American elected officials still want to give it a shot. Dear God in heaven, help us.

Not too long ago, Danny Glover, an otherwise fine actor, embarrassingly abused his uniquely American freedoms by siding with the Communist Venezuelan dictator Hugo Chavez to finance what clearly appears to be an anti-American propaganda film. Nice. Meanwhile, right there in that Communist country, old Hugo is shutting down an entire media network for daring to challenge his heavy-handed, corrupt, dictatorial policies. This is a leader in South America who has proudly sided with terrorist support groups, and Danny Glover gives him a big hug. If a Venezuelan citizen were to do the same with President Bush, \I am confident that Hugo would not respect that individual's right to

continued

★ ★ ★

free expression. Venezuelans have no right to free expression. Danny must be blinded by the trees in that forest.

Examine the agendas of the liberal party of peace. They clearly don't believe you and I are smart enough or capable enough to make our own choices in life. While conservatives "live and let live," the Left arrogantly thinks they know better than we do and will burden "We the People" with more government control until we are taxed to death. Watch them. Listen, pay attention, and blow whistles. Educate your family, neighbors, friends, coworkers, and hunting buddies about how dangerous such control is to the American Dream of individual pursuit of happiness. Throw off the shackles of government-run slavery, and stand up for individual independence. Enough is enough. Hey Hugo and Obama, leave me alone.

CHAPTER THREE

"A good man has got
to know his limitations."

★ ★ ★

Inspector Harry Callahan, *Dirty Harry*

So quoteth Sir Dirty Harry. It's always worth repeating and remembering. I am the first to admit that I am just a guitar player, but my life, family, home, and property are well under control—and totally managed and conducted in such a way to be meaningfully beneficial to our fellow man. We don't take, we give.

All it takes is hard work, genuine thoughtfulness, honesty, goodwill, decency, heart and soul, and some sacrifice. And pretty much everyone we know can say the same. We tend to hang with the best of the best.

Unfortunately, the same cannot be said of our government and a growing segment of the American people. Nobody we know considers "pimp," "whore," or "welfare brat" to be legitimate job descriptions. And therein lies the rift. The logic and common sense that guides the best, most productive Americans seems to be dwindling, and in the case of government, is in its death throes.

If America operated in the same manner as the Nugent family, the spiritual suicide wreaking havoc upon us would simply not exist. As the head of my household, I instinctively know what to do. If I were president of the United States, I would carry those instincts to the job at hand and in my first 100 minutes, I would do or have Congress do the following:

★ Instruct the U.S. Military warriors to do their job—win the global War on Terror right now and eliminate all threats from all sources by any means necessary.

★ Take appropriate oil and gas from Mexico and the Middle East as payment for all debts we are owed by them. End all foreign aid except in cases of extreme natural disasters.

★ Refuse to pay one red cent more to the UN until other nations pony up their fair share—but maintain membership just to keep our eyes on the bastards.

★ End diplomatic immunity.

★ Make English the mandatory American language.

★ End taxpayer healthcare for elected officials.

★ Refuse to fund healthcare for people who don't care about their health—those who choose to live lifestyles universally considered unhealthy (like intentionally ingesting poisons like tobacco to the point of cancer, drugs, alcohol to the point of cirrhosis, bad food to the point of obesity, etc.). No insurance provider is obligated to cover them until they begin caring about their health.

★ Eliminate all welfare except temporary benefits for military personnel and their families. Able-bodied Americans who refuse to work will be sent to Cuba, Mexico, England, and France.

★ Decree that the Second Amendment is a national concealed weapons permit for all non-felon Americans.

★ Eliminate all gun-free zones.

★ Announce globally that anyone who is armed who invades America through unauthorized ports of entry will be shot on sight.

★ Institute a national castle doctrine encouraging all American citizens to shoot-to-neutralize any and all unauthorized invaders of their homes and places of business. Give Presidential Medals of Freedom to those who do.

★ Create a $100,000 reward for any U.S. citizen who shoots and kills a paroled felon during an assault or home invasion.

★ Instruct all law enforcement officers, hospitals, government agencies, and the public to identify all illegal aliens and immediately deport them with the guarantee of severe prison time if ever caught illegally being here again.

★ Instruct the Attorney General to issue federal arrest warrants for any elected official who has created or supported a sanctuary city. Immediately suspend all federal dollars to these cities.

★ Demand that Mexico and all foreign countries release all American citizens from their jails immediately.

★ Make it legal for armed U.S. law enforcement officers with just cause to enter any nation—especially Mexico and Canada—in pursuit of any wanted criminal.

☆ Eliminate the IRS, institute a national sales tax, and force the U.S. government to live within a budget tied to actual revenues.

☆ Pass a constitutional amendment limiting citizen employment in federal, state, or local government jobs to 5 percent of the U.S. workforce.

☆ Eliminate any cushiness, comfort, or convenience in all jails and prisons. Make prisoners clean up America and plant trees.

☆ Remove and open all levees and dams in New Orleans and make people live on high ground. Give no more handouts to cover stupid mistakes of any kind.

☆ Eliminate the EPA, ESA, FEMA, OSHA, FDA, USDA, BATFE, NEA, TSA, and all affirmative action and racial quota systems.

☆ Fire every teacher whose students have bad posture or hygiene, who cannot properly speak, read, write, converse, or balance a checkbook by the fourth grade.

☆ In every school in America from the fourth grade on, show films on the Nazi concentration camps and the Japanese military atrocities, along with the unedited French documentary of September 11.

☆ In every school in America, make a mandatory core curriculum that covers all the topics we should never neglect.

☆ Offer courses in hands-on firearms and archery history and safety, basic hunting and fishing skills, and the basics of sustain-yield, habitat-carrying capacity, wildlife population dynamics, and respect for wildlife through utility in all schools.

☆ Teach hardcore auto mechanics, carpentry, plumbing, welding, general construction, farming, and ranching in grade school, high school, and college.

☆ Issue an Executive Order that the government cannot nor will not pay for treatment for any self-inflicted damage when citizens riot and destroy their own neighborhoods.

☆ Thoroughly prosecute Janet Reno, Louis Freeh, Bill Clinton, and all federal agents involved in the assault, murder, and illegal use of military force against the Waco Branch Davidians and at Ruby Ridge.

MANDATORY CORE CURRICULUM

Nutrition, personal hygiene, the U.S. Constitution, the Bill of Rights, slavery in America, the atrocities against the American Indians (including Wounded Knee, the Ghost Dance, the Trail of Tears, and the government slaughter of the American bison), the Bataan Death March, the Rape of Nanking, the Nazi regime, Communism, dictators (including Stalin, Lenin, Pol Pot, Idi Amin, Kim Jong II, Charles Taylor, Mugabe, and Nelson Mandela), the KKK, the Black Panthers, the Zodiak Killer, the amount of chemicals and poisonous preservatives, pesticides, fire retardants, and dangerous carcinogens used in the production of our foods, homes, clothing, carpets, bedding, soaps, shampoos, deodorants, automobiles, tires, air fresheners, detergents, fabric softeners, and children's toys, the Tulsa race riot of 1921, the Detroit riots of 1967, the Watts riots of 1965, and the Rodney King riots.

★ Make it illegal to sue any business simply for the criminal misuse of their legal product.
★ Criminally prosecute and sue any judge or prosecutor who knowingly interferes with evidence in any trial.
★ Permanently eliminate the death tax.
★ Permanently eliminate capitol gains tax.
★ Eliminate all gun registration records.
★ Rescind the ban on new citizen machinegun ownership.
★ Require vehicles registration only one time per ownership.
★ Hold judges, prosecutors, and attorneys accountable for the crimes of criminals they facilitated being released, paroled, and plea-bargained.

★ Encourage all states to expeditiously execute all convicted child molesters.

★ Instruct states to charge parents of children who have blubber or bad hygiene with child neglect.

★ Wage a real war on drugs, including implementing the death penalty for first-time meth, crack, heroin, and opium dealing.

★ Legalize hemp.

★ Encourage states to make drinking and driving a felony with two strikes equating to a life sentence crime.

★ Make two years of service in the military mandatory for all Americans upon graduation from high school.

★ Make it policy that law enforcement can disable any evading vehicle by any means necessary.

★ Treat attempted murder the same as murder, giving no breaks just because the perpetrator missed vital organs.

★ Call on Michael Moore to return his documentary award till he makes a documentary.

★ Honor Chesty Puller as a great American war hero.

★ Make killing game animals by government hunters illegal. Make game animals available to America's licensed hunters wherever surpluses are found, including in national, federal, and state parks and monuments.

★ Encourage states to eliminate shooting hour and minimum age restrictions for hunting and fishing.

★ Legalize Sunday hunting nationwide.

★ Legalize dove hunting wherever doves are found.

★ Eliminate the requirement to use plugs, limiting shots at doves and waterfowl.

★ Encourage the open drilling, exploration, and cultivation of gas, oil, coal, shale, sugar cane, and prairie grass ethanol, bio fuel, wind, solar, hydro, nuclear, waste, and any and all alternative energy sources in the United States with the goal of becoming energy independent ASAP.

And then I would have breakfast.

SOULLESS IN AMERICA

What is this ugly, dehumanizing condition of soullessness in America that I have the audacity to point out? Look around yourself. It exists, and is killing this once great nation. The scramble to hide from these embarrassing conditions is at the root of the pandemic of apathy that is metastasizing in the social landscape of my beloved America. The emperor has no clothes indeed.

God gave man a soul; a powerful, instinctual moral and intellectual True North compass that completely differentiates us from all other living creatures. Animals stomp, kill, and eat each other, even their own, in a primal instinct to survive. Man has the power of reason, calculation, dreaming, and a thought process to *choose* to do good, not just for himself, but for the predictable benefit of family, fellow man, and the good earth. Respecting the gift of life and the power of responsible choice, man can pursue complete happiness while being a positive force for allthings. When man seeks to benefit from wrong choices, at the expense of others and the environment, he has lost his soul. His misdeeds will eventually catch up with him.

In the meantime, the majority of good people will be forced to perform damage control for bad people's failure in quality control. In this feeble and pathetic condition of soullessness, all mankind should fight and strive to banish those who so callously disregard the good of others. Apathy shows no soul.

It is soulless to purchase blingbling, tobacco, booze, and excess, then claim that you can't afford a sandwich and an apple for your kid's school lunch. Let the government waste some more tax dollars on your cruel soullessness.

It is soulless to forbid a good citizen the right to carry a gun for self-protection while you dare to actually charge that citizen (subject) to pay for your armed security detail.

It proves you have no soul when you quote Mao Tse Tung that you will "take those profits…" from an American corporation and redistribute it to your blingbling infested, irresponsible constituents, Obama.

Your soul is clearly gone if you walk past numerous "help wanted" signs on the way to pick up your welfare check—understand, Hillary?

Your soul, God's greatest gift to you, has rotted away if you make meth, sell meth, use meth, or know anyone who does and you do nothing to put an end to it. Your sheeplike soullessness is complicity.

To partake in a court system that continually paroles and plea bargains child molesters back into America's neighborhoods is as soulless as it gets.

Supporting the obscene practice of taxing families' after-tax savings upon death proves you have no soul.

To intentionally poison yourself with tobacco, alcohol, drugs, and enough junk food to beach a sperm whale, then expect health care from others is an ugly, soulless condition.

To provide billions and billions of dollars for the lie of (conduct driven) AIDS research while U.S. Military heroes go without is both soulless and foolish.

For any person to wake up in America and plan a day of crime against fellow Americans is criminally soulless.

For a government to reward slovenly, irresponsible behavior with a check actually encourages soullessness.

The depth of soullessness necessary to believe that animals have the same rights as human beings is beyond measure.

For a government to turn its back on the ever-increasing invasion coming across our borders is braindead, suicidal, and soulless.

A REASONABLE MAN

Must I repeat yet again that I am just a guitar player? Do I really have to explain the lyrics to Wango Tango, again? Will someone please step up with some meaningful, constructive critique of substance of my wonderful, wild life? Please! My flaws are many, but nobody has said a word about them. All I hear is transparent squawking about nothing. Does the fact that 1 + 1 = 2 really confuse that many people? Can ineptness truly be so celebrated that Obama qualifies as an American presidential candidate? Are there that many stupid Americans amongst us? Are pigs flying yet?

Here it is in nutshell; I've got life nailed. Damn near perfected. And I'm not all that clever. With all due respect, I don't need anybody to give me jack squat. Logic and excellence continue to drive my American Dream, and affirmative action would be an insult in any way, shape, or form. I have a ringing in my ears and it sounds like this: I ask not what my country can do for me, but rather, I demand that I do all I can for my country. Call me wild, but rugged individualism still turns me on. Don't Ted on me.

In the final, honest analysis, you must admit that a neighborhood, even a nation, is the sum of all its parts, and the very condition of those parts will determine whether quality of life comes from the government, or rather, from the soul of the people. I know the answer like a ring of the bell. 1 + 1 does indeed equal 2, my sweet Penelope, no matter how irritating that doggone *dos* digit may be. Get over it. It looks like this:

All members of the Nugent household are rather productive and clearly benefit one another, our communities, and this great nation. We pay way more than our fair share of taxes and we are confident that all

continued

things Nugent reside squarely in the asset column of life. We demand excellence of ourselves for our country. Call us crazy, but we truly give a damn.

The Nugent household has never had any invaders. No unauthorized persons have ever made it through our borders, or for that matter, ever even attempted it. We give off, shall we say, a *vibe* that such criminal activity has, shall we say, *consequences.* I, the lowly guitar player, have succeeded in securing my borders. Call me an extremist, please.

There is no crime in the Nugent house. None. No crime in the Nugent family. No wasted tax dollars needed for increased security, parole officers, psychologists, court appointed anything or anybody, and no new prisons need to be built on our behalf. The Nugent cops are not outgunned and don't need any special training. We have total, complete, and perfect gun control. Logic, goodwill, and decency are all working hand in hand to keep us on the straight and narrow, thank you. How *do* we do it? Call us weird.

We all woke up early again today. Some strange fire keeps burning in our guts, driving us to be productive, to work hard before we play hard. Not a single welfare check has ever been fondled by a Nugent. We simply do not believe in it.

We have flawless gun control. Literally flawless.

Do not throw any more wasted tax dollars at the Nugent's education. We teach each other to read, write, and speak properly and how to balance a checkbook, thank you. It's almost miraculous considering the modern American education fiasco.

Our gas bills and electric bills are insane like everyone else's, but we do use our heads and conserve energy at every opportunity. We use less so it costs less. We are environmentally conscientious; we have

continued

always recycled and do our damnedest to wisely use everything and waste nothing. We treat our pets humanely and with utmost care, and our precious wildlife is balanced and flourishing on our sacred wild ground. Then, of course, there are all those trees we plant each spring. I wonder how many Sting planted this year?

Recently, we helped some more wounded warriors of the U.S. Military, delivered a few tons of venison to homeless shelters and soup kitchens, and took a dying young man on his last hunt. No need for government programs here. We know exactly what to do and we do it better.

And global warming? Please. We are looking forward to getting one of those increased polar bear hunting permits from the Inuit's this year in order to procure a beautiful white bear rug to put in front of the fireplace where we burn logs for heat, harvested from the huge forest of trees we have been planting for more than thirty-five years. We will celebrate our bear steaks with a nice, big salad from the increased produce derived from the lengthened growing seasons due to the natural warming cycle we just so happen to be in. We have invited Al Gore over to the BBQ but haven't heard from him yet.

Health care? We practice health care by actually caring about our health. That pesky quality control weirdness at it again. Who *do* we think we are?

A thinking soul would at this juncture have to ask himself; if a goofy Motor City Madman guitar player can do all this, why would I need Obama to hold my hand or provide for me? Write this down: ***you don't***.

Your soul is gone if you board your private jet on the way to preach to others that they must use less energy.

For an American to have to push "1 for English" is a soulless, downward spiral from the American Way.

To force unarmed police cadets into the streets of Manhatten is soulless, Mayor Bloomburg.

Suing the manufacturer of a legal product when illegally misused by criminals is soulless.

To claim that war is not the answer after 3,000 Americans were murdered by foreign invaders is soulless.

You would have to abandon your soul to spend more than you earn.

Knowing that a healthy diet and ample exercise is the basic recipe for good health, but still allowing blubber to destroy your life anyway is embarrassingly soulless, and a surefire ticket to a painful, agonizing, unhappy life and an early grave.

Reading the warning signs of cancer on the package of a product, and then actually purchasing and using that product is soulless and expensive for everyone.

For a government agency to pull elderly, wheelchair-bound Americans out of line at the airport for x-ray screening is soulless and counterproductive.

To forbid American citizens the right to harvest our natural resources on our lands, but then hire others to do so with our tax dollars is insanely soulless.

Overall, it is the abandonment of common sense, logic, and self-evident truth, which is adhered to by the majority of good, conscientious, productive Americans that has brought about this incredibly stupid suicide of the American soul. People actually feel comfortable making these chimplike choices, and those of us who know better must galvanize everyone to stand up and put pressure on those ruining things for us all. Indecent behavior and choices must be demonized and condemned; those guilty must be ostracized from our society. We respect all pursuits of happiness unless that pursuit forces the costs upon others. The Declaration of Independence is the celebration of the soul of man. Celebrate soulful independence.

CHAPTER FOUR

POLITICS AND RELIGION

"I believe in the dream. I believe in you.
If you believe in me, ya know just what to do."

★ ★ ★

"CumNGityaSum-O-This,"
Craveman, 2002

There is an age-old piece of advice that claims that we should never discuss religion or politics with our friends. That advice is stone-cold, dead wrong.

Religion and politics drive many of the cultural and social decisions we make on a daily basis as countries, societies, and individuals. To not discuss these important topics and issues with your family, friends—and enemies—is to ignore the very conditions that impact our lives.

The biggest curse affecting America today is apathy, which is why I don't wait for these conversations to begin. Around my campfire, we turn up the heat on these pivotal issues so as to face down the beast before it gets too threatening. Initiating such dialogue is the cure for the pain caused by looking at the wart-riddled, naked emperor, for surely, he has no clothes.

It doesn't matter to me what you believe or do not believe regarding religion or politics. As an American, it's your choice and First Amendment right to exercise your individual religious and political beliefs. Freedom of speech, freedom to assemble, and religious freedom are the cornerstone of this experiment in self-government. If you do not have these most basic human rights, you live in a slave state like Mexico. I say kill tyrants, slave drivers, and dictators. I'm going to smoke a Cuban cigar when Commie Castro finally crawls into a rat-infested hole and dies. Do the world a favor, Fidel, and blow your human rights-violating brains out. On second thought, die a slow and painful death. You deserve it.

> ★
>
> **Do the world a favor, Fidel, and blow your human rights-violating brains out.**

Divergent opinions and beliefs should not only be tolerated in America, but should be encouraged and celebrated regardless of which political or religious camp you have pitched your tent in. You might not agree with me, or I with you, but the history of America is one where disagreement has been as important as agreement—maybe more.

Celebrate divergent thoughts and beliefs and then go like a mad, howling wolf into the not-so-mean streets of America to hunt down your unique American Dream. Call me if you need help. I'm real good at busting down barriers and making bureaucratic idiots squirm in a puddle of confusion and fright. I'm a free man, it's my job, and I like it.

Winston Churchill once said that democracy is the worst form of government on earth, but compared to the rest, it was the best. That's wisdom, folks. Winston was one of my biggest fans.

Politically, I'm no fan of big government, which, for the last forty years has meant the Democratic Party, though the Republican Party hasn't been any better of late. Big government has caused incalculable harm to Americans and America. It wrecks lives, communities, and businesses. Should we make the mistake of putting the Democratic Party back in power in the fall of 2008, they will tax us more but give us much less. Underline that last sentence and then come back to it in four years if we elect the Democratic Party. Big government fails at everything and it will continue to fail. It is designed to be unaccountable. It is the model of inefficiency, complacency, waste, and excuse-making. It is about more control, not about more freedom. Less government is real progressive reform. The free market rocks. We need to roll.

The free market rocks. We need to roll.

We have politicians representing us, not statesmen. Make no mistake; there is a huge chasm between the two. A statesman is an elected individual who sees beyond the years and votes and does what is best for America and future generations of Americans, not what is best for a demographic constituency, him or herself, or select lobbyists. Our Founding Fathers were statesmen. They were men of high integrity, incredible wisdom, unquestionable love of country, and a shared common vision of creating a republic that would last through the ages. They saw beyond their own lives when they wrote and signed the Declaration of Independence and our mighty, unprecedented U.S. Constitution. In fact, they put their very lives and fortunes at risk to give birth to our fledgling republic that, for the first time in history, would demand freedom and liberty. The incredible bravery of these statesmen must never be forgotten by anyone who treasures freedom. What these brave men did by giving birth to America may very well be mankind's most shining achievement. We may have a few statesmen left, but none come to mind at the moment. They are that rare.

There will be politicians who claim to be statesmen, but they are not. They are professional bureaucrats interested in one thing: sustaining and growing the political bureaucracy. In doing so, these professional punk politicians are pissing on the vision, bravery, and sacrifice of our Founding Fathers. These professional politicians are sucking the very life out of America. We are trillions of dollars in debt because of insane entitlement programs—such as Medicare and Social Security—that professional bureaucrats created to get re-elected and increase their control over us. The size of these entitlement programs has exploded into a financial blob that is unsustainable unless taxes are even *further increased* or the promised benefits slashed to almost nothing. May the professional punk politicians be damned.

> ⋆
>
> **I'm real good at busting down barriers and making bureaucratic idiots squirm in a puddle of confusion and fright.**

If you are pissed off about where you see the country going, remember this: you are to blame. Terminal apathy runs amok even amongst those who often squawk the loudest, because you're squawking at the wrong people. Your own congressman and senators have blown it for the simple reason that so many Americans have outright failed to give their elected employees any direction whatsoever. Read that again. There isn't an elected official in America that doesn't know what the Nugent family stands for and expects from our political employees. I'm such an extremist that I have the audacity to actually communicate regularly with my employees, politely demanding what I expect from them. I actually participate in this glorious experiment in self-government. I am a wildman.

Do not be manipulated by smooth-talking political punks into voting for them. These bureaucratic punks do not have your best interests at heart by any stretch of the imagination. They care about nothing other than getting re-elected and will do or say whatever it takes for you to vote for them—including selling this country down the toilet. They are master manipulators and liars. Do not trust any of them. My cynicism and skepticism of these punks has never been

> ━━━ ☆ ━━━
> **Despite politicians' stunning failure to do their jobs, Americans continue to re-elect the very professional political punks who are ruining our country.**
> ━━━━━━━━

higher. Yours should be too. Polls indicate that no one trusts these windbag, self-serving bureaucrats. Polls also indicate that congressmen and senators continually score at the very bottom of the trust barrel. Even shady used car salesmen score higher than our professional political punks. And our congressmen and senators are the ones to blame for this mess. Term limits happen when you enter the voting booth. Get angry. Be defiant. Let's toss out every last one of them. Let's clean house. Literally.

Despite politicians' stunning failure to do their jobs, Americans continue to re-elect the very professional political punks who are ruining our country. Amazingly, roughly 95 percent of all incumbent congressmen and senators are re-elected. It is so rare for an incumbent to be defeated that when it does happen, it makes national news.

Our incumbent politicians spend incredible amounts of time fundraising for the next election. In 2004, the average amount of money spent by incumbent congressmen over his or her challenger was

$700,000. In the Senate, the typical senator outspent his or her challenger by four million dollars. And we have the audacity to believe this is a government of the people, by the people, and for the people? Sorry, Abe, but what we have here is a complete and total klsterphunk that even the mob would be in awe of. Maybe the mob is running the joint.

Here's a common-sense idea born of freedom and liberty that our professional politicians will surely scoff at, and which rank and file Americans will surely support: every new law passed by Congress must eliminate five other laws previously passed. This common-sense, freedom, and liberty idea would restore some dignity and honor to an institution that is currently viewed by the majority of Americans as a corrupt, self-serving den of liars, manipulators, cheats, and thieves. Republicans and Democrats are both guilty as charged. In the not-so-distant past, these people would have been tarred and feathered.

⭐

Lapel pins may be trendy and cute, but they don't fix anything.

We shouldn't be guided by our feelings in these matters. Feelings be damned. In matters of public policy, rational, objective reasoning smothered in facts should be our guiding light. I think long and hard about problems and then get after solving them by working to correct them. Who doesn't? Repeat after me: there is no Plan B. See a problem and fix it. Caring about a problem doesn't solve a damn thing. Activism, sweat equity, and hard work solve problems. Period. Liberals care about problems; conservatives fix problems. Ask yourself this basic question: if I had a problem, would I rather have a group of liberals or conservatives help me solve it? Welcome to the Home of the Conservative Activists.

Don't ever make the mistake of believing I'm a shill for the Republican Party. I'm a rugged, independent son-of-a-bitch who makes up my own mind based on pragmatism, facts, truth, logic, common sense, and unlimited historical evidence. Granted, the Republican Party is a damn sight better than the Democratic Party, but I am much more disgusted with the Republican Party than I am the Democratic Party simply because I expect better from Republicans. I know what the Democratic Party is going to do—tax more and spend more. The Republican Party, however, has lost its conservative soul on many important issues. The Republicans on Capitol Hill have walked away from Ronald Reagan's legacy and probably make paper airplanes out of old copies of the 1994 Contract with America. I doubt many of the Republican congressmen have even read the Contract with America. Why isn't there a Contract with America II? Who the hell is in charge in D.C.? If this is what the Republican Party calls conservative leadership and principles, they had better get used to saying President Obama.

> ☆
>
> **I may not agree with you, but I respect your right to say and believe it.**

I'm well aware that our constitution was written to protect the rights and privileges of those holding the minority opinion. Though the majority rules, attempting to silence those with a minority viewpoint cuts against the grain of a free and democratic society. Again, I may not agree with you, but I respect your right to say and believe it. I even support allowing the animal rights crowd to spew their intellectually bankrupt and scientifically void ideologies. Interestingly, while liberals are supposedly the vanguards and stalwarts of free speech, they are the ones who try to shout down and silence conservative speakers. Liberals are the ones who throw pies in the faces of conservative speakers on college campuses—because when you have lost the intellectual debate, the only thing left is to throw pies and shout and scream. However, I prefer to advance my thoughts and opinions in the arena of ideas where facts vanquish emotionalism. If you can best me in the arena of ideas, I will tip my hat to you. But I would pack a lunch if you want to take me on. Bring your A game. My truth/logic crowbar does not gently weep.

RELIGION

Let's shift gears to religion. I believe that the ultimate question of mankind has always been: is there a God—an architect of the universe—a supreme being? There are only two answers to this question: yes or no. Maybe is not an answer. And no one knows for sure. Only death unlocks that mystery, but unfortunately, only for the dead guy, and he ain't talking.

Some people believe science can unlock all of the mysteries of the universe. I don't think so. I've heard a lot of hypothesizing and scientific gobblygook, but Darwin doesn't do it for me. If Darwin was right, Mike Tyson would have evolved. Others have an unwavering belief in God, but even Thomas and Christ's other disciples had their moments of doubt and they lived with the guy. From a religious perspective, as far as I am concerned, you can stand on your head in the corner and claim to have deeply religious experiences with God. Rock on. In America you have that religious freedom and we should all be very drunk on it and exercise it as our religious souls see fit. Our Founding Fathers recognized that religious freedom is pivotal to free societies. As founding father and redcoat-slayer George Washington stated, "It is impossible to rightly govern a nation without God and the Bible." Let's see, where have we heard God, Guns, & Rock 'n' Roll before?

> I am not an American who takes a shine to being pushed.

If you are an agnostic or atheist, you have that right and I respect your decision. No American should ever try to force another American to believe in something. Sincere persuasion should always be welcome, but that's different from coercion. That is religious bigotry and intolerance, and freedom does not work that way. I encourage open discussion and dialogue on what people believe or do not believe, but there is a fine line between discussing your beliefs and pushing them on the rest of us. Don't cross that line with me. I am not an American who takes a shine to being pushed.

Similarly, atheists and agnostics should respect the religious decisions and beliefs of religious people. To mock the religious beliefs of others is also intolerant, disrespectful, and rude. According to a U.S. Religious Landscape survey that I read today, 92 percent of Americans believe in God or a supreme being. There is room for polite debate and disagreement between atheists and religious people. I enjoy a spirited debate much more than the next guy, but mocking a group of people ultimately reduces an argument to that of petty name calling and bickering. There is no big bang in that.

I am a huge fan of science, intellectual stimuli, challenge, and objective reasoning. Science has blazed the trails that have improved our health, taken us to the moon, created the world-wide information sharing forum, and enabled us to drop precision-guided laser bombs literally on the heads of terrorist assholes. Scientific advances and discoveries in the not-so-distant future will shock us in a mostly positive manner. Through science we will continue to unlock the mysteries of the

> ☆
>
> **"Science without religion is lame. Religion without science is blind."**
> **—Albert Einstein**

universe while creating new technologies that will improve our lives— and the key to gaining them is more science, more technology, and more research. I prefer what Albert Einstein had to say about the matter of religion and science, "Science without religion is lame. Religion without science is blind."

Religion is different than being religious. Religions are man-made institutions. Being religious is not a "group think" exercise unless you wear purple robes and commit mass suicide in the hopes of hopping on the tail of a comet. By the way, just how much Grateful Dead music and LSD does it take to believe you can hop on the tail of a comet?

Associating with others who share similar religious beliefs is one thing, but in the end it is between you and your creator. No cash changing hands at the time of your death is going to purchase you a first-class ticket into heaven. There is no cash in heaven, no caste system, and no politics.

I get the concept of fellowship. I'm sure that associating on Sunday morning and periodically throughout the week with others who are on the same spiritual journey helps to fortify, bolster, and strengthen your faith. If that's you, more fellowship power to you.

I fail to understand the magnificent and opulent churches, mosques, and synagogues that I see. From a Christian perspective, I have to wonder what Jesus would do with all that money being spent to build grandiose houses of worship. I don't get it. I am highly suspicious of religions based on such outrageous materialism. Jesus preached in gardens, on mountain sides, and on the sides of roads. The good work the religious could do for the poor with all that money being used to build lavish churches, mosques, and synagogues would be tremendous. I think it was Gandhi who once said (and I'm paraphrasing) that he liked this Jesus guy, but he didn't understand Christians. Me, too.

> ☆
>
> **I think it was Gandhi who once said (and I'm paraphrasing) that he liked this Jesus guy, but he didn't understand Christians. Me, too.**

I stay out of big, opulent churches because they remind me more of cash-strapped businesses, or spiritless "faith for sale" scams than houses of worship. If you feel comfortable with hundreds or thousands of other Christians on a Sunday morning, go and get some of it. There is plenty to be had. As for me, I prefer to sit quietly in forests and fens, climb trees in the woods, stay grounded on the ground, and take natural, soul-cleansing, predatory stalks in His gardens while watching the sun peek over the horizon and into my soul. *And He walks with me, and*

He talks with me. In-a-gadda-da-vida, baby. I will be more than happy to get you some venison.

Most of the Christians I have met are fine, decent, and honorable people of goodwill. They are humble and hard-working family people who go about their good lives quietly. They are not demanding, are not bloodsuckers, and believe in helping those who want to help themselves. They give their time and donate their money much more than most and they expect no praise or anything else in return. They are condemned, lampooned, scorned, and made fun of on television, on the radio, and by so-called comedians for their beliefs, yet you rarely hear one of them complain. These are good people, the bedrock of America.

Christian institutions and customs have been under increasing attacks for at least the last decade. Television stations rarely run spots during Christmas time wishing their viewers a Merry Christmas. Many of us now wish each other the bland "Season's Greetings" or "Happy Holidays." Some public school concerts no longer include Christmas songs. They have been replaced with songs about winter, even though Christmas is a national holiday celebrating the birth of Christ—for

> ★
>
> **Why should the majority have their values trampled upon to appease a weirdo?**

which they will certainly take the time off. Afraid of their own shadows, some denial-entrenched public school administrators have even banned Christmas trees. The American Civil Liberties Union (ACLU) has forced city parks and court houses to remove Ten Commandments monuments and displays. Our courts rule for the ACLU because of "separation of church and state" though this concept is not mentioned in our constitution. If one overly sensitive person is offended while thousands are affirmed, why should the majority have their values trampled upon to appease a weirdo?

This is no longer the America I grew up in. The minority now dictates policy to the majority. Do not be surprised if the "In God We Trust" motto is soon removed from our money. The culture war against Christianity is raging. Onward, Christian culture soldiers. Never give up fighting for your values.

Christians get angry when they hear about monuments of the Ten Commandments being removed from their city parks, but I suspect 99 percent of Christians couldn't list the Ten Commandments if their eternal salvation depended on it. Their faith is an inch deep and a mile wide. This isn't entirely their fault. In an effort to build a bigger, opulent tent to attract a larger congregation and more money, some church services sound more like new-age, self-help conventions

> ⭐
> **This is no longer
> the America
> I grew up in.**

than meetings to explore the scriptures containing the gospel of Christ. I recently saw a very popular television preacher who has a bestseller out on how to build a better you. I watched for a few minutes. I don't think I heard the guy mutter Christ's name once. Interesting. I'm not implying the gentleman is not a man of God, only that I did not hear him evoke Christ's name while I was watching. I am convinced he did not do so in order to avoid scaring a certain type of people away. I turned the channel.

I can't offer you my thoughts on Buddhists, Hindus, and others because I know zip about their faith and beliefs. I mean no disrespect, but I'm just not interested in learning about these faiths. I have other more productive and interesting ways to spend my time than exploring other world religions. If I'm interested, I'll ask.

Because of September 11, we have all been exposed to the ugly underbelly of the Muslim faith. Killing people or dying in the name of Allah is beyond bizarre to anyone with a love of mankind and respect for the sanctity of life. Blowing yourself up to please your god is difficult for the Western mind to process. Western values and mores are polar opposite those held by Muslims who worship death in return for forty or so virgins in the afterlife. That's some weird voodoo there, Achmed. If they worship death and want to bring harm to America or our friends and allies, we should give them death they could have never imagined. I support a rain of fire. We must do whatever is necessary to protect America and western culture. We are in a religious-culture war with radical Muslims who want to destroy our way of life. Let us grind our enemies underfoot. Let there be much wailing and gnashing of teeth. The world should not stay bound and gagged.

Democracies must never roll over to religious beliefs. If a Muslim woman wants to wear a total head scarf for her driver's license photo, then she gets no driver's license. Period. Amazingly, the Archbishop of Canterbury recently advocated that England adopt parts of Sharia, the Islamic law that is based on Muslim religious doctrine. The Archbishop should be excommunicated for advocating this idiotic position that would weaken the principles of democracy. In much of the Muslim world, the Archbishop's head would be severed for his beliefs.

I thought it would be interesting and amusing to play a word association game with myself. This will provide you with a few of my basic political, social, and religious beliefs.

BIG BANG THEORY: 500 S&W MAGNUM

Sin: Unloaded guns, dull knives

Democrats: Socialist slave masters

Republicans: Where are they?

Fast food: Mallards, woodcock, doves

continued

Rock and Roll: Irreverent, defiant, uninhibited, explosive, greasy, outrageous, boisterous, obnoxious, loud sexjuiceluvsongs

Heroes: Rosa Parks, Paul Tibbets, Fred Bear, Dirty Harry

Death penalty: Support at the scene of the crime. Dial 9-1-1 for a dustpan and a broom

Gay marriage: Disagree with unless both women are gorgeous

Black: Is beautiful. James Brown, Chuck Berry, Albert Collins, Ted Nugent

White: People who can't dance, cue balls, don't fire until you see the whites of their eyes.

Televangelists: Religious pimps

Alcohol: Legalized poison

Gay Rights: I have always supported Enola Gay rights

America: Last best place

Music: Universal primal scream of African origin

Good: Sheriff Joe Arpaio, Glenn Beck, John Lott, NRA, U.S. Military, gunpowder, venison

Bad: Michael Moore, Al Not-so-Sharpton, Jesse Jackass, United Nations, socialists

Ugly: Death tax, bloodsuckers, current condition of much of Africa

Smoking: BBQ pork, melting gun barrels

Jesus Christ: The first freedom lover; the alpha and omega

American Dream: Pursuit of excellence in all endeavors

Leadership: Chesty Puller, George Patton, Ronald Reagan, Billy Graham

Memory: Remember the Alamo!

continued

✯ ✯ ✯

Evil: Nazis, KKK, racists and apathy

Bored: Goal of SnapOn drills

Nickname: Uncle Ted, the Nuge, Reverend Theodocious Atrocious, The WhackMaster, but "Hey Asshole!" gets my attention

Integrity: Not for sale at any price

Humor: Too many people are looking for ways to be offended instead of laughing at obvious jokes. Damn shame. I'm the new Lenny Bruce, Sam Kinison, and Richard Pryor rolled into one.

Political correctness: Brain dead

Love: Shemane, family, dogs, freedom

Forgiveness: I ask for it daily

Patience: Bowhunting, setting rocks on fire

Politics and religion are critically important issues. Open up a dialogue with your family, friends, neighbors, and co-workers regarding these two pivotal topics. Be polite, respectful and willing to learn, but be prepared to do a little teaching of your own. Hold your ground. Discussions and debates are healthy and wise. Don't forget to pack a healthy sense of humor and never give up.

CHAPTER FIVE

**"I'm American made, American born,
from my hands my flag will not
be torn away. No way."**

★ ★ ★

"RawDogs & WarHogs,"
Craveman, 2002

A wise man once said that if you want peace, prepare for war. If you would be so kind as to indulge Gunny Sgt. Nuge briefly while I slightly modify this otherwise brilliant statement: If you truly want peace, give the assholes of the world a 2,000-pound, laser-guided bomb for lunch. Lasting peace can only be achieved through the application of relentless and superior fire power. No Rodney King, we cannot all just get along.

Good people are nearly fed up with negative, dangerous bastards like you, and I say it's time to drop the proverbial hammer. Straighten up, or deal with our righteous wrath. No more tolerance for evil choices. I wage war against evil in my life, and I say it's about time America goes full on crush. Each morning I bow down on bended knee in reverence to the Almighty and offer a humble prayer for good bombing weather. Let us all pray for good bombing weather. The history of man is one of warfare, not peace. Read that again. Now that may upset the leftover delusional peaceniks out there, but a quick study of history will tell you that warfare is mankind's modus operandi; always has been, always will be. This is reality and I deal in reality, not utopian superlatives. Doped up, logic-challenged peaceniks and their foggy ideologies are dangerous. "Give peace a chance" will get you killed. John Lennon was wrong. Imagine that.

> ⋆
>
> **Lasting peace can only be achieved through the application of relentless and superior fire power. No Rodney King, we cannot all just get along.**

AMERICAN HATERS

I recently watched a gaggle of tie-dyed, stuttering, glazy-eyed, Jerry Garcia-wannabes feebly attempting to articulate their hatred for war and warriors on TV, and just felt sorry for them.

Their pathetic cluelessness was on display when they condemned U.S. Military heroes while exercising the uniquely American freedoms

provided and protected by those heroes. And small wonder—if you fry
your brain enough with chemicals and poisons, you get to imagine anything as long as it makes you feel good and self-righteous.

Take the People's Republic of Berkley for example. Since the 1960s,
Berkley has been a hotbed of
liberal toxicity, so it should
come as no surprise that there
is an effort within that blinded
city to shut down the U.S.
Marines Corps recruiting
office—never mind that the
Marines are the very people
who have fought and died for
these Berkley hippies' First
Amendment-guaranteed rights
to express their LSD-fueled
ideology. This inconsistency will not surprise clear-thinking Americans
who don't sprinkle marijuana in their brownies and read Karl Marx for
inspiration.

> There are evil, maniacal people
> and governments in the world who
> would love nothing more than to
> see America brought to her knees
> and defeated. Amazingly, there are
> left-wing nutjobs in this country
> who would also rejoice over
> America being defeated.

As is typical of left-wing ideologues, the socialist hippies in Berkley
detest divergent political opinions and attitudes. Their transparency is
intellectually bankrupt, though I must admit amusing. Hippies generally hate the military, cops, me, common sense, conservatives, rugged
individuals, entrepreneurs, and anyone else who does not subscribe to
their Mao Tse Tung ideology. They also smell bad—it's what you get
when you drop out of Personal Hygiene 101. I suppose Michael Moore
has got to have followers like him, though. The U.S. Marine Corps has
a lengthy record of heroism, bravery, and patriotism. These Devil
Dogs—the world's largest and best trained gun club—proudly fight and
kill anyone who would take our freedoms away and subject us to tyranny. The decision to deny a recruitment office to these great warriors in

Berkley must surely have been made in a haze of pot smoke while genuflecting at the "we the sheeple" altar of denial. These punks are unwor-
thy to stand in Chesty Puller's shadow.

I support military conscription for the anti-freedom vandals who destroy military recruiting offices. Send them straight to the front lines of the global war on terror where they can be properly introduced to an enemy who will savagely behead them in a flash if given the opportunity. Even the most avowed anti-military hippie will start shooting back once the bullets start whizzing by their heads. Shooting back would do them some good. Bathing, too.

> ☆
>
> **These punks are unworthy to stand in Chesty Puller's shadow.**

TOTAL WARFARE

If we commit our brave young men and women to combat, we should do so only if we will commit to total, overwhelming, victorious warfare. I want to see acres and acres of smoking piles of rubble and dust—not a single pane of enemy glass should remain unbroken. And then we should drop even more bombs on the rubble to ensure that all living things are vaporized, and then hose down the entire area with the most potent weed killer we have. That's my kind of rock 'n' roll shock 'n' awe. Make the rubble bounce—completely wreck the joint.

Regrettably, I did not serve in the military upon graduation from high school. For that I am truly sorry. I did not volunteer. Two painful, failed dynamics were at play in my life in 1967 that guaranteed I would be hopelessly ill-equipped to do the right thing. You see, I graduated from a failed U.S. education system that in many ways made me what I was by the age of eighteen.

I had not learned a thing about how America was born by waging war against the British slave drivers to declare our "We the People" independence from tyrants once and for all. I was also never taught a lick about The Indian Wars, the U.S. Civil War, WWI or WWII, or a place called Vietnam. Nothing about communism was taught in any classroom that I attended for twelve years. I don't recall any lessons with any mention of the precepts of good over evil. I could not have told you who Stalin, Lennon, or Pol Pot were. Insane but true. Hell, I couldn't balance a checkbook.

Added to this life hidden from any information about the historical necessity of waging war against evil, was the fact that my father, like the vast majority of World War II and Korean War heroes, never uttered a word about his military service or the war to end all wars. I suppose the Greatest Generation wished to move forward and escape the horrible memories of this tragic, painful event in their lives, having held their dying, mutilated American BloodBrothers in their young arms. The sacrifices were too burdensome to bring forth, I am sure.

> ★
>
> **If you fry your brain enough with chemicals and poisons, you get to imagine anything as long as it makes you feel good and self-righteous.**

This is perfectly understandable. But it is also terribly irresponsible, for to hide such life and death, discomforting information from the next generation is to assure a condition of abject, total, unprepared helplessness when the inevitable encounter with evil arises that every generation will indeed have to face.

I am convinced that my ignorance about good over evil is the exact same self-imposed ignorance that ultimately made America so vulnerable to the incremental assaults upon us that culminated with the September 11, 2001 attacks.

I admit to self-imposed, near-total insulation from worldly truth and the reality of Vietnam or even the landing on the moon. My American rock 'n' roll dream kept me in the world of killer music and on the road for 300 or more days a year. As an eighteen-year-old kid, I never read a newspaper. There was no CNN or FOX News to turn on in the hotel room. There were no cell phones or Internet. I didn't receive mail, much less e-mail. My parents usually didn't even know where I was. Waking up in a different town each day in pursuit of my musical dream insulated me from not only Vietnam, but my family and even my cherished outdoor lifestyle to a great degree. There were a few years in the late 1960s that I hunted only a few days each fall. There was literally no time in between touring, practicing, recording, my nonstop media jihad, and getting very little sleep. I didn't know if I was coming or going. I literally did not have a home of my own or an apartment. I slept on many a floor. I didn't know anything, including how I got paid or even if I got paid for my music. I was that young and naïve. This is no excuse for my woeful and deep disconnect from the critical events of the world—and I don't offer it as one—but it is the truth.

There have been many prices I have paid to be a traveling musician, but the worst consequence was that I did not serve my country in the military. Truth be told, I didn't begin to start becoming aware, paying attention, and reading about current events until the Iranian hostage crisis in 1979. That deeply angered me and I spoke out vociferously on radio, television, and newsprint that we should respond with the full weight and force of our military. I wrote a song titled "Bound and Gagged" that captured my frustration and anger.

Take a look at the situation
I don't believe in negotiations
You would think that they would back up you and me.
So when you're proud of this great nation.
We got to have us a confrontation
that's the only hope that we stay free.

We should never stay bound and gagged.
We will never stay bound and gagged.

Take a look at our constitution
We must demand us some retribution
How the hell did they take our embassy?
We should've had armed guards up and down the stairways
fighter jets flying through their airways
that would guarantee that we stay free.

If we don't, we will stay bound and gagged.
We should never stay bound and gagged.

Got to face those consequences.
It's time to strengthen our defenses.
Got to tell them right now that we are still tough.
There's a nation there just off the border
and all they know is law and disorder.
Now's the time to scream we had enough.

No way we will stay
bound and gagged
bound and gagged.

We refuse to stay
bound and gagged
bound and gagged.

You see we have always been there to pick up the pieces
we make all the sacrifices and what do we get in return.

You would think they would show us a little respect wouldn't ya
wouldn't ya
but no they take us hostage.
They kidnap our leaders, they kill our advisors
they burn our flag.
Now just who the hell do they think they are
who do they think they're messing with anyhow.
I think we've had enough yeah I think we're fed up.
We've had enough we refuse to stay
bound and gagged.
All the way we are the U.S. of A.
we will never never stay
no way no way nuh nuh no way
bound and gagged.

Mine is right.
We're willing to fight fight.
Bound and gagged.
Fight fight fight.

Just who
I think we had enough.
We had enough, we refuse to stay
bound and gagged.

—*Nugent*, 1982

In order to provide some sort of restitution for my youthful disconnect, I have done what I can over the years for members of the armed
forces. I have many wonderful and happy memories of meeting with
military members and their families and expect to create many more.

There are also things I have seen that are painful and very personal. Suffice it to say, the absolute best people I have ever met have all worn the uniform of the U.S. Military. May the Good Lord bless each and every one of them.

My enlightenment, though slow in coming, eventually arrived. War is the answer, unless you believe that evil should control you. Me, I say wipe out those who would deprive others of their peace and freedom. Wipe them out. Just as I do not allow cockroaches in my home, I do not believe we should ever negotiate with or talk to the world's cockroaches. Step on them and then spray their remains with giant cans of Raid.

> ☆
>
> **Just as I do not allow cockroaches in my home, I do not believe we should ever negotiate with or talk to the world's cockroaches. Step on them and then spray their remains with giant cans of Raid.**

Of course, I will be opposed in my policy of total warfare by well-insulated Washington, D.C. policy wonks—proverbial hand-wringers that they are—who endlessly question and debate what little America manages to do. These vacuous idiots are more concerned about how the international community would view us than they are about the security of our nation or the lives of our brave soldiers, sailors, airmen, and Marines. Not me. An ounce of blood from an American GI is worth more than ten thousand gallons of enemy blood. Any American who finds fault with that statement is aiding and abetting the enemy.

Press the red button for common sense, Koko. I could not care less what the United Nations would say about America grinding our enemies underfoot. The United Nations is a den of socialists, despots, slave drivers, crooks, scoundrels, Marxists, thieves, commies, gangsters and anti-American punks from flea-infested countries, many of which are the worst violators of human rights in the history of man and blatant supporters of terrorism. To hell with what the United Nations says or does in response to America exterminating our enemies. The United Nations is anti-freedom and is as useless as teats on a boar hog. It is the largest gang of worthless humanity the world has ever witnessed. I, for one, refuse to take direction or advice from any people who still wipe their asses with their bare hands.

★

> **The United Nations is anti-freedom and is as useless as teats on a boar hog. It is the largest gang of worthless humanity the world has ever witnessed.**

Total warfare is hardly a new concept. History is replete with numerous successful military scorched-earth campaigns. During our Civil War, General Sherman's famous military campaign known as the March to the Sea in 1864 was designed to break the will of the Confederacy by employing this proven and logical concept of total warfare. General Sherman burned the South's crops, destroyed their railroads, took thousands of animals, and generally wrecked everything along the way. General Sherman's march worked. It broke the back of the Confederacy. Next. Just sixty years ago during World War II, America used total warfare to crush, destroy, burn, and vaporize Germany and Japan in an effort to bring about their surrender. It worked. Total warfare reduced these military superpowers to broken nations in just four years, which saved American lives. From bases in England, our bombers flew night and day over Nazi Germany and carpet bombed their military installations, factories, railroads, and cities. Our heroic flyboys literally wrecked the place. What they didn't destroy, the U.S. Army and Marine Corps did. Our Navy owned the Atlantic Ocean in just a couple of years from the time we entered the war. It was costly beyond imagination, but in its own way, beautiful. The war finally ended in Europe when the laughable, goose-stepping, animal-rights punk Hitler finally came to his senses and put a bullet in his warped brain. The Third Reich, which the Fuhrer touted would last for a thousand years, was destroyed in four years from the time America entered the war to the time of his little 9mm Lugar boogie. Germany was wrecked, and their people taught a very painful, if not eternal lesson. Can I hear a loud and proud "never again" and "hallelujah" please? We did the same to the Japanese. We literally vaporized them at Hiroshima and Nagasaki by dropping atom bombs on them. God bless Colonel Paul Tibbets who recently passed away. He and his crew of the Enola Gay dropped the atom bomb on Hiroshima on August 6, 1945. Just so you know, I support Enola Gay rights.

A few days later on August 9, our flying fortress B-29 bomber Bockscar piloted by Major Sweeney reduced Nagasaki to baked rubble. Pearl Harbor reciprocity times a thousand, anyone? The heat from the nuclear blasts were reported to have been so intense that shadows of people were literally seared into the sidewalks. I've never done that with my guitar. I will have to work on it.

> ⭐
>
> **Just so you know, I support Enola Gay rights.**

While our nukes vaporized the Japanese, the less renowned fire bombing carnage of Tokyo caused more casualties than either Hiroshima or Nagasaki. The fire bombing of Tokyo was a scorched-earth policy. Recognizing that we were committed to total warfare and the complete and total destruction of Japan, Emperor Hirohito ordered the surrender of Japan on August 15. Total warfare works, and in the final analysis, in this case it saved hundreds of thousands—some estimate millions—of GI lives and who knows how many millions of Japanese lives. That's how ya do that. Total warfare is designed to utterly and completely break the will of the enemy. It changes evil minds to peaceful minds in a hurry. Just ask the Japs or the Germans if you doubt me. They got the message in World War II and responded appropriately.

Now they are, by and large, our friends as it should be. Instead of cutting and running in Somalia in 1993 after our outnumbered brave warriors mowed down thousands of thug warlord Adid's henchmen in the streets of Mogadishu, we should have evacuated our forces expeditiously and then given the city twenty-four hours to evacuate their own. Exactly twenty-four hours later, the fiery glow that was once Mogadishu should have been seen had you been standing on the moon. I am convinced that had we done this, along with flattening a couple of terrorist-infested Middle Eastern cesspool cities in retaliation for the 1983 U.S. Marines Corps barracks bombing in Beirut by Islamic jihadists, the horrible events of September 11, 2001 would not have happened. I am absolutely convinced of it.

> ━━━ ☆ ━━━
> **Ill-conceived "feel good" diplomacy has gotten us in a ringer, and for no good reason whatsoever. Never again.**

Our cowardly inaction after the Iranian hostage fiasco and the bombings of the Marine barracks in Beirut...the World Trade Center in 1993...the U.S. embassies in Kenya and Tanzania...and the USS *Cole* in 2000 confirmed to the allahpukes that America had become a spineless paper tiger. Even these uneducated, Darwin-challenged, camel jockey, goat-herding, unclean sandboys figured they could do us harm. Sickeningly, they were correct. This may very well be the most unforgivable failure in American history. Just a thought.

Carter's embarrassing failure to crush Iran within hours of the hostage fiasco there was to be expected from such a goofball. But if, on his first day in office in January 1981, President Reagan had ordered the flattening of Tehran for holding our hostages for 444 days, we would not be facing war with Iran today. As much as I admire President Reagan, I believe he failed in his responsibility to wield a big stick against Iran and severely punish them for criminally taking and holding American hostages.

We should have thoroughly shattered their will to ever again mess with America right then and there. Ill-conceived "feel good" diplomacy has gotten our ass in a ringer, and for no good reason whatsoever. Never again.

The Mideast terror problem we face today is directly tied to our lack of resolve to immediately cause so much death, destruction, mayhem, and devastation that the Arab community would themselves have stamped out terrorists living and training in their midst. Instead, countries like Iran and Syria laugh at us and boldly poke their dirty fingers in our chests. What do we do? We run to the anti-American United Nations and ask for more condemnation and sanctions. Unbelievable. Where did our backbone go? I know the U.S. Military's laws of armed conflict and what they say about proportionality.

We can thank the lawyers for this legal quagmire that puts American troops and America itself in danger. The law of armed conflict ties our hands and keeps us from doing what needs to be done to solve problems—so they fester. Iran is providing arms and training to Shiites in Iraq to kill American soldiers. They run their attack speedboats close to our Navy ships and took some British Marines hostage. Intelligence states they will have a nuclear weapon that could be used against Israel within a year. President Ahmadinejad has repeatedly called for Israel to be wiped off the map. Iran is a rogue, criminal nation who supplies and trains ter-

> ★
>
> **I'm not interested in winning the hearts and minds of the Arab world.**

rorists. It is a wart on the world. For us to continue to kick the Iranian problem down the road for future generations of Americans to deal with is irresponsible.

Now is the time to hit Iran very, very hard, especially before Iran gets their hands on a nuclear weapon. I'm not interested in winning the hearts and minds of the Arab world. I'm interested in breaking their will to ever dare harming America. Secretary of Defense Rumsfeld and

TOTAL WARFARE

Our State Department should issue a shortly worded press release to all of the rogue nations in the Middle East. I propose the following: "The use of a weapon of mass destruction against America or its allies will result in the complete and total extinction of a number of your cities whether your nation had anything to do with it or not. When we are through, you will think Guantanamo Bay is a Caribbean resort. Have a nice day."

company blew it by thinking we would be treated as liberators when we walked into Iraq. We should have leveled a few cities and killed tens of thousand of Iraqi soldiers before any of our tanks or infantrymen ever entered the country. That would have been my kind of shock and awe. Instead, we used precision strike weapons to take out tactical military targets. That didn't break their will. In fact, it emboldened many of them. By failing to employ total war, we have extended the war and put the lives of American soldiers at risk. Deterring the use of a weapon of mass destruction (nuclear, chemical, or biological) is not so difficult so long as we have the resolve to do what is necessary if we are hit. Researchers and some government officials believe it is only a matter of time before a U.S. city is attacked with a weapon of mass destruction that could kill or severely injure hundreds of thousands of Americans. The answer to this problem is not nearly as daunting as what you may believe.

Believe it or not, I am not a warmonger but rather someone who believes that if we are going to put our brave men and women in harm's way, we should employ total warfare and break the will of our enemy as soon as possible so that they will remember for decades the carnage we brought upon their nation. America should walk tall and carry a big stick. We must always be willing to swing that big stick and crush our enemies underfoot. I subscribe to General Patton's view of war: "May God have mercy upon my enemies, because I won't."

I LOVE REAL ASSAULT WEAPONS

The huge, jagged crater from yesterday's IED blowout could have swallowed up our Humvee, but my U.S. Marine driver did what U.S. Marines do so well—he improvised, adapted, and overcame the cavernous sinkhole as we motored vigorously into Fallujah, Iraq. My Kevlar helmet banged back and forth against the bulletproof interior of my military ride, and my heavy flack vest cushioned the bodyslams against the door and frame. With a mind-jolting loud bang, the door violently swung open and I frantically grabbed and pulled it back instantaneously, but it would not latch shut. Bouncing wildly now like a Baja 1000 off-road ragdoll, our convoy cruising at high speed through the pitch black corridors of this dangerous, God-forsaken warzone, I yanked my belt tool from its pouch and set to jimmying the broken door latch of my Hummer, hanging on for dear life. I felt a bit cocky knowing that the old guitar player from Detroit had just jury-rigged a busted military vehicle on the fly, and the USMC hero warriors winked and smiled with snickered approval, humoring me I'm sure.

Though I never officially served in the U.S. Military, my U.S. Army drill sergeant father's gung-ho parental discipline was as close to boot camp as you can get, legally. Barely legally, I'm sure. But here I was in Iraq with the Marines, rockin'. I instinctively knew what to do. It felt good.

Proudly yet humbly representing the great United Service Organizations charity, I spent two wild weeks on the frontlines of the War on Terror with American BloodBrother Toby Keith, hanging with and learning from the bravest souls that ever lived. In the unnamed mountain passes of Afghanistan, the sandpit deserts of Iraq, the third-world hellzones of Baghdad, Tikrit, Taji, and Kandahar—and in U.S. Military camps too numerous and remote to identify, I was honored and privileged to share campfires and tented mess-hall meals with the best of the best. There is no question that these young American men and women are the finest, most dedicated, intelligent, well-trained, highly disciplined, absolutely capable warriors the world has ever known. And that's really saying something, for the Greatest Generation from World War II would be hard to beat. Yet an upgrade on even that amazing level of commitment has been lauded upon today's War on Terror U.S. combatants for freedom. Thank God we have a U.S. commander-in-chief who understands the self-evident truth that America's only hope is to confront evil over there, in its face, instead of waiting for the terrorists to call the game elsewhere and otherwise. It's shameful how so many fail to grasp this proven truism. That there exists an American alive today that is so entrenched in ignorance and denial that the putrid and soulless words "*war is not the answer*" could possibly be spoken is beyond comprehension. I feel like an idiot that I have to ask them what could possibly have been the answer when the Japanese and Nazi monsters attempted to enslave the world? Could anyone be so conveniently disconnected as to not understand the essentiality of waging war against evil? Could the very concept of good over evil not register with some human beings in the inescapable historical evidence of genocide, tyranny, kings, emperors, and Hitler-type murderers? Meanwhile, the U.S. Military warriors sacrifice on. God bless them all.

Being an honorary member of the 101st Airborne, and having the amazing experience of training with various elite commando units of the U.S. Military and law enforcement, I can truly say I have been to the mountaintop of freedom. To be in the presence of such absolute greatness reminds me to dedicate myself to being the best that I can be every day, if only in honor of the ultimate sacrifices of these heroes. Though we humans can, and do, stumble, I learned long ago that a good man gets right back up, dusts himself off, and learns from his errors. This I do. It is the essence of quality of life and survival. When great men and women are dying so we can be free, it is the least we can do.

To ultimately drive this Discipline 101 home, there surely is no better routine than firearms training with these masters. As a hunter and registered gung-ho gun nut, I will never apologize nor waste my time defending my God-given right to keep and bear arms. The more and bigger the arms, the better. Which brings us to the ultimate fun guns of all-times: the hot brass rainbow party of fully automatic machineguns. And I am not talking about your basic deer rifle that Sarah Brady and all the antigun nuts call assault weapons and wish to ban. I am talking about real, honest-to-God, military type assault weapons, the kind that we carried in Fallujah that night to defend ourselves and freedom with. Which of course, makes them "defense weapons" not "assault weapons." But I like the term "assault weapons" better, if for no other reason than it causes Nancy Pelosi and her anti-American gun-grabbing cult of denial clan that much more grief. If they are so hyper-dedicated to pretending that all guns are bad, I wish to increase their unfounded, denial-riddled anguish, thank you.

> ☆
>
> **There is no question that these young American men and women are the finest, most dedicated, intelligent, well-trained, highly disciplined, absolutely capable warriors the world has ever known.**

If idiots accept you, then you must be an idiot. Idiots hate me.

On the official military firing range in the secured Green Zone of Baghdad, Toby Keith and I settled in for an afternoon of machinegun fun with the professionals. The lovely M60, beltfed .308 can only be described as a piece of mystical ballistic artwork, its black finish and skeletal framework begging for a solid grip and downrange hosing of hot lead. The mighty M16 .223 battlegun is also a thing of beauty. Firing the behemoth .50 caliber sniper rifle was truly amazing, registering consistent headshots on the two hundred-yard badguy target to rounds of cheers and celebration. All in all, as is the case every time civilian families gather back home in the good old U.S. of A., the joys of shooting provided even these frontline warriors a gratifying relief from the insane stress of their volunteered life and death workload. Much laughter, high-fives, and shared stories of hunting and fishing back home took us all to a much better, incredibly needed escapezone of better times. For a moment there, evil did not exist outside the fort walls. Remember the Alamo indeed.

> ⭐
>
> **If idiots accept you, then you must be an idiot. Idiots hate me.**

So on numerous occasions each year, I gather around the Nugent family home campfire here in Texas and back in Michigan, and we shoot machineguns. Like hundreds of thousands of law-abiding American families—military, law enforcement, and civilian—we shoot literally hundreds of millions of rounds of ammo through these amazing creations of ballistic art.

Legally owned in most states—more than a half million are legally owned by more than 250,000 American families without a hitch—the lies about scary guns couldn't be more intentionally deceptive than what is misreported by the media in this country. Number of injuries and deaths each week during machinegun fun with all of us? None. Zero, zilch, nada. Go figure.

All I know is that when it comes time to have one hell of a fun, laugh infested Uncle Ted Texas family BBQ party, heroes of law enforcement and military join us for some challenging machinegun competition. It is all good. We are busy paving our driveway in assorted brass these days—an environmental upgrade if ever there was one.

BLOOD ON MY BOOTS

Toby Keith and I stood at the bedside of Private First Class Todd Bolding of Central Texas. We had just landed via BlackHawk battle chopper on the tarmac of Landstuhl U.S. Military Hospital in Germany. Visiting with wounded heroes of the world's greatest warriors from the U.S. Army, Navy, Air Force, National Guard, and Marine Corps, we were deeply humbled by not only the obvious sacrifice and courage of these amazing men and women, but their astonishing commitment to get their shattered bodies repaired and back into fighting shape as soon as possible, to, in their own words, "grab my rifle and get back to the front-lines to fight with my buddies." God bless America.

It was the last stop of our trip of a few fascinating weeks with these heroes, hanging out, eating, shooting, talking, patrolling, sharing hunting and fishing stories, celebrating the American music that bonded us, and doing our best to keep a stiff upper lip and a positive attitude as we emotionally dealt with such sacred time with many warriors with life threatening injuries. We were moved.

I was glad to be there. After hearing such bullshit from people who claim to support the troops but condemn and even dismiss the war on terror, I was totally fortified in my confidence that the cause was without doubt just and proper. You see, I'm just a guitar player, so instead of guessing or relying on uneducated emotion, I believe my opinion should be based on the best information I can find on any given subject, particularly when the subject is freedom and justice, and the real story behind those heroes willing to volunteer and possibly sacrifice their lives for such noble causes. The last thing I want to do is to improperly or irresponsibly misinform anyone listening to my statements in the

continued

media, in my writings, speeches, or conversations, which may or may not affect policy, so that cheap hunches and a selfish need to protect one's ignorant feelings screws things up. That would be deadly.

So I put my heart and soul into digging as deep as I can, researching the facts and evidence to the best of my ability and finding those souls most dedicated to the truth, those actually in the heat of the hot zone. Historical and current evidence scrutinized is surely a good basis for opinion, but nothing quite compares to information shared by actual hands-on combatants in the war on terror's frontlines. I so respect these bright, incredibly sophisticated, gung-ho military professionals who obviously put their hearts and souls into researching the post-September 11 world, that maybe, just maybe, their decision to volunteer after looking into all the facts themselves, would draw conclusions more meaningful than some U.S. bashing punk like, say, Michael Moore, Pam Anderson, or their disconnected, insulated ilk.

The intimate, inside dialogue that these brave men and women share with me brings me to a single conclusion: the terrorists and those who support them in any way must be destroyed at all costs. Peace and love and security are procured by killing those who would interfere out of hatred for our free way of life, and that is exactly what the U.S. Military heroes are doing. Fighting the evil terrorists and tyrants who have held Muslims and that entire region of the world in bondage to an unjust life of misery, locked hopelessly in the seventeenth century, is right. This is clearly the only hope we have to beat down the maniacal religious extremists who have vowed to destroy America and all dissenting innocent lives around the globe. That is what our troops are doing where they are doing it, and most people are smart enough to see this.

continued

With the horrific, mind-numbing images of those planes flying into the twin towers, the Pentagon, and crashing into a Pennsylvania field still fresh in our minds, we must never forget the depth of evil that they represent.

Todd Bolding bled to death before my eyes. I saluted many flag-draped coffins over there. I flew home with the flag-draped coffin of Lt. Col. Eric McRae and communicated with his family to say thank you. I said thank you on behalf of all Americans who know how we got here. I remember the Alamo. I remember D-Day. I remember Iwo Jima. I remember Pearl Harbor. I remember the Battan Death March. I remember 9-11-01. I remember Todd Bolding and all who gave everything so we can be free. I side with those who face the beast. They know best. Godspeed warriors.

CHAPTER SIX

"If you make any money,
the government shoves you in the creek
once a year with it in your pockets,
and all that don't get wet you can keep."

★ ★ ★

Will Rogers

In my wildest nightmare scenario, I could not dream up an uglier joke than our current tax system. It is arbitrary, punitive, wasteful, confiscatory, counterproductive, cumbersome, confusing, burdensome, idiotic, wrong-headed, and ugly—heavy on the ugly. Nothing about it makes any sense whatsoever. Oh yeah, and it's unconstitutional, by the way.

We are taxed so much because we have surrendered our economic freedom to the government. Plain and simple. So you can bitch, whine, and complain about taxes but you have nothing to say if you then vote for your incumbent congressman or senator. Boggles my mind. Until you realize that your congressman and your senator are to blame, nothing will change. The game remains the same and we lose every time because the government will take even more of your money to pay for more ineffective, inefficient, and bloated programs. I'm just a greasy guitar player and I figured that out. Why haven't you?

Well, maybe some of you have begun to figure it out. Maybe there is hope for America. A May 20, 2008 Rasmussen poll found that sixty-two percent of voters support fewer government services and lower taxes. Best news I've read all year. Amazingly, the same poll found that one third of Americans would rather have more government and higher taxes. Boys and girls, these useful American idiots are known as socialists who despise the free market, capitalism, entrepreneurship, and economic freedom. If they had the strength of their anti-American convictions, they would set sail for Cuba. In fact, I propose that conservatives donate money to buy a large boat and offer to sail liberals to Cuba free-of-charge where they can live out their socialist dreams. Not one of these anti-American socialists bloodsuckers would get on the boat.

President Obama's stated program is to eliminate the tax cuts of President Bush, to raise the top marginal tax rate on the so-called "wealthy" who already pay the vast amount of income taxes, raise Social Security taxes, and provide tax dollars to fund private retirement programs. He supports throwing more tax dollars into the government's feed trough to gobble up. Not me.

Before I get started on throttling our modern tax mess, a quick but very important history lesson is in order. This unique experiment in self-government was started in 1776 by a bunch of uppity, defiant, logic-addicted rebels well pissed off over the British Crown's onerous, old world taxes. Does "no taxation without representation" ring any Liberty Bells inside your head? Facing the largest, most well trained army in the world at the time, our forefathers risked their lives and fortunes and began killing King George's Redcoats over taxes. Please, a moment of silence for our rebel forefathers killing Redcoats. They were rebels with a cause. God bless them for killing Redcoats. Their defiance and love of freedom changed the world.

Upgrade starts simply by being honest. We all know what is good and bad. Do good, don't do bad. That's a tuffy!

Our founding rebel fathers despised the very concept of income taxes, or direct taxes, which is why the confiscatory concept of income or direct taxes is not mentioned in our constitution. Without an income tax on Americans, our government paid all its bills by levying indirect taxes on imports. An income tax was proposed around 1815 but with anti-tax rebel blood still coursing through their veins, Americans promptly shitcanned that offensive idea.

During the Civil War the government forced an income tax on Americans to help fund the war, but the tax expired after the war. Imagine that, a tax that actually expired as the new bureaucrats said it would! In a rare stroke of black-robed brilliance, the Supreme Court then struck down an attempt to create an income tax of just two percent in 1894. Finally, in 1913 the tax and spend bureaucrats got their way and passed the Sixteenth Amendment, which permitted taxation of individuals and companies. The rest, so they say, is an ugly, ugly history of confiscatory and increasingly unjust tax rates on our incomes.

No one looks forward to paying taxes, even those hypocritical liberals who have never seen a tax they did not support. If liberals were true to their big government convictions they would all be sending in stacks of extra cash to the IRS to fund their favorite, bloated, inefficient government agencies and programs. But we all know they don't send in any extra money, which makes them hyper-inflated hypocrites. Liberals are elitist windbags who must never be taken seriously, and should be used only for entertainment purposes.

―――― ☆ ――――

**Warning:
Use liberals only
under close
conservative
supervision.**

―――――――

The amount and variety of taxes Americans are forced to pay is staggering. Every area of our personal and private lives is governed by taxes. There are federal income taxes, state income taxes, property taxes, death taxes, sales taxes, any number of not-so-hidden taxes in the form of permits, licenses, reviews, registrations, codes, safety checks, gas taxes, social security taxes, various county and city taxes, etc., etc., etc. Who in God's name comes up with this stuff, and worse, how long will we bend over and take it? I smell one hell of a tea party on the horizon.

As the Institute of Policy Innovation has pointed out, many of the taxes we pay are hidden from us. Each and every one of us pays an additional $2,642 in hidden taxes in the form of gas taxes, travel expenses, sin taxes on booze and cigarettes, on hotel rooms, and even more. The government makes more in taxes on a pack of cigarettes than the company who produced the cancer sticks makes in profit. The same goes for booze. As we struggle with high oil prices, it may interest you to know that roughly thirty percent of the cost of a gallon of gas is from taxes. It makes me sick.

According to the Tax Foundation, Tax Freedom Day was April 23, 2008. In 1900, it was January 22. Tax Freedom Day is the day when you quit working to pay your tax burden and begin working for yourself and your family. Scott Hodge, Tax Foundation president, states on their tremendously informative website that, "Government continues to dominate the American taxpayer's budget. Americans will spend more on taxes than they will spend on food, clothing and housing combined." Thanks, Scott. Now pardon me while I puke.

Fundamentally, the reason Americans pay so much in taxes is simply because we have surrendered our economic freedom and choices to the ever-expanding, horribly inefficient Nanny State. Instead of relying on the free market to provide our services and sundry wants and needs, we permitted the Nanny State to intrude into virtually all areas of our lives. In my opinion, the socialist bureaupunks lack the constitutional authority to do it and have zero financial acumen in managing what they have taken. Big mistake, Kemosabe. If you want a service to become more expensive, more inefficient, more burdensome, and as wasteful as humanly possible, let the Nanny State take over. She is a pig.

When you are in a hole, the first thing you need to do is to quit digging. Our government's response is to demand a bigger shovel and to hire more diggers. Take Social Security, for example. Never intended to be a retirement income, Social Security has ballooned into a nightmarish fiscal blob that is on its way to bankruptcy in the next fifteen to twenty years unless benefits are drastically cut, means testing is done, or, you guessed it—the Social Security tax level is raised on workers. This socialist program should be tossed on the trash heap of stinking socialism and Americans told that they are responsible for their own retirements, not for other American workers. Any financial analyst will tell you that if you invest even a small amount of your income over a lifetime of working that you will amass a small fortune. Damn right I support opting out of Social Security for young workers and privatizing the entire program, not just the one to two percent that President Bush advocated but then weaseled out of. Imagine the money you could have amassed if you would have been able to invest the money automatically confiscated by the Nanny State so that a Social Security check can (maybe) be sent to another American. Everyone would be financially independent. Bloodsuckers would starve. So be it. Instead, Social Security has created poverty by reducing the incentive for people to save for their own futures. This is mental retardation on parade. I am not responsible for you and you are not responsible for me.

Even the guitar-playing, maniac, master lovesong author of WANG DANG SWEET POONTANG and LOVE GRENADE knows that cutting taxes generates income. The more taxes are cut, more income is available to Americans to start small businesses, invest, donate to charities, or spend at their leisure on other commodities and services. Alternatively, raising taxes takes money out of the economy because Americans have less of their cash to spend. Always support tax cuts. Tax cuts give you back your money instead of letting the Nanny State blow it. Everyone with me so far? The only people against tax cuts are Nanny State socialists, as they ardently believe they know better how to "invest" (meaning spend) your money than you. This isn't flawed economic logic. It is no logic. By the way, whenever you hear a politician use the term "invest," watch your wallet because the Nanny State is trying to pick your pocket yet again.

> ★
>
> **I support trashing the current tax system.**

Most American families manage their personal finances rather adroitly, even with burdensome tax rates. They understand that spending more than what you bring home is a sure way to commit financial suicide—yet that is exactly how our gluttonous, unaccountable, runaway Nanny State manages its finances. It routinely spends more than it brings in and then borrows money from other nations to pay for its insane spending ways. As such, the national debt now stands at over nine trillion dollars and we are spiraling further into debt at a rate of roughly 1.5 billion dollars each day. Deficit spending, meaning the money the Nanny State spends over the amount it brings in, continues unabated. America does not have a Balanced Budget Amendment because the Nanny State bloodsuckers do not want to be legally bound to practice sound financial management with OUR money. Angry yet? If not, you are no friend of mine.

TAX REFORM

There are two major tax reform programs that have caught fire: the Flat Tax and the FairTax.

"Both the FairTax and the Flat Tax are 'consumption taxes.' In other words, people are taxed for spending money, not earning it. The Flat Tax would require citizens to file tax returns as they do now, paying tax on all spent money (income minus savings).

The FairTax would rely on merchants to collect tax at the point of sale, as they now collect state and local sales taxes.

Both would eliminate the estate and capital gains taxes.

Both plans are single tax rate systems that eliminate double taxation.

Both plans would dramatically reduce compliance costs and the tax system's deadweight loss to the economy."

—Scott Hodge, Tax Foundation

Either one would be better than our current 55,000-page tax code nightmare. Somebody get me a match. I know a book that needs burning.

I support trashing the current tax system. Throw the IRS baby out with the tainted bath water. Let's start anew with the goal of making taxes as easy to understand and as simple as possible. No lawyers, accountants, Washington, D.C. lobbyists, or elected bureaupunks are necessary or wanted. They will only screw things up, which will make me unleash my oil-soaked, Andy Jackson hickory stick and start playing the drums on their skulls like a possessed African medicine man.

Now while I support dumping the current tax system, don't for a second believe I don't support some type of tax system. What I support is overall, real, honest-to-God tax reform. Taxes are necessary evils. But the ultimate goal is to reign in the out of control Nanny State. Tax cuts without reducing the size of the Nanny State are largely meaningless and temporary, stop-gap measures. That's like bringing brass knuckles to a gun fight. Wrong tool. We must work to reduce the size of the Nanny State. That's first order of business. Once that is accomplished, the flooding Nanny State River will be put back in its channel and your tax burden will be reduced. Failing to reduce the size of the Nanny State will continue to increase our tax burdens. This is one of the most important reasons why you should never vote for a Democrat. Interestingly, there is a strong corollary between the size of the Nanny State to our current tax rates. The larger the government has grown over the years, the more we have paid in taxes. By the way, we don't have the best government you can buy unless you are a Washington, D.C. lobbyist.

THE DEATH TAX

I am compelled to shine the biggest spotlight I can get a hold of on the ultimate tax cockroach of alltimes; the incredibly unfair Death Tax. Let me see if I get this right; so a family busts their asses for a few generations, struggling and sacrificing to establish, build, and maintain a successful family business. For the sake of example, let's say it is a built-from-scratch, expanding dairy farm that through painstakingly hard

ECONOMIC FREEDOM

I'm incensed at the recent Bush/Pelosi $150 billion so-called economic stimulus package. You should be, too.

Sending us a token check for a couple of hundred bucks is a pandering joke and an economic slap in our faces. Hopefully you are smart enough to see through this economic smokescreen.

Even if you spend all of the money (your money) coming back to you, it will do little, if anything, to improve the sagging economy. Sending Americans a check is economic flash over substance. If our professional politicians really wanted to improve the economy, they would do a couple of key things.

The first thing that needs to be done is cut the size of the bloated, wasteful federal budget by ten percent or more over the next couple of years. The blob-like federal government has grown to such a size that it is now eating itself with a nine trillion debt and billions in deficits, smothering economic opportunity. If you want real economic stimulus, it can not be accomplished until the federal beast is reigned in and is put on a financial diet. Although I am no economist, this is so fundamental to improving our economy that I am surprised so few of the talking heads have discussed it as a way to improve the long-term American economic condition. I have always lived within my means, and my government should too.

Second, small businesses need tax relief. We must create incentives for small businesses to expand and hire more people. This can be accomplished by getting the onerous, unaccountable IRS off of our backs. The majority of Americans work for a small business. Small businesses are the backbone of the American economy. Strangling them

continued

★ ★ ★

with taxes and stacks of regulations, rules, and requirements sucks the life out of our economy. We must do whatever we can to assist small businesses and encourage them to grow.

Putting money back in the pockets of Americans is a good idea only if the money is in the form of permanent tax cuts. Americans keeping more of their money creates more economic choices. Socialists and bloodsuckers aside, I have yet to meet an American who does not favor tax cuts and keeping more of his or her money.

Instead, the professional bureaucrats who run our government want to give you some of your money back in hopes that you spend it on blingbling, big screen televisions, and other indulgent garbage. Even if everyone blew through the money, it would do little to prop up our economy. Bailing water on the Titanic may have sounded like a good idea at the time, but you would have drowned anyway.

Robbing and spending our grandchildren's tax dollars today is surely a recipe for economic disaster. We can not tax our way out of this economic mess without pushing the middle class further into the economic abyss. The only way out of this is to grow our way out of it, and that can only be accomplished by reducing the size of the federal beast, doing whatever we can to help instead of hindering small business, and giving all Americans permanent and meaningful tax cuts.

As the American presidential primary juggernaut roars down the political track, there are two key economic questions you need to ask yourself when considering who you are going to support: Do I really believe that federally controlled health care will improve the quality of health care? Do I believe that more or less government intrusion is the right approach?

continued

America remains an economic powerhouse. Our economy is four times that of China, but China, India, and other burgeoning economies are nipping at our economic heels. If we continue down the path we are on, China will eclipse our economy by 2030. That's not good.

The foundation of freedom is economic freedom. You know far better than others how to spend your hard earned money, how to invest it, and how to take care of your health. Vote for your economic freedom. The economic fate of our country is your hands.

work (is there any other way?) has grown to encompass adequate acreage to hold and feed their large herd of cows. Their business accommodates a milking operation that constantly requires upgrading and includes an expensive fleet of high maintenance refrigerated tankers that haul the precious white liquid to market. Overall, it is a costly operation that over many years represents many millions of dollars worth of stuff, which is all taxed to the hilt every damn year.

Then gramps or dad dies.

I want to meet the human being, much less the American, who is willing to look me in my eyes, and the eyes of sensible people anywhere, and dare to explain how the government has a right to one red cent of this family's lifetime of after-tax savings. That is *after-tax savings*! As in "they already paid all their taxes" every year, but now must pay a huge, business-destroying, suicidal tax on what they were able to save AFTER paying exorbitant annual taxes. Dear God in heaven, how can this be? Who supports this evil, criminal confiscation of personal property? In many heartbreaking cases, many of these family businesses simply cannot afford such an unfair burden, and the business goes under as assets are sold in a fire sale to pay off the biggest, baddest, extortion gangster of alltimes: Uncle "Al Capone" Sam. Incredible.

The Death Tax is the ultimate indicator of a government out of control, robbing its most productive citizens (subjects) to finance their immoral, out of control spending orgy. That no meaningful effort is underway to accurately expose this criminal tax abuse and bring it to an end once and for all is a conclusive indictment to the gangster mentality running amok in the U.S. government today. Shame on these pigs. The death tax penalizes success, productivity, entrepreneurialism, and professional business management, and that is downright crazy. Meanwhile, the pimps, whores, and welfare brats would be rejoicing if they weren't so drunk on the blood of the working class.

The questions that cause my brain to swell are, who the hell came up with this insanity in the shadows of the night, and what sort of sheeplike America is so stupid as to allow it to continue?

Who other than socialist extortion artists could possibly think this is compatible with the American way? I guarantee you one thing, the list is made up mostly of democrat punks that must think economic freedom is unacceptable. It breaks my heart that brave Americans are dying for the American Dream, while a gaggle of anti-American bureaupunks are doing this. God help us all.

CHAPTER SEVEN

UNCLE SAM IS A PIG

"You don't know where you come from.

You're not too wise.

You got nowhere to run to.

You are paralyzed."

★ ★ ★

"Paralyzed,"

State of Shock, 1979

Judging by outcome, the modus operandi of our federal government must be to look for stacks of our hard-earned tax dollars and then set them on fire. The bureaupunks then try to put out the fire ... by throwing more stacks of our tax dollars on top of the blazing inferno. Insane.

There is basically zero accountability in the way our tax dollars are wasted.

The Government Accountability Office has the specific mission and responsibility to be our "We the People" watchdog over the federal government and how it spends our money, but the amount of runaway pork spending and mismanagement is off the charts. We have a federal government that has run amuck in fraud, waste, and abuse of our tax dollars. Name one big-time bureaupunk who has been fired or charged with a crime for either wasting our precious tax dollars, or worse, not knowing where our tax dollars went in their so-called "budgets." Private auditing firms have literally given up trying to audit some government agencies because the financial records are either nonexistent or so screwed up that they could not complete their audit. If the financial records of public companies were as mismanaged, incomplete, or missing in the same manner as many government agencies, CEOs and other company officials would be—and have been—justly charged with fraud and various other crimes and sent to prison. The same standard should apply to federal officials, but it doesn't. They tread on us with impunity and it must stop now.

> There is basically zero accountability in the way our tax dollars are wasted.

Our former president stood at the podium, shook his finger, and sternly warned private industry that the voluminous weight of the federal government would come down on them for mismanaging the financial affairs of their companies. And while the president was lecturing and threatening action against private industry, Bill O'Reilly opined on his television program that 50 percent of every tax dollar the federal government collects from us is wasted or can't be found. Sadly, after doing a modicum of research on the Internet on government waste, I suspect Bill was much more right than wrong. What say you, Mr. President?

The Internet is brimming with example after example of billions and billions of dollars of government waste. Type "government waste" into any internet search engine and get prepared to become nauseated and fist-pounding-on-the-table angry at what you find.

Remember the infamous Bridge to Nowhere? Just a couple of years ago, Senator Ted Stevens of Alaska slipped a couple of earmarks into an appropriations bill. They funded the building of bridges in Alaska that basically went nowhere. At a cost of 230 million taxpayer dollars, one of the bridges was

> **I love my Alaska BloodBrothers in the wilds of Knik and beyond, but they live there because they love it wild.**

from beautiful Ketchikan (population 9,000 or so) to Gravina Island (population almost 50 or so people). That proposed bridge was almost as long as the Golden Gate Bridge and taller than the Brooklyn Bridge. Another bridge for about the same price was going to be built from Anchorage to Knik.

I love my Alaska BloodBrothers in the wilds of Knik and beyond, but they live there because they love it wild.

If you want a bridge, build one, but leave my hard-earned tax dollars alone. Fortunately, thanks to a few good old-fashioned whistleblowers, logic and some rare justice prevailed and these wasteful bridges were cancelled by embarrassed politicians caught in the act. (Though Alaska did still get the money.)

Unfortunately, thousands of wasteful earmarks slide right on through the federal funding process like greased pigs.

You need look no further than Martin Gross's wonderful book *The Government Racket: 2000 and Beyond* for some of the ugliest and most reprehensible examples of government waste ever cataloged. Go out and buy this book and study it. It is wonderful intellectual ammo. Lock and load. A couple of examples from this book worth noting:

★ A two-year study by the Government Accounting Office (GAO) in 1998 found that virtually the entire federal government was guilty of bad bookkeeping. Anybody think that if the GAO did the same study today that the results would be any different?

★ The same GAO study found that the IRS could not verify three billion dollars of expenses. The IRS has got to go.

★ Although this book is already eight years old, Mr. Gross estimated that government waste accounted for 375 billion dollars a year in 2000 and that eliminating this waste could have meant a 40 percent cut in our taxes.

Martin Gross is a national treasure and if just one of our politicians had any sense of decency, character, or integrity, Mr. Gross would be nominated for a Presidential Medal of Freedom for his work in exposing government waste. God bless Martin Gross. America needs more patriots like him.

As I write this, my hunting buddy Ward Parker in Nebraska e-mailed me to let me know that fellow turkey hunter Senator Ben Nelson recently earmarked $500,000 for security cameras in Omaha public transportation buses (that, reportedly, hardly anyone rides). Since when is it my responsibility to pay for security cameras in public transportation in Omaha? Isn't that the responsibility of my taxpayer buddies in

Omaha? He also told me that former Nebraska senator Bob Kerrey slipped the city of Omaha fourteen or so million of our tax dollars in the Transportation Bill a few years back as a parting earmark gift for the Cornhusker citizens to build a walking bridge over the Missouri River. More pork, more fat, more waste.

Out-of-control pork spending is everywhere. Just today (Feb 27, 2008), there was an article in the *Washington Times* that stated the Department of Defense has paid out a little over forty-two million dollars to the families of Iraqis accidentally killed or whose property has been destroyed since the beginning of 2005. Let me see if I have this straight: over 4,000 brave Americans have lost their lives in this war and almost 20,000 more wounded isn't enough payment? And if it wasn't enough of a sacrifice to liberate Iraqis from the brutal dictator, Saddam Hussein, let us not forget that America has spent hundreds of billions of dollars on this war to also capture or kill Hussein's evil henchmen, and build Iraqi schools, sewers, electrical grids, hospitals, roadways, waterways, and more. Now, we are paying Iraqis some forty million more dollars so that they won't be mad at us! I'm the one who is mad as hell and so should you be.

Politicians bring home billions and billions of pork (formerly known as your tax dollars) to their districts and states by including spending "earmarks" in otherwise often legitimate bills. What they're trying to do with this wasteful spending is buy your vote with your own money—your own money for goodness sake! Senator Robert Byrd of West Virginia is the "King of Pork," having brought over one billion of our tax dollars home to West Virginia for any number of wasteful projects. According to a June 2007 CNN report, Congress approved 29 billion dollars in earmarks in 2006. If that is not a mob-style racket, what is? And I thought dead people voting in Chicago were unique. Al Capone lives and he is running the U.S. government.

Get this: In the same June 2007 report I mentioned above, CNN asked every member of the House for information about their earmarks for fiscal year 2008. Sixty-eight of our illustrious representatives refused outright to answer the CNN request; 315 more didn't respond at all. When I read this story I couldn't believe it. These people work for us. We are their employers! How dare these holier-than-thou shysters refuse to give their employers information on the job they are doing for us? Too many of our elected employees know no shame. And unless the Supreme Court reverses itself (thanks a lot, *Clinton* v. *City of New York*), our president will never be able to use a line-item veto to eliminate wasteful spending projects from otherwise sound bills.

GRANTS

You can sprinkle all the perfume you want on a bloated, greasy pig, but at the end of the day it is still a nasty, skanky hog. So it is with federal grants. The federal government doles out grants to pay for various projects, studies, and programs to cities, schools, private organizations, and individuals. Federal grants work something like this: say a county police department needs more money so that they can have more road officers out patrolling and writing you and me speeding tickets on Sundays. Instead of asking county taxpayers to ante up more tax dollars, the county police department fills out a federal grant application and Uncle Sam comes riding to the rescue with a federal grant. The county then keeps the extra traffic fine cash from the additional speeding tickets they are able to write.

Follow the money here. I pay county taxes, some of which is given to the county police department. I also pay federal taxes. Some of my federal money comes back to the county in the form of a federal grant so that the county police department can have more road officers out patrolling on Sundays and writing me speeding tickets. The county gets to keep the money from the speeding ticket. What did the federal government get for their grant? Absolutely nothing. Non-scrutinized federal grants cost U.S. taxpayers outrageous amounts of wasted tax dollars each and every year. The fleecing of the American taxpayer will never end until We the People raise enough hell to bring it to a much overdue halt. It is time.

Even more of our money is wasted by our federal politicians who fly all over the world on "fact-finding missions." While some of these trips may be legitimate, others are surely vacation junkets for congressmen paid for with our tax dollars. Doubt me? Ask your congressman in a public forum such as at a town hall meeting if he or she believes every "fact-finding" trip congressmen have taken has been legitimate and the wise use of our tax dollars. Put them on the spot.

Embarrass the thieves. They deserve it. Then vote them out of office.

Our government is spending America into bankruptcy. In a matter of just three

★

Embarrass the thieves. They deserve it. Then vote them out of office.

decades, America has gone from the world's largest creditor (lender) to the world's largest debtor. America is now over nine trillion dollars in debt and going further into debt at a rate of 1.8 billion dollars each day, 365 days a year. To a get a sense of how large this debt is, the entire federal budget for 2008 was 3.1 trillion—the largest federal budget in history. We are literally borrowing money from the Chinese and others against the tax dollars of future generations of Americans. That is certainly immoral and should be illegal. Currently, every man, woman, and child's share of this debt is over $31,000 and growing. You can see it for yourself if you go to www.debtclock.com to watch the federal debt grow by tens of thousands of dollars before your eyes. It is one of the most depressing websites on the Internet.

I expect bureaupunks and those who make their living lapping up our tax dollars to claim that my analysis of wasteful spending is too simplistic, that much of this pork spending is used to provide jobs for people, and that pork barrel spending is just a drop in the bucket of the entire federal budget. They are wrong, of course. There is never any justification for waste or irresponsibility with public funds. Those responsible for how our tax dollars are spent should be held to as high, if not higher, ethical, legal, and moral standards as those in private industry. Those politicians who violate the public trust by knowingly wasting our money on pork projects should be sent to prison. Case closed.

In defense of my common sense argument, Congress would be wise to heed one of its own members, Davy Crockett—the famous American frontiersman and defender at the Alamo.

According to *The Life of Colonel David Crockett* by Edward Sylvester Ellis, Congressman Crockett received a lesson from a constituent on how Congress should spend taxpayer dollars:

Several years ago I was one evening standing on the steps of the Capitol with some members of Congress, when our attention was attracted by a great light over in Georgetown. It was evidently a large fire. We jumped into a hack and drove over as fast as we could. In spite of all that could be done, many houses were burned and many families made houseless, and besides, some of them had lost all but the clothes they had on. The weather was very cold, and when I saw so many children suffering, I felt that something ought to be done for them. The next morning a bill was introduced appropriating $20,000 for their relief. We put aside all other business and rushed it through as soon as it could be done.

The next summer, when it began to be time to think about election, I concluded I would take a scout around among the boys of my district. I had no opposition there but, as the election was some time off, I did not know what might turn up. When riding one day in a part of my district in which I was more of a stranger than any other, I saw a man in a field plowing and coming toward the road. I gauged my gait so that we should meet as he came up, I spoke to the man. He replied politely, but as I thought, rather coldly.

I began: "Well friend, I am one of those unfortunate beings called candidates and—"

"Yes I know you; you are Colonel Crockett. I have seen you once before, and voted for you the last time you were elected. I suppose you are out electioneering now, but you had better not waste your time or mine, I shall not vote for you again."

This was a sockdolger….I begged him tell me what was the matter.

"Well Colonel, it is hardly worthwhile to waste time or words upon it. I do not see how it can be mended, but you gave a vote last winter which shows that either you have not capacity to understand the Constitution, or that you are wanting in the honesty and firmness to be guided by it. In either case you are not the man to represent me. But I beg your pardon for expressing it that way. I did not intend to avail myself of the privilege of the constituent to speak plainly to a candidate for the purpose of insulting you or wounding you.

I intend by it only to say that your understanding of the Constitution is very different from mine; and I will say to you what but for my rudeness, I should not have said, that I believe you to be honest."

"But an understanding of the Constitution different from mine I cannot overlook, because the Constitution, to be worth anything, must be held sacred, and rigidly observed in all its provisions. The man who wields power and misinterprets it is the more dangerous the honest he is."

"I admit the truth of all you say, but there must be some mistake. Though I live in the backwoods and seldom go from home, I take the papers from Washington and read very carefully all the proceedings of Congress. My papers say you voted for a bill to appropriate $20,000 to some sufferers by fire in Georgetown. Is that true?"

"Well my friend; I may as well own up. You have got me there. But certainly nobody will complain that a great and rich country like ours should give the insignificant sum of $20,000 to relieve its suffering women and children, particularly with a full and over-flowing treasury, and I am sure, if you had been there, you would have done just the same as I did."

"It is not the amount, Colonel, that I complain of; it is the prin-ciple. In the first place, the government ought to have in the Treasury no more than enough for its legitimate purposes. But that has nothing with the question. The power of collecting and disbursing money at pleasure is the most dangerous power that can be entrusted to man, particularly under our system of collect-ing revenue by a tariff, which reaches every man in the country, no matter how poor he may be, and the poorer he is the more he pays in proportion to his means.

What is worse, it presses upon him without his knowledge where the weight centers, for there is not a man in the United States who can ever guess how much he pays to the government. So you see, that while you are contributing to relieve one, you are drawing it from thousands who are even worse off than he.

If you had the right to give anything, the amount was simply a matter of discretion with you, and you had as much right to give $20,000,000 as $20,000. If you have the right to give at all; and as the Constitution neither defines charity nor stipulates the amount, you are at liberty to give to any and everything which you may believe, or profess to believe, is a charity and to any amount you may think proper. You will very easily perceive what a wide door this would open for fraud and corruption and favoritism, on the one hand, and for robbing the people on the other. No, Colonel, Congress has no right to give charity.

Individual members may give as much of their own money as they please, but they have no right to touch a dollar of the public money for that purpose. If twice as many houses had been burned in this country as in Georgetown, neither you nor any other member of Congress would have thought of appropriating a dollar for our relief. There are about two hundred and forty members of Congress. If they had shown their sympathy for the sufferers by contributing each one week's pay, it would have made over $13,000. There are plenty of wealthy men around Washington who could have given $20,000 without depriving themselves of even a luxury of life.

The congressmen chose to keep their own money, which, if reports be true, some of them spend not very creditably; and the people about Washington, no doubt, applauded you for relieving them from necessity by giving what was not yours to give. The people have delegated to Congress, by the Constitution, the power to do certain things. To do these, it is authorized to collect and pay moneys, and for nothing else. Everything beyond this is usurpation, and a violation of the Constitution.

So you see, Colonel, you have violated the Constitution in what I consider a vital point. It is a precedent fraught with danger to the country, for when Congress once begins to stretch its power beyond the limits of the Constitution, there is no limit to it, and no security for the people. I have no doubt you acted honestly, but that does not make it any better, except as far as you are personally concerned, and you see that I cannot vote for you."

I tell you I felt streaked. I saw if I should have opposition, and this man should go to talking and in that district I was a gone fawn-skin. I could not answer him, and the fact is, I was so fully convinced that he was right, I did not want to. But I must satisfy him, and I said to him:

"Well, my friend, you hit the nail upon the head when you said I had not sense enough to understand the Constitution. I intended to be guided by it, and thought I had studied it fully. I have heard many speeches in Congress about the powers of Congress, but what you have said here at your plow has got more hard, sound sense in it than all the fine speeches I ever heard. If I had ever taken the view of it that you have, I would have put my head into the fire before I would have given that vote; and if you will forgive me and vote for me again, if I ever vote for another unconstitutional law I wish I may be shot."

The only real difference between the $20,000 Congressman Crockett voted for the Georgetown fire and the over $2,000,000,000 Congress approved to rebuild New Orleans after Hurricane Katrina is the number of zeroes. The principle of Constitutional authority remains the same. So long as Congress believes they have a right to appropriate our money for charitable purposes, they will continue to give our tax dollars away or waste them with impunity.

It's true that Hurricane Katrina was a disaster of untold magnitude. However, disasters do happen periodically. Small towns in the Midwest are literally picked up and blown away by tornadoes, floods are routine occurrences, massive fires burn cities to the ground such as Chicago in 1871, and earthquakes level cities such as San Francisco in 1906 and 1989.

Just as sure as I'm typing this, more disasters will befall us. There will be more hurricanes, floods, earthquakes, and fires. Do you expect the federal government to appropriate tens of millions of dollars and rebuild entire communities each time a community suffers massive damage? If so, we are not from the same planet. When you live in a flood plain without flood insurance you are a dunce. When your house and all your belongings float away in the aftermath of a hurricane, you should not expect the federal government to soak up the water with wads of federal tax dollars. Davy Crockett learned that lesson and we would all be wise to learn a lesson from him.

I urge each of you to attend your congressman's town hall meetings. These meetings are specifically designed for you to have an open dialogue with your congressman. Take advantage of these opportunities. Ask your congressman-employee what legislation he has specifically proposed to reduce the size of the federal government and how he proposes we pay off the national debt. Let him or her know if you aren't pleased and that you will fire them if they aren't good stewards of our tax dollars.

There are many outstanding private organizations and lobby groups on the front lines, working to expose and eliminate government waste every day. They can use your help in the good fight for responsible stewardship of our hard-earned money. Do your homework and stand for what is right, not for what is politically expedient.

The government does not have the right to waste your money. We the People have the *responsibility* to ensure that they do not.

CHAPTER EIGHT

GET A DAMN JOB

"I'm workin hard to earn my way,
but lucky me my work is play."

★ ★ ★

"Workin Hard Playin Hard,"
Cat Scratch Fever, 1977

Years ago I stated I never graduated from college because I was too damn busy learning stuff! Now mind you, a higher education is almost always a better thing, and although I'm no college educated professional economist, fiscal conservatism is instinctual to this simple, thinking, American Dream guitar player. I have made a few dollars over my lifetime so far, and clearly understand the pragmatic, responsible economic basics of profit and loss, debt and balance sheets, and most importantly, living within your means. Debt and sloth are bad, work ethic and profit are good. Living within your means puts you squarely in the asset column of America.

I work like a man possessed throughout the year, rocking all summer long each and every year for the past forty plus years, and I don't take a dime home until everyone else is paid first. From hard earned salaries and per diems for the best rockband and road crew in the world, to the rawcrude suckfest for our big trucks and buses, state of the art sound and lights, daily catering, professional security, hotel bills, food costs, airfare, guitar strings, and a myriad of outlando other things. Expenses must be covered first. Everyone knows that no apples get to market unless the orchard is well managed and cared for. That's how successful businesses and all responsible families operate.

> ★
> **Debt and sloth are bad; work ethic and profit are good.**

After expenses are paid, mean ol' Uncle Sam picks my pocket for half of what is left for its masterful orgy of waste, and I get to keep the rest. Just as a welder could not make sparks fly if there was not profit to be made, I could not do what I do without conscientiously and vigorously managing my music affairs, producing our *Ted Nugent Spirit of the Wild* and other various television programs, or even writing this book if I was thoughtless enough to operate in the red. Amplifiers, elk hunts, and machineguns are not cheap.

Unless you are Uncle Sam, you don't get up in the morning and go to work to get further in debt at the end of the day. If you are in the asset column of America, you bust your ass every day to make all the money you possibly can, and you want to make more of it as efficiently as possible. Plan B is for chimps. Excellence has its rewards. That's the American way.

If you work harder than the next guy, or hone a skill, product, or service that is in demand, and put your heart and soul into being the very best that you can be, then you stand to make more money. More money and more profit is good. Pretty simple stuff if you ask me. Only socialist punks and stoned welfare bloodsuckers fail to grasp this self-evident economic truth. Therefore, from an economic and spiritual perspective, nonproductive people intentionally make the choice to be liabilities and are a scourge in America and stand against all that is good. They know it, you know it, and Hillary knows it. The horror is, they don't give a damn. Great. Hey Obama, give me something for nothing. We all know you do that; unfortunately, a growing number of Americans clearly do not give a damn. "Ask not what your country can do for you" has sadly become "ask not what you can do for your country."

The only things you need in America to be successful and happy are a dream, a dedicated work ethic and an alarm clock. Everything else is elementary. Surely one of the most powerful forces in the universe is a determined American. We invented "kick ass." Our willingness to sacrifice, dream, cultivate intense creativity, pursue success with a pure animal drive, and persevere with our red, white, and blue warrior can-do spirit propels us past the competition everytime. Always has, always will. The fact that Toyota became #1 in the auto industry is due more to

The only things you need in America to be successful and happy are a dream, a dedicated work ethic, and an alarm clock.

Americans losing this spirit of pride and excellence than anything else. It can be fixed if we dig deep and take charge with that age-old, intense determination again. Instead of negotiating for more benefits and coffee breaks, maybe the unions should negotiate for better productivity and quality control. My team does, and it works. I'm unleashing the greatest, most intense concert tour of my life. My career defies gravity. Next.

Ever notice that productive Americans are never satisfied? Bill Gates constantly tried to improve the Microsoft brand by developing new software and new features. My money says Bill worked no less than seventy hours a week—and he's one of the world's richest men. Americans like Bill Gates, the guy down the road who owns the Rusty Star barbeque restaurant, or so many other small business owners who are the real catalyst behind our economy have a relentless drive to constantly climb new and more dangerous mountains in pursuit of personal excellence and their glowing, unstoppable American Dream. They never give up. Some go broke but they pick themselves up, dust themselves off, and try again. These are true visionaries who will never quit. We all have that instinctual drive deep inside to succeed. But some are strangled by feeble excuse-making by liberal democrats and socialists. For all intents and purposes, it is a form of slavery. Soulless.

> ⭐
> **The path to success is not easy, cheap, or quick. It will require getting up an hour earlier and going to bed an hour later.**

It breaks my heart to see any American giving up on his dreams, hopes, and aspirations simply because someone convinced him that the path to success is either too hard or he would rather sit on the couch and watch his favorite television program. That's no life for me or anyone I know. The path to success is not easy, cheap, or quick. It will require getting up an hour earlier and going to bed an hour later. It may require going back to school to learn a new skill or trade. In my case, it meant practicing the guitar until my fingers were raw and bled. And then I practiced some more. For years I had a welt across my chest from leaning over the guitar during daily marathon jam sessions learning the stunning licks of my heroes, Chuck Berry, Bo Diddly, Duane Eddy, Dick Dale, Lonnie Mack, Keith Richards, Jimmy McCarty, Eric Clapton, Jeff Beck, BB King, Freddie King, Albert King, George Harrison, Junior Walker, Gatemouth Brown, and many, many others. Learning to play the guitar was the hardest thing I have ever done. Every other young guitar player I knew way back then could outplay me on every level, but I never gave up. I merely practiced more.

My path to success meant constantly stepping over stoned, stinky, nasty-ass hippies, punching out crooked promoters, chasing down fraudulent bootleggers, firing band mates who couldn't keep up, being away from my family for extended periods of time, traveling over six million grueling miles, not getting enough sleep, losing my hearing, playing 6,000 over-the-top outrageous concerts, but never compromising my musical vision one spit. I still push myself to the limit and jam everyday. No one has ever gone to a Ted Nugent concert and said that I did not give it my all. I beat myself into a tortured frenzy of gushing sweat and sheer exhaustion every night on stage because I owe you that, not to mention that I enjoy pushing myself beyond known scientific human capabilities. Even after all of that I'm still looking for that elusive perfect tone, the perfect sound, and the next magical grindmaster guitar statement. I can do better and I will do better. I'll rest when I am dead. I kick ass in my sleep.

> ⋆
>
> **A responsible American only uses credit to buy a home and car. Everything else should be cash only. For every dollar you earn, the goal should be half saved.**

Let's get one thing straight upfront: no one owes you a job or a paycheck. This isn't France. For anyone to expect that someone or some company owes you a job is *Planet of the Apes* buffoonery and sinfully anti-American. You are paid what you deserve based upon what you are worth to your employer, nothing more, nothing less. Get that? If you bring in tens of millions of dollars to the company, you are compensated accordingly by the board of directors. If you lean on a broom all day and expect the automobile industry to continue to pay you $32.50 an hour because you are a member of a union and have been around for twenty-five years, get ready to join the ranks of the unemployed. The Japs and Chinese are kicking your ass.

A responsible American only uses credit to buy a home and car. Everything else should be cash only. For every dollar you earn, the goal should be half saved.

Give your employer $100 worth of effort for every dollar you are paid and you will never be without a job. I find it amazing how many Americans fail to realize this, especially young people. They all-too-often do the zombie shuffle and look as though they are about to fall asleep. They then act as though they are doing us a favor by doing their jobs and waiting on us. I correct them every time. Sgt. Nugent reporting for duty. Much to the chagrin of my lovely, patient wife, I politely but sternly tell these young people to speak clearly, smile, and make me feel welcome. I tell them that I am the customer and they receive a paycheck to provide professional, attentive, quality service with a smile. Try it; it's an amazing concept and it pays off.

I hear some Americans complaining that they do not have enough money to make ends meet yet they have sixty-inch plasma televisions and cable or satellite channels, chrome wheels on their pimped-out automobiles, cell phones, iPods, wear the latest fashions, get their hair and nails done, own enough assorted blingbling to sink a sperm whale, have pets, own laptop computers, and basically live like they are millionaires. All of this indulgence is waste any way you cut it, even for rich people, yet some goofy Americans somehow believe they are entitled to

IT'S NOT RIGHT

"I stopped to get some groceries last night. Didn't have too much to get, just some stuff I forgot when I did the regular weekly shopping.

The lady in front of me had a cart brimming with stuff. No big deal, I don't mind waiting. Her total was something like $285. She hands over a state welfare access card, and all of the sudden her total is $25. WTF? I thought I was mistaken, until I saw her fumble through a bunch of cash to hand over a 20 and a 10.

I'm not normally one to bitch about that kind of stuff. When my middle son was an infant, it was medically necessary for him to be on Neocate, a prescription and very expensive formula. Our insurance and the WIC program split the majority of the bill. At $40 per can it wasn't something we could afford ourselves at that time. We got help when we needed it with that. When my oldest was a baby we also had free insurance from the government for him until hubby got a job that offered medical benefits (we were very young and totally unprepared). Got help there too.

But this pissed me off. It's not like she was buying almost $300 worth of staples or necessities. Pop, snacks, junk food, pet food, unnecessary garbage from hell, etc. All on welfare. YET she was in brand new nice shoes, coat, and clothes...with a bunch of gold rings decorating her fingers. When I get outside, she's loading her free groceries into a brand new SUV, yacking away on her cell phone. It is just not right."

—Maryn, TalkBack, tednugent.com

these material creature comforts even though their wages cannot support this non-essential junk. This lifestyle causes them to slide further and further into out-of-control debt.

The average American owes almost $8,000 on credit cards. Instead of stopping the financial hemorrhaging and living intelligently and responsibly within their means, some Americans deliberately continue to commit economic hari-kari. Unbelievable. This is analogous to repeatedly stabbing yourself in the eye and then complaining that you can not see. Weird.

It boils down to wants and needs. Take care of your real needs first and if there is money left, spend it as you see fit. The problem is that Americans have confused wants and needs. Needs are things such as quality sustenance without waste, basic clothing, simple and affordable shelter, reasonable insurance, and gas for essential travel. Everything else is blingbling. Those of you who actually believe you need cigarettes, booze, dining out constantly, cable television, multiple cell phones, a new jacket despite a closet full of them, and more, who then "can't afford" a nutritious school lunch for your kids are just plain rotten human beings. And the more bizarre amongst you want the rest of us to pay for your health care while you waste money on dog food, getting your fake finger nails polished and painted, along with other, too numerous to list, gluttonous indulgences. My advice: eat the dog and clip your own damn nails. To paraphrase Pogo's eloquent statement from many years ago: I have seen the enemy and he is us.

> ★
>
> **My advice: eat the dog and clip your own damn nails.**

Want more blingbling? How about getting a second or third job? Now that's a novel thought. If working forty hours does not provide you enough money, then work sixty hours. I see "help wanted" signs everywhere. Surely you see them, too. Bust your hump and go get another job. Last time I counted, I had about a dozen jobs. Seriously. On a good night, I get six to eight hours of sound sleep. The remaining fourteen to eighteen hours a day is spent making music, rehearsing and recording

"JUST WHAT THE DOCTOR ORDERED"

I got my guitar when I was
    10 years old
Found a love in rock 'n' roll
Now I'm on the verge of a
    nervous breakdown
I'm gonna give my body and
    soul

It's so crazy
But you know that I like it
I've found a cure for my body
    and soul
I've got me an overdose of rock
    'n' roll

I jammed everyday
I jammed everynight
I practiced till I knew all the licks
Now I'm on the verge of a
    nervous breakdown
I don't know the meaning of quit

It's so crazy
Yes you know, but I like it
I question my health, my brain is
    on the border
But this is what the doctor
    ordered
Yes, it is

I jammed everyday
I jammed every night
I practiced till I knew all the licks
Now I'm on the verge of a
    nervous breakdown
I don't know the meaning of quit

It's so crazy
But I like it
I question my health, my brain is
    on the border
But this is what the doctor
    ordered

—*Ted Nugent*, 1975

with my band, preparing tours, touring, conducting media interviews, filming and editing my television programs, guiding hunters, writing books, newspaper editorials, and articles for over 40 publications, filming movies, doing charity work year-round, running my trapline, training dogs, shoveling kennels, fixing fences, sweeping garages and barns, filling feeders, clearing brush, planting trees and foodplots, speaking at universities and various public events, writing songs, tending to Mrs. Nugent, raising kids, scaring politicians, and more. Show me a busier human being and I will come over to your house, do your laundry for a week, and then eat your pickup truck. Your house plants will wilt and die in my vaportrail, then we will eat them.

> ✫
>
> **America is not at war. The U.S. Military is at war. America is at the mall.**

Welfare is for liars and people too lazy to work. If you are angry with that statement, good. That would be guilt. If that pisses you off, you are either on welfare or you are an anti-capitalist socialist enemy of America who believes the homicidal commie punk Che should have been given the Nobel Peace Prize. Do us all a favor and take the first boat to Cuba. Only a numbnut would disagree with a policy that all able-bodied men and women should work. Not forced, so to speak, by government or physical coercion of any kind, but by the forces of goodwill and decency and the rewards of dedicated productivity versus the pain, suffering, and anguish of self-inflicted dependency. Instead of a society rewarding good and punishing laziness—conditions forcing people to either work or starve—we have created an institutional, wasteful, anti-human system that has stripped people of their pride, their work ethic, and their independence. Damn shame.

Welfare has created and rewarded a sub-human underclass of underachievers. What is even more pathetic is that welfare has become a runaway, generational entitlement program. Instead of getting off of welfare, we now see generations of welfare recipients who have come to consider it their right. Lovely, just lovely. These dogs are too damn lazy to scratch their own fleas yet they squaller and whine about how the rest of us owe them. Dogs have no souls.

We do not need to reform welfare, we need to abolish it. Not only is there no reference to this foolish concept found in the U.S. Constitution, (for clearly it is outside the realm of "self-evident truth"), but by all honest review, it is a false "feel good" system that begs for corruption and waste. Allowing the feds or state government to have any financial responsibility in helping the needy is analogous to hiring a staggering drunk to manage a liquor store. They created the problem in the first place! The definition of insanity is doing the same thing over and over again and expecting different results, and unless we want to compound the problem by continuing to throw our hard-earned tax dollars into the welfare abyss of zero accountability, it's time shed all government welfare programs like a cheap suit. End it now, all of it.

All welfare programs should be shut down tomorrow at noon. Welfare recipients should be handed rakes, brooms, shovels, paint brushes, picks, and hoes. We did this very thing in the 1930s under the Works

> ★
>
> **We do not need to reform welfare, we need to abolish it.**

Progress Administration in order to give people jobs so we could climb out of the Great Depression and save the world by throttling the Nazis and the Japs. We damn sure could and should do that today. When given the choice between starving and eating, people will make the choice to eat. Every time. Those that don't do not get to breed. Hey Darwin, I got your natural selection right here.

The real curse of this current system of blind welfare is that (inevitable) corruption and deceit have funneled so much money to

"CRAVE"

A simple life, I will not have
It doesn't satisfy me
I don't believe in the status quo
It kinda leaves me weak,
A mountain high is what I climb,
I swim the river deep
And if ya crave the time of your
    life,
Try to keep up with me

I'm gonna live I'm gonna fly
I'm gonna soar till the day I die,
On the wings of a Byrd of prey,
Hey hey hey,
You're absolutely what I crave,

Look at me,
I got a smile on my face
Ya know it don't come cheap,
Sure I live the American dream,
Go ahead and crucify me

I'm gonna live I'm gonna fly
I'm gonna soar till the day I die,
And all the wings of a bird are
    prey,
Hey hey hey,
You're absolutely what I crave,
Crave,

I'm gonna live I'm gonna fly
I'm gonna soar till the day I die,
And all the wings of a bird are
    prey,
Hey hey hey,
I'm gonna live I'm gonna fly
I'm gonna soar till the day I die,
And all the wings of a bird are
    prey,
Hey hey hey,
You're absolutely what I crave
Crave

—*Craveman*, 2002

redundant administrational boondoggles that the truly needy end up with the short end of the stick. Meanwhile, many able-bodied Americans have become so depraved that they view taking advantage of the system as a badge of honor. They are actually gleeful and proud that they have robbed their neighbors and sucked blood from their fellow Americans. Shame on them. We have seen too many examples of welfare brats loading up with expensive bling while we pay for heating fuel assistance, foodstamps, school lunch programs, transportation, housing, healthcare assistance—the disgusting list goes on—while they end up with bigscreen TVs, horses, pimpmobiles, pedicures, liposuction, and an incredible pile of superfluous bullshit. And their insane, unaffordable shopping sprees are paid for by hard working America. Bizzarro.

It is true, though, that some people, through no fault of their own, need a temporary helping hand. Like millions of generous, loving, giving Americans, I will be the first in line to offer them my assistance, as does the average American who donates to more community charities than any people in the history of humanity. (Liberals, not so much.) Indeed, Americans in real, honest-to-God need will always be cared for by family and the plethora of generous charitable organizations across the land. The Catholic church alone is worth a few trillion dollars in gold, silver, jewelry, art, real estate and God knows what, even after the few billion dollars they were forced to dole out defending the in-house gang of pedophiles amongst their "spiritual" brethren. They gave a few billion bucks more to the families of their demonic sexual abuse, yet still the basket is passed each Sunday to bilk the hardest working members of the congregation.

> **If people in their communities are experiencing genuine times of need, let the churches help them out.**

Mind-boggling really. If people in their communities are experiencing genuine times of need, let the churches help them out.

Instead of building new, multi-million dollar additions with donated cash, more churches should act more like Jesus and do what he commanded us to do: help the poor. It is possible to find people who need help in any community in America. Only the guilty churches and congregations should feel guilty for if the church you attend is active in helping the needy in your community, you are doing the Lord's work and should be very proud. There is much work to do. Let your spirit faith move mountains.

Civic and community organizations should also be challenged to step up. Instead of holding annual banquets, slapping each other on the back, and giving one another meaningless awards, these organizations should focus their resources on those in the community who legitimately need the help. Again, only the guilty need feel guilty. I realize there are many excellent organizations and charities that are staffed by volunteers. These people do a tremendous amount of heavy lifting behind the scenes and generally do not get, expect, or want any recognition. These are the people who make America great. I salute you.

> ★
>
> **If you do not know your neighbor, stop reading this book right now, and go introduce yourself.**

Neighbors must step up, too. If your neighbor has fallen on hard times, the neighborly thing to do is to offer a hand of assistance. Neighbors helping neighbors helps build strong neighborhoods, communities, and ultimately, our country. If you do not know your neighbor, stop reading this book right now, and go introduce yourself. Get to know them. No need to be best friends with them, but remember that neighbors looking out for neighbors is the American way. Coming home from work, pulling into the garage, shutting the garage door, walking inside, and turning on the mind-control box won't cut it. I could not be more convinced that if everyone in America committed to the simple act of just getting to know their neighbors, crime and poverty would be dramatically reduced, drug dealers would end up behind bars where they belong, kids would be staying in school instead of dropping out, and literally, lives would be saved. We must all commit to doing better if we want to make our neighborhoods and communities safer places to live, work, and play. Do this now. It is that important.

Give America the best you got by busting your ass and never accepting mediocrity.

By keeping assistance at the grassroots person-to-person level in the community, we are better equipped to provide specific assistance as required and to better identify those dishonestly abusing the system. If that isn't the goal, then what in God's name is? The problem and solution is incredibly obvious to me. There will be naysayers who claim I'm being too simplistic in my observations, analysis, and recommendations. These are the kind of people who want to study a problem for years (with taxpayers' dollars, of course) and then offer no real solutions. Meanwhile, the problem only gets larger, stinks more, and ruins more lives. They are bureaucrats whose only real mission in life is sustaining and building the bureaucracy. I get more done during a cold, wet morning in a deerblind than these bureaupunks will get done all year.

America horrifically and mistakenly gave the left-wing social engineers a free ride for forty-five years and all they did was make a complete mess of things while burning through a couple of trillion dollars with their Great Society and other left-wing bullshit. Give some true reformers (they are known as real conservatives) a week and we'll fix it. We'll restore dignity, pride, and independence in people. Guaranteed. If a socialist house gets in our way, we'll burn it down. This is the America I was raised in and still believe in. Give America the best you got by busting your ass and never accepting mediocrity. Mediocrity is poison. Excellence must always be the goal. Be an asset, not a liability. It is a simple choice no matter what anybody says.

CHAPTER NINE

BLACK LIKE ME

"The ultimate measure of a man is not where he
stands in moments of comfort and convenience,
but where he stands at times
of challenge and controversy."

★ ★ ★

Martin Luther King, Jr., 1963

As a large, in charge, ruggedly independent, angry black man, oh-so-reverently genuflecting at the Funkbrother Altar of Motown, I believe it is time for black people like me who give a damn to take back our pride, our lot in life, and our communities. We all must do whatever we can with our unlimited positive power to lead our families and communities to the Promised Land which Dr. Martin Luther King, Jr. so eloquently celebrated in his last speech to the nation so many years ago. Follow me, brothers and sisters, and let us work hard to restore our hopes, dreams, and aspirations.

Black is beautiful. To quote the Godfather of Soul, "Say it loud; I'm black and I'm proud." Mayor Kwame, thanks for nothing. You are the enemy of black America. My priority has always been to focus on a flat tire instead of admiring three tires full of air on an otherwise fine vehicle. So while February is designated as the month to celebrate all things good with black Americans, we should also identify the bad and the ugly in order to effectively pursue upgrade.

> ★
>
> **Black is beautiful. To quote the Godfather of Soul, "Say it loud; I'm black and I'm proud."**

It is important to understand our true black history if we are to identify where we are going. The history of blacks in America is a rich and colorful portrait of family, dedication, sacrifice, strong work ethic, belief in God, discipline, love of country, patience, and above all, a desire for our offspring to have a better life than what we have had. Many brothers and sisters maintain these wonderful time-honored values that were born of the sweat and prayers of our forefathers who toiled their lives away as slaves. I say never again. We are after all, "free, free at last."

Freedom. It is a wonderful word...a liberating word...the dream with letters. It's a word to be eternally fought for, cherished, celebrated, embraced, demanded, and passed on to our young people. Only by fully embracing freedom, which ultimately means taking responsibility for our own destiny and the actions that accomplish it, can we then begin to fully realize our potential, climb that mountain, peer over the precipice, and drink from the cold, refreshing spring waters of the Promised Land.

Sadly, others in our community have turned away from the values our forefathers embraced. They have embraced a culture of soulless rot, ethnic suicide, and self-imposed death and destruction. They will never see the Promised Land. We must ask why, we must demand the truth, and we certainly must be willing to do whatever is necessary to stop the plague of violence, hopelessness, and poverty that permeates so many of our communities. While I do not have all of the answers, I am sure of one thing: more government departments, agencies, and programs are not part of the answer. These are the very well-meaning institutions that contributed to the destruction of black America by eroding our family, community, and cultural foundations.

As brother President Reagan once said, "Government is not the answer, it is the problem." Regardless of their words, the federal government has never been about helping blacks. Instead of studying their laws and the rules of their programs, we should focus on their deeds and actions. If you do, you will find their actions have hurt, never helped us. They did the same to Native Americans. They wrote long, flowing treaties with Native Americans and then promptly ignored the treaties and butchered their people. Those treaties were written in suffering and signed in blood.

> **As brother President Reagan once said, "government is not the answer, it is the problem."**

Prior to the era of big government in the 1960s, black families were strong and proud, our communities were vibrant, our young people studious and polite, drugs were rare and the exception rather than the rule, and prisons and jails were not nearly as full of young black men as they are today.

Today, many black families are in ruin. Seventy percent of our young people are being raised in single parent families; fathers are an endangered species. In many cities—such as my hometown of Detroit—well over half of our young people do not even graduate from high school, thereby sentencing themselves to a life of poverty. Our inner cities are virtual war zones, not vibrant, peaceful communities. Our young people kill each other over the color of the clothes they wear, drugs are everywhere, and over half of the prison populations in America are made up of black men, though we constitute only 12 percent of the American population. Like it or not, this is the horrible condition of black America. Can I hear a "Hallelujah! Preach on Brother Nuge!"?

There is a movement in our communities to refuse to cooperate with the police and it is the wrong move. Whether it is out of fear of reprisal from black punk criminals or because we believe the police are racists, or both, failing to cooperate guarantees more violence and death in our communities. Only a coward or another black thug would not cooperate with the police. If we want peaceful and safe communities, we must cooperate with the police.

> **White racism did not put them in prison; their own poor choices locked them in cages because that's where they belong.**

Our prisons are full of young black men because they turned to a life of crime in the absence of black America's most powerful traditional force of family, love, discipline, and guidance. White racism did not put them in prison; their own poor choices locked them in cages because that's where they belong. Once let out of prison, many will return to a life of crime. They will victimize more people—mostly other blacks. Many black thugs have been in and out of prison numerous times and have a list of crimes that is lengthy, despicable, and horrendous. They belong in cages, not in our communities where they will surely prey upon us. They should be left there to rot as an example to our young people that crime leads to cages.

"THE BLACK MAN, HE RUNS THROUGH HIS AFRICA."

"TOOTH, FANG & CLAW,"
SPIRIT OF THE WILD, 1995

White, wealthy, liberals have long been our enemy, though too few of us have recognized, or, I believe, dared to admit it. Instead, we have embraced our enemy as our friend and swallowed their political poison. In the process, our families, institutions, communities, and pride have been vanquished. White liberals of the Democratic Party, not white Republicans and conservatives, have, and are continuing to destroy the Black people. These liberals propagate racist policies that are based on the assumption that we are too stupid and lazy to take care of ourselves and they try to convince us, often successfully, that we need Big Brother to give us handouts. But we do not need handouts. We can take care of ourselves and we know it. Welfare in all its forms is the new slavery and this Funkbrother refuses to play that game.

White liberals are snakes. While they claim that they want to do good, what they really want is to buy our vote to keep themselves in power in order to make themselves, not us, more wealthy. And we insanely give these political racists our support in overwhelming numbers. Traditionally in the presidential race, Democrats receive 90 percent of the black vote. Without this kind of support from black voters, the Democrats would never again win a presidential race. Can we be bought and paid for like this? I say no way.

Liberals have conditioned black people to believe that we are unable to do and provide for ourselves. They have habituated us to the belief

continued

☆ ☆ ☆

that the Great White Liberal Father in Washington, D.C. is our only salvation and that we need to be taken care of. Hogwash. Dr. King didn't believe this and neither do I. Neither should you.

Dependence on social programs creates a cycle of poverty and unfulfilled dreams unbroken from generation to generation. Black people are being used as pawns for white, liberal snakes to move on their political chess boards as they see fit. Liberals are the political enemies of black people, pure and simple. To fail to grasp this truism is to misunderstand how the political game is played. Liberal politicians control many of our cities—and look at their condition. They are war zones. Our young children cannot even play outside in many areas of these cities without fear of being gunned down, beaten, raped, or robbed *by our own kind!* From my hometown of Detroit, to Philadelphia, to even Washington, D.C., the home of the federal government, the nights in our communities are not filled with laughter or song, but rather the terrifying sound of gunfire throughout the liberals' dreamed up *gun-free zones*! How much more white liberal bullshit are we willing to take?

These are not white people shooting and killing blacks; this is not the evil KKK. This is, astonishingly, blacks shooting, murdering, and raping other blacks. You will not be mugged in our communities by a white thug—only by black thugs. Most crime against blacks is committed by blacks. This is unbelievable and heartbreaking. Haven't you had enough?

We gather to mourn, cry, and march when another one of our young gangsters is gunned down in the street. We shout out on our marches that the violence must stop, but deep down inside we surely know that tomorrow will bring more violence, more drugs, and more death. And the same will happen the day after, too. Our marches are meaningless.

continued

> While marches against violence may make us feel as though we have accomplished something to save our communities, the cold, hard fact is that no lives have been saved because of a march. Not one.

Despite knowing that numerous, violent thugs with lengthy arrest and conviction records are living in our communities, some black community leaders and pastors claim that easy access to guns is to blame for the violence and crime in our neighborhoods. They must be drunk on sacramental wine. The real problem is that not enough law-abiding black citizens in our neighborhoods have the ability to defend themselves. If more law-abiding citizens in our communities had guns and legally carried them to protect their loved ones, the black thugs who prey on us just might think twice about attacking. Taking back our communities begins with being able to defend ourselves. Dialing 9-1-1 will get you killed.

⋆ **Dialing 9-1-1 will get you killed.**

The nation's first gun laws were aimed at blacks as Jim Crow ran amok. Those days should be over. Do yourself and our communities a favor by getting a gun and a concealed carry permit, practicing often, and defending yourself from criminal thugs who want to harm you. Refuse to become a victim.

Many of our young people are stupid. It is not their fault. Many of their parents are stupid, too. Their parents placed no value on education and passed this trait on to their children. With high school dropout rates at 70 percent or higher in some black communities, we are sentencing our young people to a life of poverty and despair. In a widening world of the "Haves" and "Have Nots," they will be the latter. Their opportunities are severely limited and they will be confined to taking jobs on the lowest rung of the economic ladder. Advancement will be limited, if existent. The wages they will earn will be poverty wages—less than what they can subsist on. They will be qualified for nothing. Many will turn to a short life of gangs and crime and end up either dead or in prison. You know this to be true. Black poverty is not the result of white racism; it's the product of our failure to value education. An education is the way out. Period.

Education is not a "white" value to be shunned and mocked, but a human value to be embraced, cherished, and passed on to future generations. America needs educated blacks. We need black engineers, scientists, computer specialists, entrepreneurs, and all other professional specialties that require a college education. To ignore education is to spit on that for which our forefathers worked so hard. They wanted to have this opportunity—and they wanted it for us. Don't you dare throw our forefathers' hopes and dreams down the gutter. Don't you dare.

Everyone knows that the best chance in life is provided by a set of loving, caring parents. With upwards of 70 percent of black children being raised by single parents, we are, metaphorically, eating our young.

> ★
>
> **With upwards of 70 percent of black children being raised by single parents, we are, metaphorically, eating our young.**

Kids who are raised by single parents are much more likely to get involved in drugs, drop out of school, have sex at an early age, and get involved in crime. The data is irrefutable. This is what the black studs who impregnate our young women must want because they are absent in the lives of their offspring. They are only the biological fathers. They are not real fathers. A dad loves, guides, directs, encourages, instructs, disciplines, and is there for his children. It takes two, a mother and father, to raise a child. Let us raise our children, not grow them.

The greatest threat to our communities is the lack of sexual values in both our young men and young women. Black babies having babies with biological sperm donors who then disappear is a recipe for social and cultural genocide. This behavior poses a far greater threat to black continuity than how whites treated our forefathers as slaves all those years ago. We are killing the future of black Americans. If we want to save black America, we must confront this immediately.

So-called black leaders such as Jesse Jackson and Al Sharpton enrich themselves by fanning the barely flickering embers of racism, all the while our black communities are rotting from within. They are the first to protest and march against the rare but erroneous white injustices against black people, but they do not come to our communities to offer aid, hard and tough love, or any honest suggestions to help us. They are charlatans who advocate dependence instead of independence. Like white liberals, we must scorn the race-baiting Jacksons and Sharptons of the world, not embrace them. Following Jackson and Sharpton will cause the black condition to further deteriorate. They are wolves dressed as sheep who will lead us to further slaughter, not the Promised Land.

> ★
> **Like white liberals, we must scorn the race-baiting Jacksons and Sharptons of the world, not embrace them.**

The good news is that institutional racism is a dead, rotting corpse and has been for quite sometime. Both Jackson and Sharpton know this but if they publicly admitted it, they would both be unemployed. With the right education, skills, and abilities, black Americans are widely embraced by employers. Moreover, there are severe penalties for denying a qualified person a job based upon race, creed, color, or sex. Every employer knows this. Educated blacks are doing very well for themselves and their families. We, quite frankly, cannot be stopped. Unfortunately, we cannot legislate personal hate out of existence. If a person, black or white, hates another person based purely on the color of his skin, there is little we can do for that racist except pray. He has poisoned his heart with hate. We must all practice what Dr. King taught us, which is to judge a person by his character, not his color. If you want to be treated fairly and with respect, that's how you must treat others. To refer to one another as niggers, dogs, and hos is hateful, sad, and racist. These are not terms of endearment or respect—they are low-class, demeaning, and derogatory terms. The use of these ugly terms must end in our communities. Respect for self and others cannot be achieved by using vile and reprehensible language to describe ourselves or our brothers and sisters. And it is indefensible to condemn others for using these hateful words but then claim that we can use them because of the color of our skin. MLK must surely be rolling over in his grave.

Too many of us give Jackson and Sharpton our respect and admiration and refer to other prominent blacks who do not harbor liberal beliefs as Uncle Toms—sellouts to the white man. Supreme Court Justice Clarence Thomas, author Thomas Sowell, talk-show host Armstrong Williams, and writer/economist Walter Williams have suffered this slur. Through hard work, sacrifice, and a quest for excellence, these brethren have blazed a trail of success for other black Americans to follow. Yet they are demeaned by many blacks for embracing conservative values. Justice Thomas's *New York Times* bestselling book, *My Grandfather's Son*, should be mandatory reading by all young blacks. Our young people may think they have it tough, but they won't know the true meaning of tough until they read Justice Thomas's book.

Thomas Sowell is a brilliant author who has written numerous books on topics ranging from economics to social issues. He is a national treasure and should be treated as such by all Americans. Read Mr. Sowell's books and learn. I suspect these two fine men in particular are embraced by more whites than blacks. Why is this?

All of this leads me to the presidential race of 2008. Barack Obama, a half black man, was the nominee for the Democrats. Obama galvanized and inspired the nation with his eloquent speeches of general hope and change. Black Americans responded in overwhelming numbers to his message of "Change You Can Believe In." A majority of blacks supported Senator Obama for president. Not this black man.

Barack Obama is a black liberal. The only difference between him and his white liberal friends is the color of his skin. In fact, Barack Obama was rated as the most liberal senator in the entire senate in 2007 by the *National Journal*. As I articulated earlier in this chapter, liberals are incredibly dangerous and very destructive to black Americans. The color of their skin does not matter.

In addition to being a black-destroying liberal, President Obama has zero experience and no record of any kind, public or private, that qualifies him to be the leader of anything, let alone president. He is politically naïve, inexperienced, and believes government knows what is better for you than you do. Just because President Obama is a black man does not mean he is a friend to blacks. He is not. He is a liberal snake in the grass.

Instead of mentioning a single word about the unhealthy lifestyle so rampant in our black communities, he wants to reform health care and put the government in charge. This will destroy the most successful health care industry the world has ever known. With the U.S. government in charge of health care, pray you never get sick. Like everything else they get their hands on, "waste" and "unaccountability" are guaranteed to be the key operative words.

> ⋆
>
> **Just because President Obama is a black man does not mean he is a friend to blacks. He is not. He is a liberal snake in the grass.**

Obama has stated he would talk with America's enemies—such as Iran. Iran is a lying, terrorist regime dedicated to the destruction of the civilized world that should be isolated, not validated. President Obama's willingness to have a dialogue with one of the world's most oppressive governments shows his international inexperience. Should we sit down with the Klan so we can all just get along? I don't think so.

President Obama will raise payroll taxes to prop up Social Security, one of the government's largest liberal, out-of-control, bankrupt programs. He also supports starting taxpayer-funded savings programs for low-income workers. This, too, will result in more taxes on hard-working black Americans whom bureaucrats will eventually bankrupt. Will we ever learn? He is against us having the right to defend ourselves in our communities. He supports disarming us so that only criminals and his tax-funded personal armed security force have guns. That seems fair.

> ☆
>
> **Should we sit down with the Klan so we can all just get along? I don't think so.**

President Obama is long on windy speeches but short on substance. What we do know is that President Obama is a liberal—apparently one of the most liberal politicians alive. And we know that liberal policies, programs, and agencies have destroyed our communities, our families, and our values. Liberals can never be trusted. Barack Hussein Obama is a terrible president.

Unlike President Obama, who speaks of change but offers little substance, I prefer Dr. Martin Luther King who dreamed of a better tomorrow. Dr. King is more believable and inspiring than the blowhard, liberal President Obama.

Of all the famous speeches given by American statesmen and freedom lovers, Dr. Martin Luther King's "I Have a Dream" address delivered on the steps of the Lincoln Memorial on August 28, 1963 is one of the most powerful, inspiring, and eloquent. It's mounted on my office wall—it moves me that much.

One particular line in Dr. King's speech is as poignant and illustrative today as it was forty-five years ago when he gave it. "Let us not wallow in the valley of despair, I say to you today, my friends. And so even though we face the difficulties of today and tomorrow, I still have a dream. It is a dream deeply rooted in the American Dream."

Like Dr. King, I, too, have a dream that is rooted in the American Dream.

I dream of a day when my great-grandchildren will look fondly back on our generation and proclaim that we did not shirk our responsibilities and trials, but instead turned to face the issues of our day with courage and conviction much like the American Bison turns to face the howling winter storms. Maybe I am the Great Black Buffalo. I think so.

I dream of a day when future generations of Americans have more opportunity and more freedom than we do. I may not live to see this Promised Land, but it is my dream and I will continue to work towards achieving it. I will continue to make sparks fly in the arena.

I dream of a day, someday soon, when Americans will look in the mirror to introduce themselves to the person responsible for their station in life—instead of trying to blame someone else if they don't like that face. I am in charge and I want to keep it that way.

I dream of a day when Americans realize that we have a great government, but that America did not become great because of its government. It became a great nation

Barack Hussein Obama is a terrible president.

because of a people who refused to accept tyranny or the status quo, and who dreamed of and died for freedom.

I dream of a day when Americans shake off their cloaks of apathy, roll up their sleeves, and commit themselves to improving their own lives, the lives of their families, their communities, and America. Activism is real funk and roll.

I dream of a day when all Americans re-commit themselves to excellence and realize their American Dream can be achieved through hard work, dedication to craft, and sacrifice. There are no short cuts. None.

I dream of a day, one day soon, when parents turn off the television, computer games, and cell phones and spend more time with their children. Only copious amounts of love, guidance, and discipline will shape a child into an accountable, responsible, and courteous adult in the asset column of America.

I will never quit dreaming and working towards a better tomorrow. That is the American spirit. In spite of the numerous and weighty challenges facing our country, I still believe America's best days are in front of us if we unleash that uniquely American innovative and determined spirit that has always risen to the challenges of the day. Now is our time to rise, brothers and sisters!

President Reagan stated in his farewell address to America, "I've spoken of the Shining City all my political life. In my mind it was a tall, proud city built on rocks stronger than oceans, windswept, God-blessed, and teeming with people of all kinds living in harmony and peace; a city with free ports that hummed with commerce and creativity. And if there had to be city walls, the walls had doors and the doors were open to anyone with the will and the heart to get here. That's how I saw it, and see it still."

I see America through the same lens as President Reagan and Dr. King. I have a dream: an American Dream. Dream with me. I think I will run for president of the National Association for the Advancement of Colored People. I would appreciate your vote. Join me. Let's rock.

I remain black and proud. Say it loud. I break out, in a cold sweat. Papa's got a brand new bag. I feel good. It's a man's world. Hit me.

CHAPTER TEN

IMMIGRATION

"In the first place, we should insist that if
the immigrant who comes here in good faith becomes
an American and assimilates himself to us, he shall be treated
on an exact equality with everyone else.... But this is predicated
upon the person's becoming in every facet an American...."

★ ★ ★

—Theodore Roosevelt, 1919

ome of us Theodores sure do think alike. I love immigrants and immigration. To love them is to love America, for we all know that the very Herculean genetic profile of this amazing, strong, productive, Last Best Place is founded upon the original American breeders who came here to follow their hearts, dreams, instincts, and aspirations. The vast majority of original Americans were the most courageous, defiant Europeans from the old, unacceptable world of tyrants, kings, and dictators; and these uppity, take-no-shit forefathers of ours decided that they had had enough.

Think of the movies *The Patriot* and *Braveheart*. They knew it was time to beat feet, escape, get the hell out, unleash the beast within, and head for the promised land even if there was no guarantee of success, for their hearts and minds told them definitively that there was no way they were going to be dominated any longer. "Live free or die," "Don't tread on me," and "Shall not be infringed" roiled over in their souls. We shall take the risks and cross the big pond, for death would surely be no worse than living under the control of a king. Our brave forefathers knew there was more to life. They knew that freedom was the path to happiness. They were determined to make it on their own and live a dream—a uniquely American Dream—where We the People determine our own destiny through hard work and sacrifice. No more could evil henchmen come into our lives to do with an unarmed citizenry as they damn well pleased. It was time to rise up, seize the day, and take control. Fight the good fight. I'm outta here.

> **These uppity forefathers of ours decided that they had had enough.**

What you are about to read will get me labeled a racist and xenophobe, again. Those charges, of course, are not true, but false and libelous labels and accusations do not matter to me. I do not easily suffer fools and intellectual cotton balls. The truth is all that matters and you are about to read a massive chunk of unvarnished, unapologetic, politically incorrect, bold, full-auto nonstop truth, Nugent style, thank you very much. The truth will either set you free or break your neck— it's your choice. I am the Ropeman of Truth.

I merely bring the rope of truth to the party, and unsuspecting denial cultists never fail to toss it over a nearby rafter, noose it around their necks and jump off a chair. So be it. It is my job and I'm perfect at it. Before we get started, give me a moment to adjust my glowing, shining halo of common sense, truth, and justice. And yes, inventory my vast supply of rope. We live in a target-rich environment and I must always be prepared. The Last Boy Scout lives.

> ★
>
> **The truth will either set you free or break your neck—it's your choice. I am the Ropeman of Truth.**

During his tenure, President Bush was a coward for not having enough leadership or political will to protect our nation's borders. As a direct result, millions of illegal immigrants poured over our borders during his presidency. As Pat Buchanan states in his shocking book on criminal immigration, *State of Emergency,* America is being invaded. As Buchanan further asserts, in an earlier time in America, President Bush would have been impeached for his dereliction of this clear presidential duty. I hang my head in shame and have to agree. It not only surprises and shocks me, it breaks my heart.

Let's get one thing straight right off the bat. The people who enter America illegally have committed a crime. That makes them criminals, which is the reason why I will accurately refer to them throughout this chapter as criminal aliens. They are not undocumented workers or even illegal aliens; they are criminal aliens. Got it? A spade is still a spade in my world. Political correctness be damned.

The answers to seemingly complex problems are often not nearly as confusing and daunting as we make them out to be. By breaking a problem down into manageable pieces it becomes less troublesome. Criminal immigration is no different. Think of criminal immigration in the following terms and then apply your common sense conclusions to America's overall criminal immigration problem.

Let's say that upon coming home from work today, you enter your humble abode to find people you do not know and have not invited sitting in your dining room eating your food, rifling through your medicine cabinet, sleeping in your bed, and lounging in your family room in front of your television. What would you immediately do? Personally, I would scream rather emphatic instructions at gunpoint with a fine red dot dancing on their center mass as I force them from my home. Of course, many of you would call the police. The police would hopefully come in time and dutifully arrest the intruders. That makes perfect law and order sense. With the possible exception of the ACLU and people with cinder blocks for brains, surely no fair-minded American who respects private property and the rule of law will argue with this common sense approach of arresting the intruders who criminally entered your home. Try entering the Nugent household illegally and you will exit in a Ziploc bag wearing a toe tag. Invited guests into my home are more than welcome; invaders will be shot more than once. Know this.

> ⭐
>
> **Try entering the Nugent household illegally and you will exit in a Ziploc bag wearing a toe tag.**

People who embrace logic as their daily guidepost will easily extrapolate the previous example of the rightful protection and sanctity of their home to our nation. Those who fail to see the parallels and similarities between their home and our nation should immediately return to the first grade and begin anew. This time try to pay attention.

Regrettably—with few exceptions such as Colorado Representative Tom Tancredo and a couple others who actually care about securing our borders for the future of this country—our professional politicians have failed to grasp the fundamental concept that the rightful protection of an American's home is no different than the dutiful, legal, and just protection that should be applied to our nation's borders. Because of our politicians' apparent lack of fundamental leadership, love of country, courage, and respect for our nation's laws, America is being over-run by non-Americans. That is not debatable. The thousands of criminal aliens who are pouring over our borders on a daily basis are, as radio talk show host Michael Savage might argue, changing our borders, language, and culture. It is happening. Look around you. It is undeniable. If this invasion isn't stopped, we won't recognize America in a few short decades. The peril to our great nation is that great.

> **Invited guests into my home are more than welcome; invaders will be shot more than once. Know this.**

No one knows for sure how many criminal aliens are here or how many are breaking our immigration laws and coming to America each day and year. I have seen estimates that ten to 30 million criminal aliens are already in America and as many as one half to one million more invaders come every year. In *State of Emergency*, Pat Buchanan claims that between 10 and 20 percent of all Mexican, Central American, and Caribbean people are living in the United States. This is untenable and unacceptable, and worse, a sure recipe for disaster. Far too many of these invaders have made it abundantly clear that their allegiance is to their homelands, NOT America. That's like inviting Santa Anna's men into the Alamo for a BBQ break. Insane.

Those Americans who speak out against criminal aliens are labeled racists, xenophobes, and anti-immigration by those real anti-American forces on both sides of our southern border. Pro-criminal alien organizations attempt to legitimize their anti-American beliefs by arguing that America is a nation of immigrants and that criminal aliens actually

WISDOM FROM ANOTHER UNCLE TED

"In the first place, we should insist that if the immigrant who comes here in good faith becomes an American and assimilates himself to us, he shall be treated on an exact equality with everyone else, for it is an outrage to discriminate against any such man because of creed, or birthplace, or origin. But this is predicated upon the person's becoming in every facet an American, and nothing but an American . . . . There can be no divided allegiance here. Any man who says he is an American, but something else also, isn't an American at all. We have room for but one flag, the American flag . . . . We have room for but one language here, and that is the English language . . . and we have room for but one sole loyalty and that is a loyalty to the American people."

—Theodore Roosevelt, 1919

benefit America through their economic, social, and cultural tangibles and intangibles. Those who make these perverted and unsupportable arguments are dangerous anti-Americans whose ultimate goal is to reduce America to a third world country. They are succeeding while our disconnected politicians are inactive and paralyzed. Atlas is shrugging-because of the weight of their pathetic, political paralysis. They have damned themselves with their insubordination and dereliction of sworn-oath duty. May they become roadkill on the expressway to Hell.

In addition to these outrages, leadership in numerous American cities have actually declared themselves to be "sanctuary cities" for criminal aliens. A sanctuary city is one in which the city has forbidden the cops to work with federal immigration officials in order to arrest people based purely on evidence that they are illegal and felonious. Cities such as New York City and San Francisco have literally rolled out the red carpet to criminal aliens.

Effective immediately—and I mean immediately as in today, right now, this very minute—the U.S. Attorney General should issue felony arrest warrants for city council members and mayors who authorized their cities to become sanctuary cities. They have aided and abetted criminals. Additionally, all federal dollars allocated to these cities should be immediately halted and diverted to the U.S. Border Patrol. It's 2:00 p.m. where I'm at right now. Anyone want to sip some afternoon common sense tea with me? You can sip the tea. I'll throw mine over the side of the ship and into the harbor. That's in my defiant DNA. Uncle Ted knows how to party.

Reading *Illegals* will make your American blood boil with anger. Read it and weep for America.

States bordering Mexico such as Arizona and New Mexico have already declared states of emergency due to the outrageously burdensome social and criminal costs that these criminal aliens have created in their states. As author Jon Dougherty points out in his book *Illegals*, it is not just the state agencies and their criminal justice systems that are in peril, but working hard, tax-paying American citizens who live near the border. Dougherty gives sad example after example of American ranchers and their families along our southern border who have been murdered and brutalized and their property destroyed by criminal aliens. Dougherty also gives many other examples of U.S. Border Patrol agents being fired upon and attacked by criminal aliens. Reading *Illegals* will make your American blood boil with anger. Read it and weep for America.

By overwhelming numbers, poll after poll shows that Americans want our government to do something meaningful and sensible about criminal aliens instead of giving us lip service. Americans see criminal aliens everywhere in their communities and workplaces and tens of thousands of hardworking Americans are victimized by criminal aliens each year. Americans—especially ones living in border states like Texas, California, Arizona, and New Mexico—understand the depth of the problem, which is why they want the government to stop the flow of criminal aliens. I can say that in my nonstop travels through the American southwest, Americans of European decent appear to be the minority. When Californians did try to do something about criminal aliens in the early 1990s by passing Proposition 187 which would have ended welfare benefits to criminal aliens, an anti-U.S., black-robed, federal judicial punk over-turned the will of the people, thereby costing California and U.S. taxpayers more in wasted welfare dollars. The judicial punk should have been charged with a crime, impeached, stripped of his robe and his retirement benefits, and forced to teach English at night to criminal aliens for the remainder of his pathetic life. I've about had it. It is this kind of un-American judicial activism that reminds me why our Founding Fathers wrote the Second Amendment.

Are there any statesmen left?

Illegal immigration costs U.S. taxpayers billions of dollars each year. From welfare to free medical care to housing criminal alien thugs in our jails and prisons, the financial cost is staggering. The Internet is replete with information on the financial burden criminal aliens have placed on the backs of American taxpayers. Research it, read it, and then weep. It is almost too staggering to bear.

Roughly one in ten babies born in America is born to a criminal alien mother. The babies of criminal alien mothers are known as "anchor babies." Under a perverted view of the Fourteenth Amendment which grants citizenship to "all persons born or naturalized in the United States and subject to the jurisdiction thereof," our court system and weak politicians have conferred citizenship on illegal babies born on U.S. soil.

I'm no shifty, lawsuit-happy lawyer, but it stands to reason that criminal alien mothers or their babies are not "subject to the jurisdiction thereof," meaning the laws of the United States. By gaining U.S. citizenship, these babies (and their criminal alien mothers) are eligible for welfare and a host of other social programs funded by U.S. taxpayers. This distorted view of the Fourteenth Amendment is encouraging criminal aliens to cross our border for clear and present bloodsucking reasons. All reasonable U.S. citizens want this rectified. Once again, where is the political leadership to do what is right for America? Are there any statesmen left?

Governors of border states should mobilize the National Guard today and put them back on the border. It would be good training to complete on-going tours in which they patrol and apprehend criminal aliens invading our country. The National Guard responds in times of floods and other natural catastrophes—our border insecurity certainly qualifies as a national crisis. Operation Jumpstart in 2006 proved that the National Guard could play a valuable role in helping secure the border and that help should be ongoing. Just think—the National Guard guarding the nation. Now there's a thought. We should have troops patrolling the border by tomorrow night. That's what Americans want and deserve and that's what America needs if we are serious about securing our country. If we want to jack around, go back to the status quo.

> **Our border insecurity certainly qualifies as a national crisis.**

With the Mexican drug cartels increasing their slaughtering of Mexican cops and army troops in Mexican border towns, the need for heavily armed U.S. border troops augmented by even more heavily armed National Guard troops is imperative. A massive shoot-out between Mexican drug cartels and the U.S. Border Patrol is only a matter of time.

Congress provided the cash in the Secure Fence Act of 2006 for the Department of Homeland Security to build seven hundred miles of fence along the Mexican border where much of the invasion and drug running is occurring. The Department of Homeland Security says they will have 670 miles of the fence completed by the end of 2008. It may surprise you, but I don't want to waste any more tax dollars on a border fence boondoggle.

I don't need a fence around my property because I have simply erected a Spirit Fence. My Spirit Fence is stronger and much more effective than any eyesore concrete block and cantina wire fence could ever be. My very effective fence shouts out loud DON'T TREAD ON ME! If you do, you will face terminal consequences. I have signs posted that state "private property." I respect your private property and demand you respect mine. Just as I am convinced that an uninvited intruder onto my property or into my home has made a clear statement of threatening danger, and therefore must be dealt with according to my belief that I should fear for my life, so, too, should America treat the armed invaders that cross our borders carrying drugs, smuggling other criminal aliens, and doing who knows what else. Unarmed criminal aliens should be rounded up and locked up by the Border Patrol and the National Guard. My "threat" fence sends a message. It is time for America to send the same message to all would be armed invaders—invade and die.

> ⋆
> **Invade
> and die.**

Shooting a few armed invaders would solve even more of the problem. Shoot armed invaders? Correct. Shoot to kill to be exact. As a policy, it is flawless. I think back to the Democrats' convention in beautiful downtown Chicago that fine summer of 1968 when the hippies dared to take on Mayor Daley's finest. At the time, I wasn't sure just whom to root for, as the reputation of corruption in the Chicago police department was notorious, yet at the same time, nobody likes rioting, stinky hippies. Being both a big fan of law and order, and a huge fan of defiance and civil disobedience, young Ted was torn. Though I would be the first to club some punk throwing bags of feces and urine on me or my brothers, both sides clearly went beyond reasonable conduct. Now that the dust has settled over time, I stand with the cops overall.

However, the most powerful lesson of that historical event was the definitive line drawn in the sand by tuffguy Mayor Richard Daley when he growled his orders to the police and national guard on live TV that he gave the green light to "shoot to kill" anyone on the Windy City streets after curfew. A collective wince reverberated across America at this seemingly over the top, outrageous order. But as the sun peeked over Lake Michigan the following morning, there were no victims of police or National Guard shootings because everybody knew Daley meant it. His extreme stand actually saved lives and the small businesses throughout his beloved Chicago without a shot being fired. Cool. Works for me.

SHOOT TO KILL

The president of the United States should immediately make a public decree to all Border Patrol, National Guard, law enforcement, and private landowners that SHOOT TO KILL is the new policy for dealing with any and all armed invaders, whether they be coyotes transporting other criminal aliens across our border, drug runners, or any others attempting to enter the United States through any unauthorized port of entry.

And it would work for our border security too. We simply need to initiate a ubiquitous, global carpet-bombing public relations campaign letting the world know that on such and such a date, say sixty days from the commencement of the wallpapering PR blitz, any armed invaders crossing our borders at any and all unauthorized locations will be shot dead. And mean it. Take the heat, pound the bully pulpit, and say it like we mean it. And I am convinced that no one would be shot, because people don't want to have holes punched in them. They would simply end their criminal invasion. In my home state of Texas, that is the very system and policy by which we stop any potential invaders from invading our homes. Potential invaders know that we Texans will indeed shoot them, which for the most part, nearly eliminates any home invasion problems. Sure, a few try, and we shoot them. They deserve to be shot. As Dirty Harry once said, "There's nothing wrong with shooting, as long as the right people get shot." Is it just me, or do you also think Inspector Callahan always made perfect crime control sense. Don't invade, don't get shot. Comprende, señor?

Using the most comprehensive media carpetbombing, wallpapering blitz of alltimes, a new, bold, believable, dead-on serious promotional campaign should make it crystal clear that America will not tolerate any more armed invaders on our sacred soil. Period.

In the absence of sustained enforcement, at least we have the Minutemen. They are dedicated, brave, unarmed, volunteer, "We the People" Americans, performing an obvious, proper, long overdue duty to protect their country. They are not vigilantes, as both President Bush and former President Sly-As-A-Fox of Mexico insinuated. The Minutemen are composed of retired cops, military men, and other law-abiding American civilians from all walks of life who are spending their own money and valuable family time to watch the border and notify the U.S. Border Patrol when they see criminal aliens. They are a pure and simple neighborhood watch program for America. That is good.

Instead of being condemned by the media, elected officials, and any number of anti-American/pro-Mexican organizations, the Minutemen deserve our public praise and admiration for doing what our government will not do—secure the border. To condemn the Minutemen is analogous to condemning every Neighborhood Watch program across the country as being racist, bigoted, and somehow dangerous. Only pro-crime punks would do this and only the enemies of America would dare condemn them.

I understand why many criminal aliens come to America. If I lived in the abjectly poor, corrupt, third world country of Mexico, I, too, would want to vamoose out of there with my family. Thankfully, I don't live in Mexico or I would have to start a revolution. Actually, that's a wonderful idea. I just might move to Mexico to start a revolution. El Presidente Nuge has a nice revolutionary ring to it. Mexico could use a man like me.

> **If I lived in the abjectly poor, corrupt, third world country of Mexico, I, too, would want to vamoose out of there with my family.**

Another sure way to ultimately curb criminal immigration is to keep going after American businesses who hire criminal aliens. Once we begin busting businesses for hiring criminal aliens and handing out heavy enough fines, the incentive for coming to America goes away because no one will hire them. No jobs and no opportunity leads to criminal aliens staying home. I don't want to hear the hollow argument that without criminal aliens many jobs in America won't get done. We have plenty of lazy, otherwise able-bodied Americans who can do the jobs that criminal aliens are currently doing.

While on the subject of businesses, I find it discriminatory to both legal immigrants and criminal aliens that automated checkout stands instruct the consumer to press "English" or "Espanol" when checking out. What this practice does is encourage Spanish-speaking people to use their native dialect. That's just wrong. Since the English language is our universal tongue, continuing to encourage and allow them to speak Spanish ensures they will not climb higher on the first rung of the American ladder of opportunity. This is real racism veiled as sensitivity to the needs of Spanish-speaking people. Being inclusive and embracing all people means putting aside political correctness and doing what is right. Forcing all people to learn the English language as many of our grandparents had to who emigrated here from Sweden, Germany, Poland, and other countries is the right thing to do. It may not be the comfortable, feel-good choice, but discriminatory, racist, pandering actions that keep people from enjoying all the opportunities that America has to offer can kiss my Ted, White, and Blue American ass.

> ★
>
> **If you can't speak English, get out of the country.**

Just as we used to do on a massive scale, we should offer English classes at night in our public schools and other public buildings. Teaching legal immigrants this most basic skill will enable them to become integrated in the American experience and help them to achieve their American Dream. Everyone wins. Denying them the opportunity to learn the English language relegates them to a life of poverty. Sink or swim, baby.

So what to do about the criminal aliens already here? With a modicum of political will, we can get them to return home and not come back. America has done it before. In 1954, under President Eisenhower's leadership, the Immigration and Naturalization Service (INS) launched Operation Wetback. Operation Wetback was designed to identify, capture, and deport millions of criminal aliens, primarily Mexicans, living in the American southwest. Operation Wetback was a tremendous success. INS agents and state and local cops apprehended over 100,000 criminal aliens who were promptly deported, and estimates are that over 1,000,000 other criminal aliens fled back to Mexico of their own volition out of fear of being apprehended by U.S. authorities. Obviously, there were no sanctuary cities back then and no politically correct immigration games being played. We should have stuck to our immigration guns over the past fifty years by aggressively enforcing our immigration laws. However, where there is political will, there is a political way. We can do it again. I like IKE.

In addition to launching Operation Wetback II, the Department of Homeland Security (DHS) should build huge jail tent cities like my hero, Sheriff Joe Arpaio, has done in Maricopa County, Arizona, for various criminal scum and such. Sheriff Arpaio dresses his inmates in pink underwear, does not provide them television, cigarettes, coffee, or pornographic magazines, and has brought back the chain gang. He feeds his inmates bologna sandwiches. DHS should immediately begin the construction of numerous tent cities in our border states to house criminal aliens and model them after Sheriff Arpaio's tent cities. In less than a couple of weeks we could have facilities for them that would be as good as the facilities that our warrior men and women have in Iraq or Afghanistan. No criminal alien should be eligible for deportation until after he or she has been charged with a crime and spent some time

SHOOT TO KILL

Aztlan can also kiss my American ass. Remember the Alamo, America. And join me and Davy Crockett on the wall. If you can't help us defend ourselves, at least show the decency to shut up and help us load our guns. It's an American thing. Love it or leave it. Bloodsuckers need not apply for citizenship.

in a DHS tent city jail. At the end of their criminal sentence, they should be deported. Do not forget that criminal aliens have committed a crime by coming to America illegally. If DHS was on the ball, they would hire Sheriff Arpaio and put him in charge. Along with our new "shoot to kill" policy, building huge jail tent cities to warehouse criminal aliens would do much to create disincentives to breaking U.S. immigration laws. Sheriff Arpaio is the kind of lawman we need to fix the criminal alien quagmire. Let the Big Dog Arpaio run.

A few years ago I caused a media firestorm, which is another of my unique talents, for saying what every American believes and knows is a blazing light of the obvious and truth: if you can't speak English, get the hell out of the country. If you didn't get it the first time a few years ago, let me repeat myself: if you can't speak English, get the hell out of the country. Your choice to be a liability is unacceptable and we don't want you here.

If I lived in any other country I would feel an obligation to learn their language and respect their customs and traditions. When in Rome, act like a Roman, at least to some degree. That would be the polite thing to do. Again, that's simple enough for any idiot to grasp. Makes abundant sense to me. It is tremendously rude to go to another country intending to hold on to your native language. If a non-English speaking foreigner wants to take advantage of all that America has to offer, learning the English language is a great way to start. Holding on to a native language is guaranteed to hold you back. That is all I meant by my "over-the-top" admonition to learn the English language, the language of America. I stand by my words of truth. Those wonderful and abundantly truthful words were right then and they remain clear as the wind driven snow today.

As a senator, Obama was weak on solving criminal immigration. I have zero faith he will do anything of substance to halt the invasion of America. We will get more lip service, more political posturing, more stalling, more political correctness, more hollow statements, and more bullshit from a government that does not give a damn about ordinary Americans. On January 20, 2009, Barack Obama took an oath of service to protect and defend America. With his hand on the Bible, he was lying through his teeth.

A nation without borders will cease to be a nation. President Obama would do well to embrace this common-sense truth regarding border security, but I'm not holding my breath waiting for him to do it.

Being good neighbors starts with taking good care of your country. After all, the reason people scramble and are willing to die trying to get to America is because we are so great—the last best place. It would be insane to allow her greatness to be destroyed by the very people desperate for the quality of life so unique to America. Our love for America is what drives us to keep her strong and safe. That is what attracts everyone to her. We shall carry on, thank you.

CHAPTER ELEVEN

**HEALTH CARE—
NOT A HANDOUT**

"I'm healthy I do declare,
it's a free for all."

★ ★ ★

"Free for All,"
Free For All, 1976

The first rule of the health care industry should model the Hippocratic oath and do no intentional harm to patients. In the raging debate surrounding health care, the first question to consider is this: is it better for me to be in charge of my health care, or to surrender it to the federal government (hereafter known as Fedzilla) who can't find his ass with both hands and a roadmap? The answer to that question will tell you if you are a rugged, independent, shit-kicking American, drunk on free market competition and opportunity or a modern slave to the socialist Fedzilla system that, if given the opportunity, will exert even more wasteful and harmful control over your health.

My radar has been on full alert for years regarding the need to reform our health care system—meaning, of course, that I have paid close attention to the debate on what to do about reducing health care costs and whether to nationalize health care. You should know upfront that I am not an advocate of federalizing much of anything (though airline passengers would be much safer and healthier if their Uncle Ted was permanently deputized as a federal air marshal).

> ☆
>
> **I am not an advocate of federalizing much of anything (though airline passengers would be much safer and healthier if their Uncle Ted was permanently deputized as a federal air marshal).**

The debate over creating a nationalized health care system was settled long ago with our forefathers, who, like me, were terminally drunk on freedom. These freedom seekers wrote our wonderful Constitution which clearly articulates the roles and responsibilities of the federal government. And health care wasn't one of them.

Our Founding Fathers did not believe government-provided health care is an inalienable right. Had they believed it, they would have written health care into our Bill of Rights. Furthermore, nowhere in my readings of the writings of the Founding Fathers have I stumbled across any statement by any one of them that either directly or indirectly implies that Americans have a right to health care, as President Obama argues. Interestingly, this point is never brought up during debates on health care. Yet it should be, to provide historical and constitutional context, if nothing else. While our Founding Fathers may not have been able to fully imagine the highly technical and sophisticated world we live in today, they were no dunces. In fact, they were brilliant, learned men who saw well beyond their years when they created our government. They understood the need to define and limit the role of the federal government so that Americans would not have to live under a burdensome, bureaucratic, oppressive, centralized, out of control system— the very kind we have today that meddles in every facet of our lives. Don't ever forget, our Founding Fathers fought a war of independence to liberate themselves from this style of European government. They created a constitutional government to provide individuals maximum personal freedom and liberty while limiting the power of the federal government. Sadly, what our Founding Fathers could not have imagined is how we have compromised their dream of limited government and personal freedom. We should hang our collective heads in shame.

You don't have a right to health care. Got that? What you have is a personal responsibility for it. Read that again. This is a critical point that is largely lost during so-called health care debates and is vital if we are going to have an open, honest conversation on how to improve health care. There is a direct correlation between your overall health and the importance you place on it. If you do not place importance on your health, no amount of either private or government-controlled health care will make you healthy. How dare any bloodsucking American ask you or me to provide for his or her health care if he obviously does not care about his health? That is soulless, ugly, *Planet of the Apes*, anti-American, brain dead, Grateful Dead logic.

Allow me to state a blindingly obvious fact: when Fedzilla gets involved in anything, political motives and ideologies take precedence over everything else—including your health. Only a naïve socialist could possibly disagree. This fundamental truism would inevitably be at work in a nationalized health care program. It's true that much discussion is needed regarding the plethora of problems within the current health care system, but if the private sector entrepreneurial beast is unshackled and allowed to flourish, it ultimately will adjust its products and services to meet the demand in the marketplace. Competition lowers prices while encouraging superior products and services. Conversely, giving more control over the nation's health care to Fedzilla will not improve it. We have learned by now that the purpose of bureaucracy (the mother of Fedzilla) is sustaining and growing the bureaucracy. There isn't anything lean and efficient in the federal government. Nothing.

> **I find it ironic and suspicious that Democrats, who largely support nationalized health care, were incensed just a few short years ago over the lack of a quick and effective federal response to Hurricane Katrina.**

Fedzilla does a phenomenally lousy job at almost everything it touches. If our federal agencies and departments were run like a business, they would have been bankrupt long ago. No business can sustain the gross levels of bureaucracy, ineffectiveness, and incompetence our government agencies and departments provide to us, its employers. All clear-thinking people know this to be true. However, I find it ironic and suspicious that Democrats, who largely support nationalized health care, were incensed just a few short years ago over the lack of a quick and effective federal response to Hurricane Katrina.

Hurricane Katrina was not an exception to the rule of how ineffective and inefficient Fedzilla is, but was rather illustrative of the woeful ineffectiveness that is the benchmark of Fedzilla. Duh. If President Obama supporters and other Fedzilla supporters were so upset over the slow and ineffective response by the Federal Emergency Management Agency and other federal agencies to Hurricane Katrina, do they honestly believe nationalizing health care is going to be a shining example of an efficient and effectively run government program that will quickly provide them the medical care they want, expect, and believe they deserve? It literally boggles the mind how tremendously illogical, easily manipulated, and dumb some Americans are. But only the guilty need feel guilty. Rest easy. Dr. Nuge is here to inject you with a shot of truth serum.

Dr. Nuge is here to inject you with a shot of truth serum.

One of the largest problems with our health care system is that our government is already too involved in it via Medicare and Medicaid. Medicare is a federal program that provides basic health care for the elderly while Medicaid is a joint state and federal program that provides health care for the poor. Half of the couple trillion dollars we currently spend on health care each year in America is already being consumed by Fedzilla providing health care assistance to nearly one hundred million Americans through these two programs.

When these socialist health care programs were created in 1965, millions of Americans beat down the door to get "free" treatment while millions more signed up to have the majority of their medical bills paid by the new taxpayer-funded system. Now we have the result—Medicare is on life support and at risk of expiring in the next ten years due to unsustainable federal deficit spending and a nine trillion dollar debt. Clearly government meddling in health care has made an unhealthy situation terminal. If that's a Great Society, I would like to see a bad one. What a terrible mistake. Giving people something for nothing is never, under any circumstances, the right approach.

Expanding Fedzilla's control will exacerbate our health care nightmare. To advocate this is to use Three Stooges numbskull reasoning. I recommend President Obama call on Dr. Moe, Dr. Larry, and Dr. Curly to serve as his advisors on advancing the nationalization of health care.

In the not-so-distant past, Americans wrote their doctor a check for services rendered just like they gave money to their auto mechanic and the local grocer for their services and goods. That was a simple, effective, and free market way to pay for medical services provided by the local doctor and guess what: health care was much cheaper overall. Everyone benefited. Because they were directly paying only for the services they needed, Americans didn't run to the doctor for sneezing, nose runs, and other minor ailments as we do today. And doctors didn't have to hire staff to gag on completing all the various insurance forms. If Americans had any health insurance, it was for catastrophic illnesses. My, how the health care times have changed.

> ★
>
> **Giving people something for nothing is never the right approach.**

The majority of working Americans now have health care provided by their employers. This has created a system whereby we no longer have flesh in the game like we used to when we wrote a check to our doctors. Now that many working Americans have health care benefits provided by employers, Americans pay nominal out-of-pocket expenses per dollar of health care costs, which is why many Americans run to the emergency room when little Billy gets a scrape on his knee. So long as the health insurance industry is picking up a vast amount of the tab for physicians and hospitals, people take advantage of it and this dramatically drives up health care costs. Quite simply, because of employer-paid insurance, we are consuming too many unnecessary health services which is driving up costs.

Health insurance expenditures are the fastest growing costs for businesses. It is estimated that in 2008, health insurance costs for businesses will overtake profits. One example of our bloated cost of health care is General Motors, which already spends more on health insurance for its employees than on steel for its vehicles. If you want to know why health costs are skyrocketing, the first place you should check is the mirror. When we pay so little of our own health care costs, our perception becomes that we are getting something for nothing. And that, my friends, is a recipe for disaster.

Arguably, if consumers paid more of their health care fees out of their own pockets, we would visit the doctor less frequently for minor ailments and probably care more about our state of health. Paying for more of our health care would drive down health care costs as we became more judicious with our own money. This is the very reason Health Savings Accounts (HSAs) are an excellent way to accumulate dollars to spend on your health (just as Individual Retirement Accounts are an excellent way to accumulate wealth). These tax-free health savings accounts are attached to high deductible health insurance policies. Pre-tax dollars from both the consumer and employer are put into the accounts, grow tax-free, and can even be invested in a mutual fund for future health expenses. The consumer decides if

> ☆
> **This is a recipe for disaster.**

and when to use his funds to pay for health care services wherever he sees fit. And because it is literally money in the bank, he shops around to find the best price for routine care such as teeth-cleaning and physicals. Consumers also benefit by receiving the insurance company's discounted rate from the doctor on the services they do purchase. Consequently, HSAs put health care purchasing decisions in your hands while giving doctors a reason to compete for your business. You make the decisions on how you will spend your health care dollars. Purchasing power to the people is a healthy thing.

It would be beneficial to see even more initiatives created that put additional health-related decisions in the hands of consumers.

President Obama should commission a group of forward thinking private sector business people to analyze and make recommendations on how the private sector can drive down health care costs.

Forty years ago, when individuals paid the vast amount, if not all, of the doctor's bill out of their pocket, medical costs consumed just five percent of the gross national product. Today, medical costs suck up sixteen percent of our gross national product—and it continues to increase. Anyone see a correlation? Have a smoke and a pop tart and give it a good, long, hard look. In 2004, our health care expenditures equated to 1.9 trillion dollars; in 2007, 2.3 trillion. It is estimated to reach 2.8 trillion by 2011 and 4.1 trillion dollars by 2016—20 percent of our gross national product. The question is, why?

Something needs to be done, but eliminating private, profit-driven insurance companies and turning over the entire industry to the bloated, ineffective government to provide "free" health care is not the answer as Michael Moore argued in his anti-free market, hatchet-job movie *Sicko*. Michael Moore is an anti-capitalist socialist stooge who believes more government control and less personal freedom is the solution to whatever he believes ails our nation. What Moore fails to understand is that by giving the Nanny State control over our health care, some Fedzilla bureaupunk will determine how our money is spent and ultimately, how care is rationed—meaning who gets treated and for what diseases or ailments. That's what is sick. Dr. Nuge's advice: Avoid Michael Moore and other socialists like the plague. They are dangerous to your health.

Avoid Michael Moore and other socialists like the plague. They are dangerous to your health.

Fedzilla health care supporters such as Sicko Moore will claim that much of the money spent in the private health care industry is wasted. To be honest, they have a point—to a degree. They will argue that almost one third of all health care dollars spent are wasted on private insurance bureaucracy and that if we could eliminate these hundreds of billions of dollars of unnecessary expenditures, this money could be used to provide comprehensive health care for all Americans. Sounds alluring, but socialists rarely lay all the facts on the table. What the health care socialists fail to say is how much money would be wasted by Fedzilla in unnecessary expenditures, fraud and waste, hiring tens of thousands more employees, guaranteed mismanagement, fraud, and corruption. I have heard that roughly one quarter of our tax dollars are already wasted or cannot be accounted for. In that light, does anyone really believe a nationalized health care program would be a paragon of government efficiency? The same waste that permeates our government today would further run amok in a Fedzilla nationalized health care system, that's for damn sure. But in that case we'd be inefficient with people's *lives*.

What we will get is Moore slop for the pigs. No wonder they call it dope.

Another thing the Fedzilla won't discuss is the very real possibility that their nationalized health care system does not work. What if it is a catastrophic failure? What will we do then, keep going down the path of health care destruction and failure until complete and total annihilation is achieved? They will retort that our private system is a botched, ineffective, and cumbersome system that is bound to fail even more Americans. They will argue that America spends more per person on health care than any other country but that we are not receiving better health for our dollars. One of the most significant contributing factors to our high cost of health care is our unhealthy lifestyles and not our health care industry. Michael Moore is a perfect example. Because of his weight, he is a prime candidate for a heart attack or diabetes.

Simply taking better care of ourselves would significantly drive down costs. Why in God's name is this self-evident truth avoided at all costs?

Why do so many Americans insist on eating, drinking, and smoking their health to hell? How can this be as they bloat, get sicker, and die? Denial is pandemic.

An entertainer once said a sucker is born every minute, and surely this is the case with those who support nationalized health care. Do you supporters of Fedzilla health care really believe the limousine liberal crowd who support a Fedzilla health care are going to use the health care system they force on everyone else? Not hardly—and you know it. They are elitist

━━━ ☆ ━━━
**Denial
is pandemic.**
━━━━━━

punks. What is good enough for you is not good enough for them. Furthermore, you can not convince me that Fedzilla health care would be cheaper and more effective than even the somewhat crazy, confusing, and inefficient private sector hodgepodge system we have now. My perspective is born out of watching how inefficient and bureaucratic Fedzilla has been, is, and will be in the future. The best indicator of what something will be is to analyze how it has already been.

Eliminating waste in the private insurance sector is one of the keys to reforming health care. If you doubt this, the next time you visit your doctor's office take a look at all the support staff hustling about, completing and filing numerous insurance forms, permissions, and histories. Physicians have to hire these support staff just to complete the many insurance forms, which leads to increased overhead, which is then passed on to your insurance companies which ultimately leads to higher premiums. Estimates are that twenty percent of all health care dollars are spent by processing and shuffling insurance forms, calling insurance companies, and chasing down payment. This breast-fed gator believes there has surely got to be a better, more efficient way to conduct this business.

Individual states also share some of the burden for our rising health care costs because of the moronic mandates they have passed dictating what insurance companies must provide to consumers who want to purchase health care. Costs for purchasing health care insurance varies wildly from state to state because of these mandates, and because residents cannot purchase health insurance outside the state they live in. These mandates require coverage of "essential" things from hair loss to alcohol abuse treatment.

Legislating what insurance policies must cover and forbidding out-of-state competition is like telling consumers they can only buy cars from one auto company, requiring that company to make only two types of cars, and then dictating what options and accessories each car must include. Naturally, if you are someone who wants an inexpensive car to use only when the weather is bad, you are not going to want to pay the same high price as someone who wants a car with all the bells and whistles. These state-legislated mandates similarly force consumers to pay extra for "options" that they didn't want and may never use.

Some states have even passed mandates that require insurance companies to provide catastrophic insurance to people with pre-existing deadly illnesses. To continue the car metaphor, that's like making a car insurance company cover a known clunker that's on its last legs for what it was worth when it was brand new. Though required by law, providing that insurance raises costs for all the other consumers.

> ⭐
>
> **Point me in the right direction and I will burn the entire system down.**

This is nuts. Point me in the right direction and I will burn the entire system down. Obviously, residents of states who are not covered by employer-provided health care insurance should be able to purchase mandate-free insurance and be able to purchase health care insurance from companies across state lines. This, too, will drive down costs. Necessity is the mother of invention. In this case competition breeds lower costs and you, the consumer, benefit.

Another cause of escalating health care costs is the costly insurance premiums physicians and surgeons have to carry, which get passed to the consumer in the form of higher prices on care. This malpractice insurance protects them from bottom-feeding, shyster legal sharks such as former Senator John Edwards. While claiming to stand up for the little guy against the big, bad health insurance industry, Edwards fleeced doctors, surgeons, and hospitals for over 150 million dollars, which drove up the price of health care for everyone. If there was ever a poster boy for medical malpractice tort reform, Edwards's sniveling, hypocritical, evil, greedy bastard's face should be on the poster. Because of close similarities in piracy conduct, one has to wonder if former Senator Edwards is related to the famous pirate Blackbeard.

Instead of relying on medical facts and science which were available at the time regarding cerebral palsy, Edwards the Legal Pirate plundered the health care industry by filing over sixty lawsuits and winning over 150 million dollars for his law firm while amassing a personal fortune estimated at around sixty million dollars. Blackbeard surely never could have imagined the plunder that legal piracy could produce. Instead of flying the Jolly Roger and plundering cargo ships, Edwards the Legal Pirate convinced gullible juries that cerebral palsy was the doctors' fault, when the medical scientific community had definitively stated that cerebral palsy is rarely caused by doctors but rather, by an infection in the womb or genetics. This information was available to Edwards the Legal Pirate, but a good legal pirate will never let the facts stand in the way of legal plunder. In one case in which Edwards the Legal Pirate ripped off a hospital for over six million dollars, it is widely reported that he stated the following to a jury considering whether the

★

Millions of our health care dollars are now in the treasure chest of Edwards the Legal Pirate.

cerebral palsy a girl named Jennifer had was caused by negligence of the delivering doctor: "I have to tell you right now—I didn't plan to talk about this—right now I feel her [Jennifer], I feel her presence. Jennifer is inside me and she's talking to you.... And this is what she says to you. She says, 'I don't ask for your pity. What I ask for is your strength. And I don't ask for your sympathy, but I do ask for your courage.'" Clearly this man, who now champions a nationalized health care program after enriching himself by plundering the health care industry, knows no shame. Millions of our health care dollars are now in the treasure chest of Edwards the Legal Pirate. Quite simply, what Edwards the Legal Pirate did was legalized theft, and he surely must know it when he stares at the ceiling at night while lying in bed.

NO LOSS

If we were blessed to have gravity fail over Edwards the Legal Pirate's hypocritical head and he lazily floated off the planet, I wouldn't lose sleep over the blessed occasion.

Edwards the Legal Pirate is not the only pirate on the health care high seas who has ripped off physicians, surgeons, and hospitals and enriched himself in the process, but he is the most famous. The end result of legal pirates filing frivolous lawsuits: higher health care costs for you and me. Frivolous lawsuits filed by unscrupulous legal pirates cause the malpractice insurance premiums of doctors, surgeons, and hospitals to rise, which adds to the overall expense of health care. If we stop the pirate lawyers from plundering our health care system, health care expenses will recede. States should follow Texas's lead and pass tort reform to keep greedy, vicious, unethical, and immoral health care pirates like John Edwards from raping the health care industry.

HEALTH CARE FOR INVADERS

Criminal immigrants are also creating a tremendous burden on our health care system. Fully one out of four uninsured people in America is a criminal alien, and you and I are picking up the tab for their health care to the tune of hundreds of millions of dollars each year. Hospitals in border states like California, Arizona, and Texas are suffering tremendous financial losses from having to provide health care to criminal aliens. Dozens and dozens of California hospitals have literally closed because they could not absorb the costs of being forced to provide treatment. Other hospitals have reduced or shut down critical services such as trauma centers.

> ✩
>
> **Bloodsuckers are the enemies of personal responsibility and accountability.**

Who does this really impact? American taxpayers, as usual. To add health care insult to injury, U.S. taxpayers were recently saddled with one billion more tax dollars to be set aside for health care providers to be reimbursed for treating criminal aliens. This, ladies and gentlemen, is the clearest definition of insanity I have ever heard: taxpayers from one country must legally pay for the health and welfare of those who have broken the law to get into their country. Of the estimated 47 million uninsured people in the United States, ten million or so are people who are not American citizens. If you are not an American, you clearly should have no right to American taxpayer funds to pay for your health care or any other social welfare system. We would drive down costs by the hundreds of millions each year if we could legally stop paying for the hospital costs of criminal aliens, but thanks to an anti-American Supreme Court ruling, this won't happen. The Highest Court in the Land ruled that a person cannot be turned away from health care providers in the United States because of nationality or ability to pay. Dr. Nuge suggests America deduct the amount of health care spent on criminal aliens from the amount of foreign aid being provided to their country of origin.

According to preventdisease.com, preventable illnesses constitute 80 percent of illnesses, yet consume an amazing 90 percent of our health care costs. If preventdisease.com is correct, then indeed an ounce of prevention is surely worth a pound of cure. We are supposed to be in charge of our health care destiny, yet many Americans clearly don't care a bit about their health. Remember what I previously wrote. You don't have a right to health care, but you do have a responsibility for it. You don't need to be a physician to know that poor health habits lead to increased illness rates, which lead to escalating costs. People who make unhealthy and risky decisions seemingly want to live their unhealthy lifestyle as they see fit and then burden the health care industry and taxpayers with their health care costs when they get ill. These people are no friends of mine. They are health care vampire bloodsuckers and they surely voted for Obama for president. Bloodsuckers are the enemies of personal responsibility and accountability. Dr. Nuge is the enemy and enema of truth for bloodsuckers.

Even more evidence of unhealthy choices is the blubbering of America. Obesity rates have skyrocketed over the past thirty years. Astonishingly, roughly 60 percent of Americans over the age of twenty are now considered to be overweight and 30 percent are considered to be obese. We're talking slabs of blubber here, folks. Numerous reports have cited that obesity has surpassed smoking as the nation's number one health hazard. We are the fattest, most out of shape, most slovenly nation on the planet and there does not seem to be any desire to change these soulless, criminally unhealthy choices. I see blubber everywhere—butts as wide as 1972 Buicks. You don't have to be a nutritionist or doctor to know there are numerous health-related maladies associated with blubber, not the least of which is heart disease which ranks as the number one killer in America. And yet when I go to the grocery store, I see people so fat they have to use motorized carts to load their ice cream, cookies, soda, chips, and other fattening nonfood poisons into their carts. These people are literally too fat to walk. In addition to buying junk and driving around grocery stores in a motorized cart, I have seen that some of these land whales are allowed to park in handicapped spaces. You have also seen them. These obese people want to eat their cake and their share of health care, too. These junk food buyers have a clearly preventable problem whereby their hands shove mountains of fattening so-called food into their mouths on a daily basis while they get zero exercise. This causes them to gain weight and to become unhealthy. Case closed.

> ━━━━ ☆ ━━━━
> **These obese people want to eat their cake and their share of health care, too.**
> ━━━━━━━━━━

I see kids so fat they cannot possibly run, jump, and enjoy competitive sports or an active life. These kids have never climbed a tree, gone on a hike, gone swimming, or gone on an extended bike ride. Instead they sit inside their homes like pathetic, fat zombies in front of the garbage videobox, or play mindless, soul rotting computer games while gorging themselves on junk that will make them fatter, less healthy, and shorten their lives. These kids look like miniature versions of Michael Moore. If this is not child abuse, what is? Their parents should be arrested for child neglect. These unhealthy kids will turn into unhealthy adults who will die early, but in the process consume a significant portion of our health care dollars. Thanks for nothing, blubbery bloodsuckers. Good choices.

Fast food in my world is a beautiful, organic, delicious, God-produced mallard, pheasant, or woodcock. Junk food addicts do not share my version of fast food. Their version of fast food is the numerous fast food restaurants who serve some of the most unhealthy, fattening slop in the history of man and try to pass it off as food. I wouldn't feed my dogs this stuff. I am reminded of the movie *Fast Food Nation* in which the creator asked a hundred nutritionists how often Americans could eat junkfast food. Ninety-six nutritionists said never. Two said once a month and only two said once a week. This movie is a powerful statement regarding making proper diet decisions and considerations. If you haven't seen it, rent it and watch it over and over again with your kids. It is one of the most disturbing and enlightening films ever made. Yet while the evidence is damning and overwhelming, Americans continue to consume the Junkfast poison.

> ☆
> **Just as bartenders are held legally liable for serving too many drinks to drunks, our food industry needs to take the lead and only sell these people healthy foods in small amounts.**

Grocery stores, bakeries, junkfood restaurants, and other food outlets should start refusing service to overweight and obese people, or at least refusing to sell them fattening food. Just as bartenders are held legally liable for serving too many drinks to drunks, our food industry needs to take the lead and only sell these people healthy foods in small amounts. Like packages of cigarettes that warn smokers that smoking causes lung cancer, foods high in fats and calories should also have bright warning labels on their packages. Dr. Nuge suggests the following: "Warning: eating this will make you fat or even more disgustingly obese."

If warning banners on food packages is what it takes, then so be it. I'm a big fan of telling people what they need to hear, not what they want to hear. I have no idea what doctors tell their obese patients, but I strongly suggest the conversation begin with a head slap to get their attention. Once their attention deficit disorder has been fixed via a head slap, doctors should tell these human blimps that their lifestyle is not only cutting their life short, thereby denying the people who love them precious time, but that their unhealthy choices and lifestyle are costing everyone through higher costs in health care insurance. Doctors should tell them sternly that they shouldn't impose their unhealthy lifestyle on everyone else and that forcing others to pay for their unhealthy choices is not right, moral, or fair. Common sense, you would think.

Despite all of the information that has been available on the health hazards of puffing on cancer sticks, according to Centers for Disease Control, 21 percent of Americans were still living smoke stacks as of 2005. While I do not condone making cigarettes, ice cream, or broken glass sandwiches illegal, the health hazards of both smoking and poor diets drive up health care costs even though cigarette smokers and fat people die, on average, earlier than people who do not intentionally stab themselves to death by making poor health choices. Even though smokers assume room temperature earlier than non-smokers, paying for them to die at the end of their shortened, smoke-filled lives is still more expensive than for someone who took care of himself and lived much longer. You don't see many old fat people and you don't see many old smokers. They are all dead. Poor choices generally lead to the express lane off the planet. Preventing illness by leading a reasonably conscientious, healthy lifestyle will not only bring an immense quality of life upgrade to many lives, but surely will further drive down costs as healthy people do not visit the doctor's office nearly as often and do not demand costly treatments. Put that in your pipe and smoke it.

> **Chimp on, just don't chimp on me.**

Every public school in the country should implement vigorous exercise regimes for American kids. Enough of playing silly, grab-ass games in Physical Education classes that have zero to do with physical education or fitness. What our kids need is to sweat and get their heartbeat going. That's physical education. I recommend kids be required to briskly walk, run, or jog a couple of miles every other day before, during, or after school. Or even play on playgrounds, for a start. Our government is only now getting it. The head of the agency in charge of child wellbeing created a National Center for Physical Development and Outdoor Play to make sure kids could play on playgrounds. Maybe they could track how many fat kids slim down from simple exercise. Or from a better diet—all candy, soda, burgers, pizza, French fries, and other trash food should be immediately removed from schools and our kids instead be given healthy dietary choices.

Letters should go home to parents of students who are overweight informing them that their child's health is at-risk. There will obviously be parents who will squawk over this. They are the guilty ones. Let them bitch and complain. Pay no attention to them. The role of the public school system is to educate, not to placate, condone, or enable. Let's turn on the tough love with this. We should set a specific goal of dramat-

> **The role of the public school system is to educate, not to placate, condone, or enable.**

ically improving the health of American kids and aggressively work towards it. In one year, every one of our kids should be ready for U.S. Marines Corps boot camp.

In addition to whipping our kids into top physical condition, we should spend fifteen minutes of each school day on a health topic such as proper diet, healthy food selection, sexual choices, etc. Hit this education hard and keep it coming. From what I see waddling down the sidewalk after school, this education is desperately needed. If we care about our kids like our society claims, we will hit the physical conditioning and health education programs hard. Talking about caring about our kids and actually doing something about it are two very different things. Enough talking. Now is the time for action. If you really care about kids, then you agree with me. If you find fault with it, I suggest running to the store to buy Junior another large bag of chips and a two liter bottle of soda to wash them down with. That's what undisciplined and uncaring chimp parents do. Chimp on, just don't chimp on me.

Though I am not aware of any statistics or empirical studies to support my claim, I believe the health care cost savings America could achieve by losing weight, exercising more, and quitting smoking would have to be tremendous. By not going to the doctor as often, prices would have to fall as lower demand for services generally produces lower costs. That's Business 101—it works in other business sectors and it can work in the health care sector, too.

We have all heard the statistic that 47 million Americans do not have health insurance. If ten million of them are criminal aliens, that knocks the number down to 37 million, possibly even less. Of those 37 million Americans, how many people who could afford health insurance simply wish to spend their dollars on other products and services? How many are employed by employers who offer employer-paid health care insurance but don't take it? How many are transitory, meaning that they only lack health insurance for a certain period of time? How many Americans simply don't care that they have no health insurance? These are questions that Americans should be asking their elected officials and that the media should be asking our presidential candidates. Regardless of the answers to these questions, know that roughly 90 percent of Americans do have some sort of health insurance and, in Dr. Nuge's opinion, that is a great place to start reducing health care costs.

So what to do about poor Americans who lack health care? I'm a sympathetic guy and want to help those who truly want to help themselves. For those bloodsuckers who just want a free handout of health care, I say let them die in the streets. I'm not interested in sustaining and perpetuating dependency. For those who are generally interested in wanting to help themselves, I believe communities, not Fedzilla, are the key to health care assistance. The closer we get to the problem, the more likely it is that we can solve it. For example, churches, civic organizations, and community volunteers could raise money to provide basic health care for their needy neighbors similar to providing food to community food banks. How about Health Care Bank? I would like to believe that community doctors and nurses would donate a couple of hours a week to provide assistance. The volunteer spirit is alive and well in America but needs a swift kick in the ass every so often. Americans have become so dependent on Fedzilla to provide all kinds of assistance that we have forgotten that the volunteer spirit at the community level helped shape and build this country. Let's help our neighbors raise their health care barn so to speak, and get them on the path of independence instead of sentencing them to a life of Fedzilla dependency.

Socialists and critics will scoff and laugh at my community-based suggestion. They will claim the problem is much bigger than what communities can possibly provide, and that my suggestion is simplistic and unrealistic. I say with enough commitment, sweat equity, and American ingenuity, we can go a long way toward providing basic health needs to those in our communities who want to help themselves. The least we could do is bust our collective ass and try instead of rolling over and letting Fedzilla pick our pockets for even more taxes. Trying is the American spirit and I still believe its embers are glowing hot. Fan its flames and what we can accomplish on the local level will shock and awe even the most strident Fedzilla supporters.

> ★
>
> **Let's help our neighbors raise their health care barn so to speak, and get them on the path of independence instead of sentencing them to a life of Fedzilla dependency.**

Our annual Hunters for the Hungry program across America provides more than 250 million hot meals of nutritious venison to homeless shelters and soup kitchens following each hunting season every year. And that is just one small segment of America that refused to accept the plight of hungry neighbors. If just the hunters of America can do this, think what a truly united effort could accomplish on any level for a truly needy cause!

You don't have a right to health care. You have a personal responsibility to care about your health. It's all about choices. The right ones are on The List. Replacing the free market system with Fedzilla health care will gobble up and waste your tax dollars and not provide you any better or more efficient care. Never surrender your health care liberty to the Fedzilla beast.

I'm just a drunk-on-freedom guitar slinger and I figured that out. And so should you. It's healthy for you, I do declare. But it ain't free for ya at all.

AMERICA HEAL YOUR CHILDREN

If you love your children, what you are about to read should shock you, cause you serious pause, and hopefully make you consider the lifestyle you and your children lead.

I sat down the other day to write an exciting article encouraging parents to take their children turkey hunting each spring. It's a magical experience during a magical time of year that galvanizes families in the most dynamic ways. As you will see here, my focus turned from magic to tragic.

As a crusader for all things out-of-doors for both children and adults, I spent a little time doing some cursory research on the internet. Instead of turkey hunting statistics, what I found hit me like a thunderbolt. As I read the horror story unfolding before me, I wiped away a tear or two from my eyes.

According to the Kaiser Family Foundation, the average American youngster spends more than forty hours a week in front of the television and computer during the school year. Study after study found that the more television a young person watches, the more weight they gained, and the more likely it is they will become overweight and deathly ill. Not sickly, *deathly ill!*

We are literally destroying our children. Destroy is the right word. I can think of no word more appropriate.

Christmas 1951,
with mom and brother
Jeff, celebrating perfect
gun control at an
early age.

Maximum volume.
Maximum fun.
Total head removal.

NEIL ZLOZOWER

Beneath the clean-cut
image was a beast
about to be unleashed.

The Real Motorcity
Madman, my beloved
mother Marion Nugent.

Terminus El Bronco & Mercedes Benz.

RON POWNALL

Three dogs in heat.

Fred Bear. In the wind he's still alive…

Godbless Ma Nuge.

Love fest with
little Sasha and Toby.

Three very black guys
with a very dead lion,
Sudan 1978.

DUANE SYCZ

Kid Rock, the Predator Teditor, Sammy Hagar.

A Funk Brother
possessed by
the spirit of
James Brown.

JAMES AND MARLYN BROWN

Ma Deuce border security,
Chesty Puller style.

JAMES AND MARLYN BROWN

JAMES AND MARLYN BROWN

Teaching Toby Keith
Motown guitar licks.

Grenades and guitars can bring out the best in a guy.

JAMES AND MARLYN BROWN

MICHAEL IVES

I am the NRA.

JAMES AND MARLYN BROWN

The spirit of Sitting Bull and Geronimo lives.

I know what you're thinking… did I shoot the entire magazine or only a short burst? In all this excitement, I kind of lost track myself. So you have to ask yourself a question: Do you feel lucky? Well do ya, punk?

Stealth makes ultimate rock-n-roll.

The only photo in existence of me with Michael Moore.

JAMES AND MARLYN BROWN

JAMES AND MARLYN BROWN

JAMES AND MARLYN BROWN

My gorgeous wife
with a gorgeous gun.
God has blessed me.

JAMES AND MARLYN BROWN

I set rocks
on fire.
Get used to it.

JAMES AND MARLYN BROWN

Grandson Jack
& Poppy eating
venison BBQ.

JAMES AND MARLYN BROWN

Free machineguns for all the children.

JAMES AND MARLYN BROWN

JAMES AND MARLYN BROWN

The universal spirit of real music.

An old black guy showing two young black men the art of the kill.

JAMES AND MARLYN BROWN

JAMES AND MARLYN BROWN

Preparing for another rock and roll assault with ThunderGods Mick Brown & Greg Smith.

The Parker Brothers have left the building. Thank God.

New Mexico Rocky Mountain elk bowkill.

JAMES AND MARLYN BROWN

JAMES AND MARLYN BROWN

JAMES AND MARLYN BROWN

I don't even have to shoot deer anymore. They just come into my barn and hang themselves.

Captain BBQ ready to feed the masses.

Son Rocco, Shemane, & I with class III funguns.

JAMES AND MARLYN BROWN

Daughter Starr, husband Chris, Larry, friend, Lucas, Riley, son Toby & Jack.

JAMES AND MARLYN BROWN

Toby, Jack, and Sasha. I could not possibly be more proud.

JAMES AND MARLYN BROWN

JAMES AND MARLYN BROWN

Anchors away!

JAMES AND MARLYN BROWN

A couple of wonderful, selfless,
beautiful American warriors.

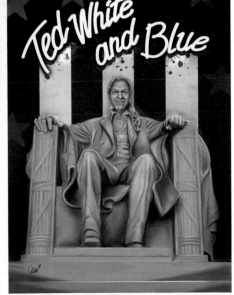

JOHN RIOS, WWW.GRAFIXJAM.COM

I have a dream.

Army trained killers. They are the best America has to offer.

JAMES AND MARLYN BROWN

JAMES BROWN

Having a riot with a bunch of the Good Guys.

A daily pursuit to promote all things guns, hunting, conservation, and common sense.

JAMES AND MARLYN BROWN

A perfect American family.

JAMES AND MARLYN BROWN

JAMES AND MARLYN BROWN

I fortify myself with family and dogs and striped protein.

Thunder,
BlackJack,
and Gonzo
on the hunt.

THOMAS KELSEY/OUTDOOR CHANNEL

I jam everyday, I jam every night.
I practice till I know all the licks.
I won't go away.

JAMES AND MARLYN BROWN

In 2002, the Centers for Disease Control (CDC) estimated that fifteen percent of our young people were overweight. In 2006, the American Obesity Association put the number at thirty percent. While our children are becoming overweight and putting their health at risk, schools across the nation lack sufficient physical education programs. This is a surefire recipe for disaster. Once a standard means of transportation, bicycle riding by kids is down 31 percent since 1995, according to American Sports Data. When I was young, back in Detroit in the 1950s, we rode our bikes everywhere. I am certain I was on my bike more than I was in front of the TV set.

The CDC found that about one third of kids between nine and thirteen years old do not engage in any strenuous physical activity whatsoever. Childhood diabetes is at an all-time high. I could go on and on. There is little, if any, good news to report. Many of the articles and research synopses I read were already five to ten years old. Just based on personal observation, I submit that the problem has only gotten worse. The numbers of overweight kids I see are staggering and heartbreaking.

We are killing our kids. Literally. No, they are not going to fall over dead in front of you, but parents are shortening the lives of their children by allowing their kids to sit in front of the television or computer for hours upon hours. This encourages a sedentary lifestyle, which leads to becoming overweight, which leads to heart disease, cancer, and other health maladies.

The problem is severe, so severe that I believe it is the single most critical problem facing our nation. The U.S. Surgeon General reported that obesity already kills 300,000 Americans each year and estimated that obesity cost the U.S. economy 117 billion dollars in 2000. The death and economic toll will continue to rise if something isn't immediately done. Immediately. Right now. Today.

It starts at home. Parents, look at your children. Do you see rolls of fat on them? Next, review their lifestyle. Do you allow them to sit in front of the television or play computer games for hours on end? If so, turn it off right now. Turn off this electronic junk and go for a walk with your child, shoot some hoops, play catch, or take them hunting or fishing. Do this every day. Get them active. Next, go through the pantry and get rid of the junk food such as soda, ice cream, and chips. Do this today. Hug them. Tell them you love them and what you are doing is for their own good.

Schools should immediately institute fundamental changes in their physical fitness programs. Each kid should be forced to briskly walk thirty minutes each day at school starting tomorrow. Physical fitness is as important as math or science class.

Loving parents and schools must reverse this unhealthy trend starting tomorrow. Failing to act now will kill our kids. Only a soulless parent and a school that doesn't give a damn will fail to act right now.

Springtime is fast approaching. It's a time of renewal, planting, fishing, turkey hunting, and pleasant weather for quality, outdoor, family, physical activity fun. Whether seasonal or a time of renewal in your life, I am certain that improvement is long overdue in many American children's lives. Healthy kids make for a healthy America. America, heal thy children.

Would someone please show me anywhere (anywhere!) in my dog-eared copy of the U.S. Constitution where the federal government is responsible for your health? You are responsible for your health, not the Nanny State. As humorist P. J. O'Rourke correctly stated, "If you think health care is expensive now, just wait until it is free." Pay for your own health care. Socialism sucks.

CHAPTER TWELVE

HIGH (ON ENERGY)

"Oh my God how I like it loud,
the stage is like a wall of sound.
More power by the hour is what I need
to help me blow the world down."

★ ★ ★

"Turn It Up,"
Free For All, 1976

That is yet just another cute lyric from one of my many hundreds of environmentally sound love ballads. Power and lots of it is my drug of choice. I am, as I write this, beyond stoned. You see, I am terminally addicted to all things maximum power. At least I admit it. I'm a Gas-O-Holic. People need me and I can't over-rock the world like I have nonstop since 1958 without magnum, raw, crude, sucking megawatts. It takes massive wads of power to create such brilliant sonic assault music, write this book, set rocks on fire, drive 55 mph in my garage, dig holes in the ground with my bulldozer, my 10mm sub-machinegun—or both, strafe (yes, that's the correct word, not surf) the internet, alter the paths of rivers with the mighty Ma Deuce .50, eat popcorn, throttle daily around my Texas ranch and pour poison on ant hills, set off explosions, conduct outrageously enlightening radio inter-views thereby causing fuzzy-headed idiots untold angst and consterna-tion, mow down trees and vast seas of puckerbrush with my chainsaw and various other weaponry, and give terminally ill children and wounded military heroes the ride of their lives through uncharted muddy swamps and other spiritual muckzonia beyondo environs in one of my many recreational neck-snapping, tooth rattling, Gonzo Buggies. Learn to enjoy me. I won't go away.

In the complex, high energy modern and urban jungles in which we live, work, play, and grill, nothing happens without power, and lots of it. Our homes, offices, and deer camps are run by it, the milk and bread we purchase at the grocery store is grown, processed, and delivered to the store by it, the lights in our home shine because of it, the food we kill, prepare, and cook requires it, and our cars, planes, trains, boats, motor-cycles, fighter jets, stealth bombers, and space rockets all move forward because of it. Power makes our ultra-sophisticated world spin around. If the lights dim in your town when I plug my Gibson Byrdland guitar-beast into my wall of overpowered amplifiers, then I have gotten just about the right amount to power urban renewal and complete head removal. I play the most powerful guitar in the world and it could blow your head clean off. So you have to ask yourself a question: Do you feel lucky? Well, do ya, punk?

Power is expensive. As I write this, gasoline is over four bucks a gallon and appears to be going even higher. The price of home heating oil, natural gas, and electricity have all risen, too, probably faster than your income. With prices escalating, consumer goods and services will continue to rise exponentially, especially those consumables such as milk, bread, and all perishables delivered by trucks operated by companies paying more for fuel. These costs are passed on to consumers, pure and simple. These turbulent economic seas will probably stay very rough for a while, making it increasingly difficult for the average American family to navigate. Tighten your belt where you can, and then tighten it some more. And while you are tightening your belt, our gang of government goons with their glowing lack of a common-sense energy independence policy is tightening the noose around the neck of America.

> **While you are tightening your belt, our gang of government goons with their glowing lack of a common-sense energy independence policy is tightening the noose around the neck of America.**

America's energy policy is this: we are dependent on foreign countries for our oil. We haven't built a refinery or a new nuclear reactor for thirty years. Following this policy will further enslave Americans to high oil prices. It doesn't have to be this way.

I'm not much for delving into the blame game, but some historical context on why we are in this energy debacle is important so we avoid making the same mistakes twice. Are you listening, President Obama? Not all of us are empty-headed, starry-eyed fools.

I agreed with John McCain when he stated, "There is so much regulation of the industry that the last American refinery was built when

Jerry Ford was president." If you want to drown an industry, throw it in a lake weighted down with burdensome, weighty, and bureaucratic government regulations.

President Obama has been running his mouth about slapping a windfall profits tax on the oil industry. This is straight out of the big government playbook of Jimmy Carter who indeed did slap a windfall profits tax on the oil industry about thirty years ago. Guess what that did? It made it more expensive for the oil industry to explore and drill for more oil. Duh. And Obama wants to do this again. This guy knows nothing of how industry works. His naiveté is astounding. It is even more shocking that anyone would pay any heed to a guy with so little experience in how the private sector operates and how government regulation kills initiative there. President Obama would do well to take a Business 101 internship down at the local donut shop to learn about profits, profit margins, overhead, payroll, taxes, and everything else businesses deal with. Here's a hint, senator: if you want more of something for less money, the first thing you must do is get government off the back of that industry. What you are proposing is socialism.

> **I have no interest in playing second guitar to some Middle East flea-infested nation stuck in the year 8 AD.**

A little over twenty-five years ago, our band of legislative idiots known as Congress passed a law that said America could not drill for oil off of our own coasts. They might as well have passed a law that said slavery would be put back into practice. It is slavery. Denying ourselves access to our oil makes us energy slaves to other nations. We are their energy bitchboys. Here's the insult to injury: the law Congress passed banning drilling for oil off our coasts is still in place. In fact, President Bush's dad, President George H.W. Bush, signed an executive order in 1990 agreeing to continue the ban on off-shore drilling. And President George W. Bush stood behind this energy suicide policy for seven and half years until he did the commonsense thing and lifted it before leaving office. He must have heard I was writing this book.

America may not have been blessed with abundant oil fields of light crude such as those of the Middle East, but we have vast deposits of oil that we are not mining. American oil production was at its highest almost forty years ago and has been declining since then. We import the vast majority of our oil from foreign countries, as do the burgeoning economies of China and India. Demand for oil resources is skyrocketing around the world like never before. Third world nations once struggling to develop are exploding into the twenty-first century with heretofore unseen gluttony. As demand for oil escalates, so does the price. Economics 101, my friends. Simple supply and demand stuff going on here. Even guitar players can grasp it.

We are a petroleum-based society. Every product you purchase moves by truck or plane and it is going to stay that way for the foreseeable future due to the distances between communities. There is no other way. None. While our automobile industry has done wonders in improving fuel efficiency in our personal vehicles and over-the-road trucks, environmentalists have lobbied Congress to keep the U.S. from building new oil refineries, drilling for oil in Alaska, and along our coasts, all of which is critical to supply ourselves with the oil we need and crave. Simpletons want to blame the oil companies for their profits but the problem is not their profits so much as it is the environmentalists who will scream and protest that drilling for oil in the Alaska National Wildlife Reserve (ANWR) will damage the ecosystem. That's patently wrong and they know it. Had we drilled for oil in ANWR over ten years ago when it was being debated (when Clinton caved in to the enviro-whackos), we would not be suffering as much at the pumps as we are today and no wildlife would have been harmed—except all that wonderfully renewable surplus protein harvested by arrow if I were providing fresh meat to the ANWR crews.

Just recently, the U.S. Senate voted once again to not drill for oil in ANWR and certain off-shore areas. Anti-American punks one and all. Who owns these bureaupunks? Their suicidal policy will continue to enslave America deeper into dependency on foreign oil. I know damn well that I am not the last American who thinks the real goal of America is to be ruggedly independent. Will someone please get off their bureaucratic ass and do the right thing for America? You can borrow my jackhammer and bulldozer. North to Alaska! Let the drilling begin.

North to Alaska! Let the drilling begin.

I have to wonder if America will ever learn that we can not, must not, rely on foreign oil. We have learned any number of lessons over the past forty years—why can't we learn that relying on foreign oil is analogous to intentionally drilling a screw into your kneecap every ten or so years to see if it still hurts? We must take aggressive action to become energy independent and we must do it now before our economy is further raped by countries that could not care less about America, our future, or the environment.

The first thing we need to do is actually commit to becoming energy independent. A little history lesson about independence is in order. By signing the Declaration of Independence, our forefathers signed their death warrants. These brave statesmen knew it and signed it anyway. They committed to becoming independent. We would be wise to follow their lead and sign a Declaration of Energy Independence—we could even do it on Independence Day in their honor. We need spirited and bold leadership in both the public and private sectors to achieve energy independence. Instead of political posturing by bureaucrats and K Street lobbyists in Washington, D.C., America needs statesmen to step forward to do what is right for America. America once again needs brave patriots and statesmen like our forefathers. Independence means rugged individualism, self-reliance, freedom, and opportunity. America must never compromise our independence to anyone. We deserve an energy policy that makes us once again independent—just like our forefathers taught us.

Let us declare energy independence with a written Declaration of Independence. I doubt our professional, windbag politicians could ever hope to accomplish writing something so simple. That would take years of debates, various committee hearings that drone on and on and accomplish nothing, multitudinous floor speeches, and then going back to committee. So the ten digits of doom guitar slinger will write it for them:

DECLARATION OF ENERGY INDEPENDENCE

To all people of the world, be it known that:

America will be completely energy independent by 2018.

In our aggressive pursuit of energy independence, we will follow the wonderful path set forth by our brave and patriotic forefathers who declared their independence over 225 years ago and established this experiment in self-government.

America will harness our own energy reserves and aggressively develop new energy technologies.

We will minimize the role and impact of the federal government in our pursuit of energy independence, as we know these bureaucrats will be a hindrance to this pursuit.

continued

☆ ☆ ☆

We will rely on and harness American ingenuity, creativity, intellect, and the free market to achieve our energy independence as we know these are the characteristics that have always created progress.

We will respect the environment in our pursuit of energy independence, but will never allow environmentalists to dictate when and how America becomes energy independent. We will provide trees for them to sit in and protest.

In our pursuit of energy independence, we will work with other countries, organizations, companies, and individuals who, first and foremost, cherish independence and freedom. We will ignore the United Nations, as many of the nation members are anti-freedom, liberty, and opportunity.

Any nation who attempts to subvert or deny our pursuit of energy independence shall be dealt with swiftly. We will fight for our energy independence just as we fought for our nation's independence. And the rubble can bounce.

Signed,

The United States of America

How's that for a Declaration of Independence? I literally wrote it in three minutes. It flowed out of me faster than greasy, bad Mexican food. I didn't need a roomful of energy consultants, politicians, lobbyists, and environmentalists to write it. Once again, I'm just a goofy guitar player drunk on freedom and logic. I see a problem and I fix it. I am Mr. Fixit, though I do admit that breaking, smashing, shooting, bending, blowing up, melting, and destroying things is my Number One specialty. I can wreck a steel ball.

As a part of an overall energy policy, we need to create financial incentives. I suggest we offer millions of dollars in prizes for entrepreneurs to engineer and develop even more fuel efficient transportation. Put enough cash in the pot and American ingenuity can build anything and solve any problem—even our petroleum problem. At a minimum, we must try. If we continue to wait, we are literally putting America's future at risk. I will be damned if I am going to be complicit in this crime. I want our energy problem fixed tomorrow before I have breakfast and get even further drunk on logic, pragmatism, and common sense. America must do whatever is necessary to secure our future. We must treat our energy needs like we approached the Nazis, the Japs, and the moonshot. Cut the big dogs loose and fix it. I have no interest in playing second guitar to some piss ass country run by ignorant, power drunk despots or by some Middle East flea-infested nation stuck in the year 8 AD. We are fighting to give the people of Iraq a shot at freedom and opportunity, liberated Kuwait fifteen years ago from Saddam Hussein's army, and have provided military protection to Saudi Arabia over the years. They owe us. Big time. Our economy is as vital to our national defense as anything and we must treat our economy as a critical national asset. If you do not understand this, call 1-800-NUMBNUT and you can arrange for Mike Tyson to come to your home and rearrange your face while he explains it to you.

> ⋆
> **I want our energy problem fixed tomorrow before I have breakfast.**

America has tremendous coal resources, and coal remains one of the world's leading energy sources of generating electricity. But coal is a dirty and dangerous energy source, much like my band. Over 70 percent of the carbon emissions dumped into our atmosphere comes from coal-fired energy generation, yet America still gets 50 percent of our electricity from lighting coal on fire. Moreover, the Environmental

Protection Agency estimates that burning coal kills about 30,000 Americans each year. I am no global warming sheeple, but when there are clearly other, more efficient, effective, and environmentally-friendly methods of generating power, I believe we have a responsibility to explore them. But until we replace these coal-burning power plants with other energy sources that will meet our demand, we will continue to burn coal at a rate of roughly 1 billion tons of coal a year. Until we develop those better methods, I say turn it up. Black is beautiful. Burn, baby, burn.

> **I have always felt guilty that we missed the killer opportunity to roast marshmallows on Richard Pryor's flaming afro. Such a waste of natural heat.**

In addition to coal and petroleum, there are other energy sources that can be tapped to provide us power—whether hydro-electric, wind, solar, biofuels, nuclear, or something we have yet to discover. Personally, I have always felt guilty that we missed the killer opportunity to roast marshmallows on Richard Pryor's flaming afro. Such a waste of natural heat.

Let's begin with hydro-electric power. This power is derived from falling or pressurized water that turns huge turbines in dams that creates the electricity that powers my amplifiers. This power source is clean and consistent, but limited. Most, if not all, of our rivers and lakes have already been harnessed, and there is little, if any, room for growth with this power source. Hydro-electric power provides America with only about ten percent of our power. Unless new hydro-electric technologies are developed, it is not likely that this energy source will ever provide us any more than that. With our energy needs and consumption increasing, hydro-electric power is not a long-term, viable solution. Well, I'll be dammed.

Harnessing the wind is another power source that can produce energy, though it is not widely embraced nor efficient just yet.

(Though our windbag Congress did vote to increase wind-generated electricity). While energy generated by wind may sound appealing, it is not a consistent energy source. When there's no wind, there is no consistent voltage, which is vital to providing the enormous electrical load balances required to power our sophisticated and demanding transmission grids.

Another problem for wind power is the flak various people in places like Cape Cod, Massachusetts have generated over the giant turbines being unsightly. Well, blow me down! With America receiving less than five percent of our electricity from wind power, the answer to our energy woes is clearly not blowing in the wind. At least, not yet.

★

Ethanol is a joke.

Solar energy was once considered a large component of solving our energy needs and had considerable popular appeal—but not so much now. It is just not economical to invest tens of thousands of dollars into the current photovoltaic cells, which capture the sun's rays and produce an electrical current. With current photovoltaic cell technology, it would take almost an acre of them to provide power for a single American home. Similar to wind power, which requires wind to produce electricity, solar energy requires…guess what? The sun needs to shine to produce electricity and that doesn't happen on cloudy days or at night. Though this technology holds some promise, right now, solar power will do little to solve our energy woes.

One of the greatest energy hoaxes and farces ever launched on America has been the bio-fuel scam, specifically ethanol. Ethanol is an energy lie in the first degree. Producing ethanol is throwing good money after bad, which, of course, is why our government provides roughly three billion of our tax dollars in government subsidies to ethanol producers. Go figure. Standard operating procedure of the "feel good at all costs" liberal fantasy police. Are they all stoned?

Ethanol is not a green fuel and is not as efficient as gasoline. The wholesale waste created by this cruel hoax has caused food prices to rise, and around the globe has caused food shortages for those most vulnerable. This may be a first, but even a few of the hippies at Rolling Stone magazine and I agree on this one. It's amazing what a modicum of research and honesty will do to the dreaded curse of denial.

In an outstanding July 24, 2007 article titled "The Ethanol Scam," *Rolling Stone* shoved a dose of common sense up the collective asses of ethanol supporters. As their article astutely notes, "Ethanol hype is dangerous and delusional." As the article further illustrates, ethanol provides only 3.5 percent of our gasoline needs, yet consumes 20 percent of America's corn crop, which has caused corn to double in price—meaning that we are paying a totally unnecessary increased cost for food stuff at the grocery store. I think that's what they call "a bummer."

It takes a tremendous amount of gasoline and water to produce ethanol. It is common knowledge that it takes more gas to produce ethanol than what ethanol generates. Ethanol is not as efficient as gasoline, meaning that a gallon of ethanol does not produce the same amount of energy as gasoline. It takes roughly 1.5 gallons of ethanol to travel as far as a vehicle on a gallon of gas. Additionally, ethanol can not travel down the same pipelines as gasoline because it picks up impurities along the way, including water. This requires ethanol to be transported by truck, which is cost prohibitive. Talk about inconvenient truth.

Talk about inconvenient truth.

Further driving up the cost of energy is America's lack of infrastructure to collect, transport, and deliver ethanol in meaningful quantities to the pump. Lastly, contrary to what Willie Nelson and other "green earth" deniers say and believe, ethanol is as dirty as gasoline and produces the same amount of pollutants as gasoline. Lovely. Only a bureaupunk interested in sustaining and growing more inefficient bureaucracy could possibly support producing ethanol. And really stoned guys like Willie.

Counting on ethanol to replace gasoline is akin to believing that rap is a legitimate musical genre, violent thugs deserve to be let out of their cages, or that animals have rights. Dogs chasing their tails make more sense than this bureaucratic KLSTRPHK. Ethanol is a joke. I'm betting Mr. Treadwell thought corn-based ethanol was a viable energy source for America—you know, the grizzly bear-lover-turned-snack-guy who thought we could all just get along?

NUKE 'EM

In the production of electricity, no energy source is more effective, clean, efficient, and cheap as nuclear energy. Twenty percent of our electricity is produced by 104 nuclear power plants in thirty-one states. Nuclear energy is the one energy source that can dramatically reverse our energy dependence, but once again, America acquiesces to "experts" like Jane Fonda and Robert Kennedy, Jr. Amazingly, a thimble-sized nuclear fuel pellet produces almost as much electricity as nearly a ton of coal. Regardless of what anti-nuclear energy, intellectually soft-minded musicians like Bonnie Raitt and Jackson Browne have to say, nuclear energy is the safest and most environmentally sound energy source we have. I have news for Bonnie Raitt and Jackson Browne and other anti-nuclear musicians and Hollywood actor activists: even Patrick Moore, one of the founders of Greenpeace, supports the facts on nuclear energy. He wrote a well thought-out op-ed in the *Washington Post* (August 6, 2006) supporting nuclear energy. Good God Almighty, what is the world coming to? Ted Nugent and a founder of Greenpeace agreeing? Mr. Moore's revelation is further proof that fact ultimately reigns over fiction, and truth conquers lies and innuendo. The nuclear truth has obviously set Mr. Moore free. Welcome to the party, Mr. Moore. I recommend that Bonnie Raitt and other intellectual light-weights leave the heavy lifting to those of us who care about the facts more than our emotions. Maybe Mr. Moore and I can share an Inuit campfire and chowdown on some fresh muktuk together soon.

Nuclear energy is created in a nuclear reactor through a process called fission. Fission splits atoms in a chain reaction. The energy produced by splitting atoms heats water, which produces steam, which powers large turbines that produce electricity which once again powers my wall of amplifiers. If you do not understand that, think of it in these terms. I play a loud guitar. The sexy, animal mating noises I make emote much happiness, which produces many smiles which creates a grand time had by all. Everyone wins and goes home with a positive glow about them with their happiness batteries fully recharged. I am the nuclear reactor of rock 'n' roll. My music is a veritable energy source.

> ☆
> **I am the nuclear reactor of rock 'n' roll.**

There are a number of erroneous fears about nuclear energy. Just like there is no Boogie Man under your bed, nuclear energy produced in America is not going to cause you to grow a third head or turn your brains to mush and make you vote for a Democrat. Much of the erroneous fears regarding nuclear power have been caused by two nuclear accidents: Three Mile Island and Chernobyl. Hollywood fueled the fear of nuclear energy by releasing the nuclear disaster movie called *The China Syndrome* right before the actual Three Mile Island catastrophe. *The China Syndrome* was as a real as the proboscis on Michael Jackson.

Though the nuclear accident at the Three Mile Island plant on March 28, 1979 was the most serious in our nation's nuclear history, no one, not employees of the plant or nearby residents were harmed by the accident there, not one tiny bit. According to the United States Nuclear Regulatory Commission's website, following the accident, numerous radiological studies conducted by the Nuclear Regulatory Commission,

Department of Energy, and several independent studies estimated the total amount of radiation released to the two million residents was less than the amount of nuclear energy released during a chest x-ray at your doctor's office. Moreover, in the months after the accident, thousands of samples of air, water, vegetation, and soil were taken. Nothing negative was ever found that concluded that the accident had measurable negligible effects on the health of the people or the fauna or flora in the area.

The Three Mile Island reactor did indeed partially melt down due to some engineering and structural errors, but the melted fuel stayed within the reactor. You and your family could have had a family picnic at the base of the reactor at the time of the melt down and not been hurt in the least. You stand a much higher risk of hearing loss at one of my Motown, rhythm and blues concerts than of radiation poisoning if you had been naked at the Three Mile Island nuclear reactor on the day of the accident.

━━━━ ★ ━━━━

You stand a much higher risk of hearing loss at one of my Motown, rhythm and blues concerts than of radiation poisoning if you had been naked at the Three Mile Island nuclear reactor on the day of the accident.

━━━━━━━━━━

Again, according to the United States Nuclear Regulatory Commission's website, the accident did produce a number of sweeping safety, structural, and oversight changes regarding nuclear energy production. Good. Safety first. There has been no nuclear accident in the United States since Three Mile Island.

Some people harbor fears that a nuclear power plant will somehow blow up and produce a giant nuclear explosion like the nuclear blasts on Hiroshima and Nagasaki. The way uranium has to specifically and painstakingly be enriched in order to make weapons-grade uranium renders this impossible. Even if a terrorist were to fly a plane into a nuclear reactor it would not explode. Al-Not-So-Sharpton's hairdo is much more likely to blow up and cause massive injuries than a nuclear power plant.

---☆---

Al-Not-So-Sharpton's hairdo is much more likely to blow up and cause massive injuries than a nuclear power plant.

Another unfounded fear is based on the waste that nuclear power produces. The overwhelming majority of the waste from nuclear power plants could be stored in your backyard with no risk to you. It is totally harmless. You could pick it up with your bare hands and not suffer any ill effects. Of the remaining nuclear waste, most of it could be recycled and used again but peanuts-for-brains Jimmy Carter banned the recycling and use of nuclear waste in 1977. Fortunately, the American voters banned Jimmy in 1980. Carter's baseless decision means that all nuclear waste we have ever produced must be stored in a nuclear waste repository such as Yucca Mountain. Thanks for nothing, Jimmy. Even in his drunkest moment, I doubt brother Billy Beer Carter would have ever made such a dumb decision.

In a December 27, 2007 op-ed on Foxnews.com, Jack Spencer identified the good, the bad, and the ugly of recycling nuclear waste. According to Spencer, France is the good and America is the bad and the ugly. Mr. Spencer highlighted the fact that we have enough nuclear waste that, if recycled, could power every U.S. household for the next twelve years. Alternatively, France has been recycling its nuclear waste and has generated enough power to run France for fourteen years. We literally have vast amounts of energy sitting around doing nothing. What a phenomenal *waste*. To compound insult to injury, I have heard nothing from our current political leadership about plans to overturn Peanut Head Carter's decision and put this energy to use. Leaders, wherefore art thou?

Only a small percentage of nuclear waste needs to be stored at a specialized nuclear waste repository such as Yucca Mountain. Intelligently recycling all that waste would free up vast amounts of storage in Yucca Mountain for the actual waste that needs to be stored there. Is logic an endangered species?

A discussion of nuclear power cannot be complete without discussing how the Soviets screwed up at their Chernobyl nuclear power plant. This 1986 blunder was primarily due to significant design flaws in the reactor and mismanagement that rivals Woodstock for getting bands on stage, on time or paying anybody. The commies did not bother to build a concrete containment structure around the reactor even though they knew it was essential. With proper construction of the reactor, the accident probably would not have happened. In addition to design flaws, my money says the commie staff at the facility was probably loaded on cheap potato vodka. Just a guess.

Estimates are that the Chernobyl catastrophe killed over fifty people within two weeks and hundreds of others suffered from radiation sickness. Over 100,000 people near the facility received radiation doses above internationally accepted levels. Interestingly, it is widely accepted that more fallout from the Chernobyl accident fell on the Three Mile Island facility than was released by the accident at Three Mile Island. Lesson: if you want something done right, never let a commie do it. Obama, booby, are you listening, young man?

There are other risks with nuclear power, namely allowing a hyper whackjob country like Iran to have access so that they could, by the smallest stretch of the imagination, build a nuclear weapon. Clear thinking people know that Iran is one of the largest terrorist-supporting regimes in the world. The free world can not let this outlaw regime develop a nuclear weapon. By their very nature, religious whackjobs do not think straight and with a nuclear weapon in hand, Allah only knows what this religious zealot is capable of. The president of Iran has made ugly and violent statements about Israel and just recently stated that Israel is a "rotting corpse" and that it will not be here in a few years. This lying and manipulative religious voodoo witch doctor is a boil on the world's butt. He is a rabid dog who routinely froths at the mouth. And what do you do to a rabid dog? You shoot them before they bite and infect someone. (Old Yeller, we love ya.) Only an idiot would try to pet a rabid dog. Enter President Obama. He has said he would open up a dialogue with this rabid dog and others who support terrorism. One has to wonder what President Obama would say to this Iranian terrorist. Would he ask Iran to stop their nuclear program and to quit supplying terrorists with weapons and safe haven? Big mistake on Obama's part, but that is indicative of his international inexperience and immaturity. Iran needs to be taught a heap big lesson and soon. To the extent Israeli, American, and other intelligence services can identify the Iranian nuclear engineers at work, they should step on them like cockroaches. In conjunction with drilling holes in their heads by snipers with silenced weapons or flying missiles into their living rooms, we should reduce Iran's nuclear facilities and all supporting nuclear facilities to rubble. Nothing would please me more than to wake tomorrow morning and watch on television giant plumes of smoke drifting to the sky where an Iranian nuclear facility once stood. I would order extra bacon for my breakfast. If the free world waits while Iran works diligently to build a nuclear weapon, we will have committed a grave injustice.

> **Maybe President Obama would take Reverend Wright along as proof that even some Americans hate America.**

Our 104 nuclear power plants provide us with 20 percent of our electricity; coal provides 50 percent. Even with producing just 20 percent of our electricity, our nuclear plants provide more electricity than petroleum, wind, natural gas, and hydropower combined. With coal burning plants dumping over two billion tons of carbon dioxide into the atmosphere, one has to wonder why international globe trotting environmentalist and Global Warming Boy Wonder Al Gore is not pushing hard for America to turn to nuclear power as a more earth friendly alternative. Ground control to Major Al. Maybe the time is too inconvenient for Al to weigh in on nuclear energy. Maybe Uncle Al is too busy purchasing carbon credits for his private jet. Al?

Nuclear energy would go a long way in reducing our dependence on foreign oil. That is good. Building more nuclear power plants is clearly the smart and common sense play. We should have at least 100 more nuclear plants in the next fifteen years. It is a damn shame that America is so late and forced to follow the lead of European socialists, but that is what we need to do as it pertains to nuclear energy.

What we need are strong, resolute leaders who actually want to get something accomplished in freeing us from our dependence on foreign energy instead of just squawking about it while being pathetic pawns of the petroleum industry. I have heard enough political yammering to gag me. I want more results and less political double-speak. Go ahead, nuke my day.

Thirty years from now when I play my 12,000th concert, I want my amplifiers powered completely by nuclear energy. I am the ultimate environmentalist and conservationist. I have personally planted more trees than any group of hippie tree huggers could ever hope to plant in five lifetimes. I support common sense environmental strategies including drilling in ANWR and expanding nuclear energy production. Never forget I am the born free, independent, Rosa Parks celebrating son-of-bitch who sets rocks on fire for fun and inspiration (with no burning permit, I might add). Live free or die. Turn it up.

CHAPTER THIRTEEN

GLOBAL "WARMING"

"Do you remember her name?
She's been here for a long, long time.
She's got the magic wand
To make it rain or sunshine."

★ ★ ★

"Queen of the Forest,"
Ted Nugent, 1975

O ne of the greatest scams ever played on Americans was Orson Welles's radio broadcast of *War of the Worlds* in 1938. Even though the audience was told the broadcast was not real, thousands of Americans within listening range bought it hook, line, and sinker that Martians were attacking and destroying America. Hundreds of hysterical citizens flooded police departments with phone calls, hid in storm cellars armed with shotguns, and generally thought the end of the world was upon them.

The *War of the Worlds* broadcast, of course, is not *the* greatest hoax ever played on Americans. It appears to be a photo finish for 1st place between the ethanol joke and its illegitimate stepsister, man-made Global Warming. The ring leader of this Global Warming farce is Al Gore, the very same guy who claimed to have invented the Internet.

Orson Welles couldn't have created the global warming hoax in his wildest imagination. Even he would have been in complete shock over Al Gore's ability to scare billions of people into believing humans are killing themselves and suffocating all life on the planet by driving their carbon-emitting cars back and forth to work instead of riding bicycles.

Never fear, the logic and truth addicted guitarboy is here. I won't go away. I'm like a bad dream to feel-good liberal idiots, only when they wake up in the morning, I'm sitting at their breakfast table. I visited a liberal buddy of mine a few years ago. The day after I left, his wife left him, his cat died, and his truck rusted off its frame. Perfection.

Nazi propagandist, Joseph Goebbels, perfected the art of the public relations lie. Tell a lie long enough and with enough passion and conviction and you can manipulate and scare people into believing anything. The goose-stepping global warming goons learned their lessons well from Goebbels. Fortunately, there remain many respected individuals in the scientific community sticking with actual science and, through the power of the Internet, they have successfully exposed the global warming chicken-little cultists and caught them in their own deceit-filled lies, half-baked truths, and toxic levels of hypocrisy. To believe Al Gore is to believe the Boogie Man lives under your bed. Everybody knows that I am the Boogie Man, and I'm too busy teaching white folks to dance properly, setting rocks on fire, and reducing Bambi to family sized portions to be a threat.

Here is all you need to know about man-made global warming: it does not exist. There is no man-made global warming. Period. It is a hoax, a sham, and an artful lie. Search out the truth and let it set you free. I recommend watching the movie *The Great Global Warming Swindle*. You can find it on the Internet. It is a factual movie based on objective, hard-hitting science unlike Al Gore's manipulative, ego-driven, anti-scientific fantasy flick. Al Gore's movie is science porno. Fortunately, the polls that I have read indicate that the overwhelming majority of Americans do not care about global warming. Godbless my logical BloodBrothers.

Is the earth warming? Objective scientists believe the earth has warmed about one degree Fahrenheit over the past one hundred years. But the question that needs to be asked is: is the earth warming because of the actions and endeavors of humans or are there other things to consider? This is where many scientists and clear-thinking skeptics— such as myself—part ways with Nobel Peace Prize Fraud winner Al Gore and company's Convenient Lies. Gee, Al Gore wins the Nobel Peace Prize, (while his "documentary" won two Oscars), Michael Moore won a documentary award, Patti Smith (who?) is in the Rock and Roll Hall of Fame, and Al-Not-So-Sharpton is a reverend under investigation by the IRS. Yeah, and I'm the grand marshal at the next gay rights parade playing "Give Peace a Chance" on the banjo. War of the Worlds, indeed.

I'm no climatologist but I am the ultimate conservationist and it stands to reason that the earth has gone through numerous periods of warming and cooling over millions of years. The earth warms and cools

AL "GLOBAL WARMING" GORE

Al Gore is an international, globe-trotting, global-warming fraud. This political punk deserves your public scorn and contempt. I get sick every time I hear or see this hypocritical political maggot.

According to the Tennessee Center for Policy Research, Al's home sucked down enough energy in just one year to power 232 ordinary American homes for a month. After it was first reported that Al's home used twenty times more electricity than the national average, Al went to work on making his home more environmentally friendly. One problem—it didn't work. He now uses 10 percent more electricity than he did before making his home environmentally friendly. The King of Environmentally Friendly's energy bill for a year was over $16,000. Through speaking fees on global warming and such, the Tennessee Center for Policy Research estimates Al's personal fortune has grown to 100 million dollars. Someone should sue him for fraud and deceit. He's no friend of the environment. He's an environmental fraud who makes stacks of cash telling you and me how we should sacrifice to save the planet while his lifestyle drains the planet. Typical liberal elitist. They can talk the talk, but they don't walk the walk. I'm getting sick just *writing* about it. Ignore Al "Global Warming" Gore.

on its own. It also stands to reason that the culprit for these warming and cooling periods is not Al Gore's energy-sucking mansion or trips in private jets. The culprit in these fluctuations is the sun, not excess carbon dioxide.

Carbon dioxide is a naturally occurring gas. Every time you breathe out you are exhaling carbon dioxide. Carbon dioxide is used by all plant life in photosynthesis, the very process that makes the life-giving oxygen that we breathe. Thanks to carbon dioxide, the circle of life is complete.

Contrary to popular belief, the natural cycle of the earth warming and cooling is due to the sun and our oceans. The oceans emit approximately 186 billion tons of carbon dioxide into our atmosphere every year—compared to the 6 billion tons from human activity. As they are warmed by the sun, they generate water vapor through evaporation. Water vapor is the largest greenhouse gas in our atmosphere. And if global warming were truly occurring (and it's not), there would be little we could do about it because we can't control the sun.

Anybody other than little old me remember the fundamental scientific fact from seventh grade science class that trees suck carbon dioxide out of the atmosphere and replace it with oxygen? I've planted more trees than any human Al Gore will ever meet. I've been responsible for an entire forest and thousands of other trees being planted, and even received an award from the Arbor Foundation for my tree planting jihad. I'm not bragging but just want to set the record straight that I know first-hand that the condition of the air, soil, and water is a barometer of the overall condition of flora, fauna, dinner-on-the-hoof, and mankind. I'm no 7th Avenue so-called environmental lobbyist that spends all day raising funds while wearing a Brooks Brothers suit. I get dirty, real dirty. I open up and fondle the dirtguts of mother earth. As a lifelong hunter, fisher, and trapper, I'm the real McCoy, hands-on, ridgerunner, swampjockey, marshboy, beaverpond muckslopper, resource-steward, supreme environmentalist, as are all real conservationists. Venison is the canary in my coal mine. Get some.

Global warming goofballs claim man-made carbon dioxide is the evil culprit for the earth warming, even though the earth is not warming significantly and, in fact, may now be cooling. They will claim carbon dioxide from your car and our factories is destroying the earth. They are the ones responsible for the soaring gas prices, as these Goebbels's protégés have been the prime manipulators in blocking efforts to build new oil or gas refineries or drill for any of the abundant energy sources off of our coasts while the Cubans and Chinese are

"SPIRIT OF THE BUFFALO"

I will not go like the buffalo
Nobody can track me down
I'll make my stand like a buffalo
Make my way to higher ground
People come from far away,
brought the plow & the will
   to stay
They broke ground and their
   promises,
now we pray for a brand
   new day.

What would ya do for the
   buffalo?
Sacrifice everything you own?
Give up your life & security,
Give them back their home?

Don't pretend that they disap-
   peared,
we killed em off with electricity
   but now they're back on a
   sacred ground,
we celebrate that spirit free...

I got the Spirit of the Buffalo,
Spirit of the Buffalo,
Spirit of the Buffalo

Welcome home the buffalo,
his return will cleanse the soul
   where he roams, the spirit
    soars,
his thunder gives us hope
    let's not
repeat the sins of our past,
show respect for the
   ThunderBeast like
   BloodBrothers we will last,
his sacred flesh will be our
   feast,
Celebrate the Spirit of the
   Buffalo....

—*Love Grenade*, 2007

drilling just sixty miles away. Is your blood boiling with anger yet? If you wonder why our economy is in a slow down, look no further than the rabid environmentalists. What the liars don't tell you is that the earth has been warming for at least the last 10,000 years. Before that, the earth was in an ice age. Moreover, long before man and his incredible inventions that improved life for mankind, many millions of years ago the level of carbon dioxide in the atmosphere was much greater than it is today. Every time a large volcano erupts, it dumps more toxins into the atmosphere than all of the toxins combined from all of our factories for a year. Clearly man-made carbon dioxide from our factories matters not in the big scheme of things. Hmmm.

The Goebbels Environmental Brownshirt Brigades will tell you that because of global warming the polar ice caps are melting, polar bears are threatened, temperatures are getting hotter (even though the winter of 2007 was one of the coldest in decades), and hurricanes and floods are more severe. It's all a pack of lies. While some glaciers are melting, others are expanding. While snow and ice may be receding on some mountains, there is zero evidence to suggest this is the result of man-made global warming. The only polar bears that arc threatened are those beautiful white rugsteaks within arrow range of my trusty bow. Other than that, their populations are thriving. Do your homework. Be a healthy, wealthy, and wise skeptic. Be a good steward of the environment by exposing environmental nazis who, if given their way, will destroy America.

The so-called environmental movement was born from the same morally corrupt, brain dead, dare I say doped up clowns that gave birth to the joke known as animal rights. These dishonest, disingenuous, typically stoned punks are void of logic and facts. Because logic and facts are not on their side, they instead try to enflame emotion to evoke fear and guilt in their feeble attempt to recruit intellectually weak adherents to their classic "feel good" cause. They tried to scare us in the early 1970s by saying another ice age was right around the corner. When that failed, these rabid conspiracy freaks next tried to scare us into believing over-population was going to ruin the environment and all of us would soon die of starvation. When that pseudo-science went down in flames, they tried to scare us into believing we would all die of skin cancer because of a hole in the ozone layer of the atmosphere. They then claimed killer bees would sting us all to death. Come again? Surely you remember these whacky claims by the environmental whackos. And now these environmental nazis are trying the same thing by promoting the hoax known as global warming.

> ★
>
> **They try to enflame emotion to evoke fear and guilt in their feeble attempt to recruit intellectually weak adherents to their classic "feel good cause."**

Environmental nazis like Al Gore and crew are not conservationists by any stretch of the imagination, but rather whack jobs who believe man is a blight on the earth, not an integral part of it. They believe the earth would be much better off if humans were not on it. Environmentalists are dirty hippies who care more about Spotted Owls (remember that fiasco?) than they do about affordable housing and energy for ordinary Americans. They care more about fish than they do about drilling for oil off of our coasts to make America energy independent. They sit in trees to protest logging while the logging companies and my hunting buddies and I plant millions of trees. They are dangerously dumb and out of touch with mainstream Americans, but admittedly effective at lobbying our hopelessly disconnected politicians. Through their dishonest lobbying, they have convinced our gullible elected officials that global warming is real, when nothing could be further from the truth. Apparently misplaced idealism is better for America than being energy independent.

A June 6, 2008 article on Yahoo News claimed that mankind needs to spend 45 trillion dollars to combat global warming. That's right—

ELECTION 2008

Senator John McCain has also bought into the global warming fraud. He's as wrong on this issue as he is on amnesty for illegal aliens and campaign finance reform. When he admits he's wrong and changes course on these issues, I might be inclined to vote for him. Of course, I would vote for the three-legged dog I saw on the highway today before I would vote for President Obama's reelection. I hope President Obama is buying carbon tax credits from Al Gore because Obama's a veritable hot air blowhard machine. Cotton candy has more fiber in it than President Obama's speeches.

---

45 trillion dollars on junk science. As the article pointed out, that's three times the size of the entire U.S. economy. This is just more alarmist, Goebbels-type scare tactics from stormtrooping leftists who hate America and want to destroy our economy and way of life. That is the goal of the global warming goon squad—destroy America. Punish her for being the last best place. Lovely.

Before you run out and replace all your incandescent light bulbs with expensive, poisonous, mercury-filled fluorescent light bulbs and turn off all the lights in your house because you have been scared, conned, and guilt-ridden into believing this global warming bunk, you first need to step back and either remember (or learn how) to think critically instead of letting someone manipulate your emotions so that you make erroneous and dangerous decisions. Brain power is free. Learn to hone it, harness it, and use it. Nuge Rule #1: Never allow your emotions to do your thinking for you. Only sheeple do that. Nuge Rule #2: See #1. Kill sheep, make wool and mutton. Next.

For example, wouldn't it be beneficial in evaluating this "danger" to know how much the temperature of the earth has risen over the past 100 years, 1,000 years, or 500,000 years, if at all? Wouldn't it be wise to ask if there are other forces besides man at play that could be causing the earth to warm—if it is? Wouldn't it be good to understand if the earth has gone through other warming and cooling cycles throughout its history? If high levels of carbon dioxide are in the atmosphere as the global warming SS Gestapo goons proclaim, wouldn't that prevent the sun's rays from warming the earth and wouldn't that actually make the earth cooler? Wouldn't it be wise to know the arguments of those who do not believe in global warming? Isn't open debate good for any issue? I think so.

Americans are constantly manipulated by our politicians and their sidekicks in crime—the complicit media, the vicious, socialist anti-American forces at the UN, Hollywood left-wing ideologues who presented Al Gore with a sham documentary Oscar award for his unscientific fiction flick, and others who prey on our well orchestrated ignorance. Until the American electorate learns to think critically about all issues, we run the very real risk of having pseudo-science continuously shoved down our throats and being conveniently manipulated into believing fiction over fact. And that's what is happening with global

OPEN LETTER TO THE SECRETARY GENERAL OF THE UNITED NATIONS

"Attempts to prevent global climate change from occurring are ultimately futile, and constitute a tragic misallocation of resources that would be better spent on humanity's real and pressing problem."

warming. The void created by a corrupt, inept, U.S. education system has left many Americans susceptible to a tsunami of pure bullshit. As long as it *feels good*, way too many Americans eat it up. Great.

When you continually press the button for more bullshit, don't be surprised when you get it. Do not be scared or guilt-ridden into believing something just because it seems everyone else is jumping on a fashionable bandwagon. Think critically for yourself. Steer clear of the herd. Always be suspicious. My skepticism radar is on full alert at all times, especially whenever I hear or read the beliefs or plans of fuzzy-headed, windbag liberals who don't think, but simply react with their emotions. These people are dangerous to you, your family, our nation,

> ⋆
> **Always be suspicious. My skepticism radar is on full alert at all times.**

and the earth. Do not even humor them. Turn on the cockroach spotlight and warm up their world. I like mine well done.

The first problem with global warming is that the global warming alarmists will not debate or open their so-called research up to scrutiny and criticism by other scientists. Isn't that how scientists are supposed to improve science? To ignore the thousands of scientists who are skeptical of global warming is to ignore the very scientific method that defines good science. Over one hundred skeptical scientists signed an open letter to the UN protesting the idea that climate change is "settled."

Thousands of climatologists and other scientists around the world have staked their reputations on global warming being a hoax—why do Al Gore and his side-kicks give them the finger? Why won't Al Gore & his global warming crew debate them? Why won't Michael Moore debate me?

Second, it is abundantly obvious to me that the media has swallowed the global warming poison. I can't think of a single news story by the dominant media whores that focused on the opposing view from any of the scientists and climatologists who have studied global warming and believe it is false and a complete sham. Other than the fact that we have a lapdog media instead of a snarling, viciously objective, guard dog media, you have to wonder why this overt bias exists. And who says our corrupt, left-tilting, dominant media doesn't have an agenda? Want to do your part to save the environment? Save a tree and don't buy leftist newspapers and magazines. Gather up the ones in your home and set fire to them in your driveway on Independence Day.

Third, anytime the United Nations is involved, know that the fix is in for America. The socialists, communists, despots, and tyrants who rule many of the UN member countries hate America and Americans with a passion and use the United Nations as a tool to wage political war against us. They know their piss-ass, corrupt, banana republic, poverty, flea, and disease-ridden countries could never take us on militarily so they use the United Nations to try to weaken America for their own, weaselly benefits. Man-made global warming is one arrow in their collective quiver to do just that.

For example, did you know that the United Nations established the Intergovernmental Panel on Climate Change (IPCC) to carry out climate research? In 2007 this panel concluded, of course, that global warming is real and that humans (meaning capitalistic Americans, of course) are the culprits. This panel of United Nations quasi-science stooges is not composed of educated, qualified scientists, and it did not do any scientific research of its own. What the IPCC did do was select certain "scientific" research that met its political agenda and used that fraud for its report. The facts, however interesting, were inconsequential to this panel of climate snake oil salesmen, but that's how the United Nations operates. Oil for food, anyone? Besides San Quentin State Prison or the Cook County Jail on a Saturday night, the United Nations is the largest gang of criminal punks and con artists that the world has ever collected in one place. Any reports produced by the fraudulent

IPCC—or the entire UN—should be boxed up and sent to Africa so poor people have something to wipe their butts with or to start today's atmosphere-polluting cooking fires. The international scam artists who work at the United Nations pose a much greater risk to mankind than so-called global warming ever will.

The pro-Goebbels, goose-stepping, Global Warming Goons point to some rather creative computer models to gauge and predict various climate indicators, but their computer models cannot predict the future effects of the sun on the earth. As I explained earlier, varying levels of heat from the sun affects the temperature of the oceans, which then produces more water vapor. Computer models used to predict hypothetical future climates should not be trusted. Hell, the local weather man can't accurately predict what the weather is going to be like three days from now. And I'm supposed to believe the computations and output from a climate computer model for the next twenty-five years? Not likely.

⭐

I was born at night, just not last night.

I was born at night, just not last night. Even if America punished itself by spending hundreds of billions on eradicating global warming, which does not exist, will China, India, and other burgeoning economies do the same? Surely no one believes that these corrupt countries would follow suit. So while America would voluntarily strangle its own economy, the rest of the world would laugh at our self-inflicted economic suicide and continue full speed ahead with their industrial revolution. It is lunacy to think the Chinese or Indians care what Al Gore or the UN has to say about global warming.

Fortunately, the U.S. Senate had enough common sense left to pull S. 2191 (the Lieberman-Warner Climate Security Act) from the agenda. Supported by the Sierra Club, this bill would have hurt America's ability to sustain and grow needed power for the coming generations by strangling our power plants with unnecessary carbon dioxide emissions restrictions. More energy efficiency and wind turbines are not going to cut the mustard when America's demand for electricity is expected to grow by over fifty percent by 2030. Self-inflicted energy wounds like S. 2191 would make America more energy dependent on other nations (many of them our enemies) and cause energy prices to rise which hurts our economy. Funny—I thought the goal was to become more energy independent. We can't achieve this by placing unnecessary burdens on our power infrastructure. When the Sierra Club talks, don't listen. Go hunting instead. Kill a polar bear for me.

> ⋆
>
> **Do not be scared and then manipulated into believing things that are not true.**

Admittedly, I am no scientist, just a skeptic who has learned to distrust leftists, socialists, the UN, various anti-American scum, and, sadly, even some of our elected officials who seem bent on making America less competitive in the global economy and more dependent on other nations. Pour large doses of rocketfuel on your skeptical fire and keep it blazing red hot. That's my advice.

There is no man-made global warming. None. Remember that, believe it. The earth has gone through various stages of heating up and then cooling down and it will continue to do so long after you and I are gone. This is because of the sun. We can't do anything about that. Mark my words, ten years from now we will look back and laugh once again at the whacky environmentalists who made dire predictions about global warming. Proven wrong once again, the environmentalists will have moved on by then to some other scare tactic like claiming our oceans are poisoned, outer space is full of space junk, we have no clean water, we're headed for food shortages, or my guitar is too loud and sexy. They're an imaginative crowd.

Do not be scared and then manipulated into believing things that are not true. I'm the real Boogie Woogie Man and I'm not under your bed.

★ ★ ★

OPEN LETTER TO THE SECRETARY GENERAL OF THE UNITED NATIONS

"Because attempts to cut emissions will slow development, the current UN approach of CO_2 reduction is likely to increase human suffering from future climate change rather than to decrease it."

I'm in your head dancing like James Brown on PCP. Learn to think critically and teach your children to do the same. Ask fundamental questions and accept nothing at face value—especially mass hysteria like global warming. Fight people and organizations who have an anti-American agenda. Stand up and be counted. It is your responsibility as an American.

I do not believe in intentionally harming our environment. I plant trees and then sit in them to hunt and kill deer while balancing the herd annually. Perfect. The cycle of life is complete. Our science has led to numerous, cost-efficient improvements, and I believe science married to the free market is the perfect, harmonious union to solve our energy woes and other real problems. I do not believe our problems can be solved by ignorant politicians, whacky environmentalists, feel-good idiots, and the anti-American UN. Like clowns at the circus, hippies can be wildly amusing. What we can't do as a society is ever let them dictate public policy. Hippies then become dangerous.

Environmentalists create problems that don't exist. The free market and scientists whose credo is objective science create cost-effective solutions to real problems that benefit people and the environment. BBQ like you mean it.

CHAPTER FOURTEEN

GOD, GUNS, & ROCK 'N' ROLL

REVISITED

"There was a time when man stood strong.
Right was right and wrong was wrong."

★ ★ ★

"I Shoot Back,"
Spirit of the Wild, 1995

As you may recall, I covered, in detail, the issue of guns in my first book celebrating logic, self-evident truth, and the facts, *God, Guns, & Rock 'n' Roll*. In light of the recent decision by the U.S. Supreme Court that struck down Washington D.C.'s handgun ban, I thought it would be appropriate to provide you with a Nuge street brief analysis of this case and remind you of your duty to defend yourself and your family.

First off, I support killing assholes at the scene of the crime. That's real crime control. Secondly, the definition of gun control is placing the second bullet in the hole made by the first bullet. Currently, I embody definitive gun control. Take my word for it.

You don't have to be a legal scholar to understand that the Bill of Rights is simply a man-made document articulating what good men know in their souls are instinctive and definitive rights. These rights are inherent to individuals that pre-existed this experiment in self-government and the writing down of such self-evident truths. The fact that four Supreme Court justices do not understand that and voted against those rights is appalling and an indictment to the dismal disconnect between we, the people, and our current so-called Supreme Court justices. It is beyond the pale.

> "A well-regulated Militia, being necessary to the security of a free State, the right of the people to keep and bear Arms, shall not be infringed."

The recent Supreme Court ruling in the case of *Heller* v. *Washington, D.C.* dealt directly with the Second Amendment. The Supreme Court ruled the D.C. gun ban was unconstitutional, but just barely. Four of the nine justices dissented. The four justices who voted against overturning the blatantly anti-freedom, anti-common sense gun ban lean hard to the left. If they lean anymore to the left, the Cuban Castro boys will ask them to pay rent.

A cursory review of the writings of our Founding Fathers regarding the Second Amendment. "A well-regulated Militia, being necessary to the security of a free State, the right of the people to keep and bear Arms, shall not be infringed" clearly demonstrates they understood the right of the people to be armed. "The people" = individual American people. They understood that an armed society is a polite society. As Professor John Lott has identified, our Founding Fathers knew that more guns equal less crime, and less tyranny. Who hasn't read this? Who doesn't understand it?

While the Supreme Court just barely overturned the anti-freedom gun ban, just a day or so before that, the leftist justices and one moderate justice (Kennedy) voted in another case that it was unconstitutional for Louisiana to execute a convicted child rapist.

So here we have it. The left-wingers of the Supreme Court vote to keep an anti-freedom gun ban in place which denies people the right to defend themselves with handguns, but votes to prevent Louisiana's executing a child rapist. Is it just me, or do you think the left wing of the Supreme Court should submit to a urinalysis test?

> ★
>
> **I embody definitive gun control.**

The first Natural Law is the God-given right of preservation of self and the lives of your loved ones. Pay attention. It's not just your right. It's your supreme duty as a father or mother, and citizen. Waiting for a court to give you that right can make you a victim, whereas my policy is to shoot violent assholes. I call 9-1-1 to request a dust pan and a broom to clean up the mess. It will be a cold day in Hell before I wait for a black-robed judge to tell me I have the right to defend myself and my loved ones. That would be as bizarre to me as having a judge tell me on which days of the week I can make love to my wife, go out to dinner, or go fishing with my grandson. Don't tread on me and I won't Ted on you.

You never hear from the co-conspirators of the left-wing media how many innocent victims are dead, raped, and mutilated as a direct result of these left-wing policies and insane anti-gun laws. That's the news story that has gone unreported. Instead, the left wing yaps on about the need for even more gun control (thereby ensuring more innocent victims) and their lap dog media laps it up like a puppy with a bowl of warm milk. They are complicit as well. Leftists enable crime. Conservatives stop crime. It doesn't get anymore complicated than that.

I like freedom. I like guns. I like it that I'm always prepared for any contingency. I like it that anti-freedom leftists, socialists, thug punks, smelly hippies, and commies hate me for believing you have a duty to protect yourself and your loved ones. Nothing makes me more proud. I'm smiling as I type this, as I've reminded myself that another pallet of ammunition was delivered just yesterday. That's right, a pallet of ammunition. You know you have achieved self-actualization and success when pallets of ammunition are delivered to your home. Please, a moment of silence for my mounting pallets of ammunition.

Guns enable freedom. Always have. Legally armed Americans are cool. Street cops have no problem with good guys being armed because street cops know they can't possibly be everywhere to protect everyone in every situation. Street cops also know that recidivistic, maggot thugs are armed and commit hundreds of violent crimes every day. As you read this very sentence, another law-abiding American is being robbed, murdered, raped, and beaten. Right now it is happening. Stop and think about that. Don't believe me? Read your evening newspaper or watch your nightly news. There will be reports today of more violence and more victims. At least with a gun you have a chance. Soon, our fellow citizens in D.C. will be able to defend themselves. This is good. Being forced into unarmed defenselessness is bad and ugly.

> ☆
>
> **Don't tread on me and I won't Ted on you.**

Try this on for size: the only good violent asshole is a dead one. That four Supreme Court justices think otherwise is supremely mind boggling. I adamantly believe a citizen who exterminates a violent punk should be given the keys to the city and a ticker tape parade in his honor. I have seen reports on the local news all across America of citizens being recognized for doing other good deeds in their communities. What could possibly be a better deed than killing a violent creep, thus making the community a safer place to live, work, and play? Go ahead, name one deed that trumps killing a violent thug. Just one. Okay, maybe killing two or three violent thugs.

Every day across America, Americans use guns to deter and stop crime. This occurs roughly two and a half million times a year, yet the good deeds of our fellow citizens are not reported. Again, doubt me? When was the last time you heard, read, or saw a story in the media that reported a citizen using a gun to stop a crime? I won't rest until I see a newspaper headline that says something like: "Armed Citizen Kills Recidivistic Asshole." When I see that headline, I know my work is done here and I can retire to killing trillions of Texas ants and daily setting rocks on fire. Until then, I won't go away. My pledge to those of you who still believe in common sense is that I will drive left-wing idiots batty.

Until I see common sense rule the day, I will become more demonstrative, more outspoken, and more committed to ensure good always conquers evil. For a civilized and just society to flourish, the very first thing that must occur is the removal of the violent human garbage. Put them in cages where they belong and do not ever release them to prey upon good, law-abiding citizens ever again. With 20 percent of the violent thugs committing roughly 80 percent of violent crime, we have an obligation to swat violent perpetrators like pesky mosquitoes at a summer barbecue. To believe otherwise is bizarre, overtly weird, and clearly complicit in their next crime.

You can't rely on the criminal justice system to keep the violent, recidivistic thugs in cages. Prosecutors routinely cut plea bargain deals to get convictions, judges give these creeps chance after chance, and even if the thugs do get sent to prison, they are released time and time again—and they are now living in our neighborhoods.

The very people who need guns the most are our fellow Americans who live in the impoverished inner cities where crime flourishes. Amazingly enough, I see many of our fellow Americans in these communities holding marches and prayer vigils to stop the violence. That's the wrong approach unless the goal is to enable more violence. The right approach is to drill holes in violent thugs. Double tap to the chest and one to the head will do the trick every time. If you don't want to live in a rat infested house, you might want to first think about exterminating the rats. Praying the rats will change their evil ways or leave is wishful and dangerous thinking. And it is downright stupid. While you pray for peace, the violent thugs are preying on you. If you are going to pray for something, pray that I'm walking down the street when a street maggot is assaulting you. It will be my pleasure to cut the maggot in half for you. If a dope-dealing maggot's house gets in my way, I will burn it down.

Four Supreme Court justices voting against giving the good people of Washington, D.C. the right to own handguns is as anti-American as anything I have ever seen in my life. That's supremely bizarre unless you also believe that child rapists should not be exterminated. I know four supremely insulated people in black robes who believe this to be true.

> ★
>
> **God gave you the amazing gift of life. Never surrender that precious gift. Be prepared to fight for it.**

How sad. How pathetic. How soulless. How supremely stupid.

Never forget you have a duty, not a right, to defend yourself and your family. You don't need a panel of judges with politically correct, dopey ideologies to give you that right. God gave you the amazing gift of life. Never surrender that precious gift. Be prepared to fight for it. That is your duty and your responsibility as a free person.

ANOTHER FINE DAY OF TEXAS BALLISTIC DISCIPLINE

My guitars are in a temporary, well-deserved state of suspended animation following the most outrageous rhythm and blues rock 'n' roll audio orgy since the invention of gunpowder. My band rocks! Forever surrounded by the world's most amazingly gifted virtuosos, I assure you that my guitar does not gently weep. Its victims do. Tears of joy, of course. Me too. Every night on-stage for more than fifty years (fifty years! Ouch!), I have celebrated nonstop, gungho musical adventure, the likes of which could erupt only from the primal inspiration of my black heroes: Muddy Waters, Howling Wolf, Mose Allison, Chuck Berry, Bo Diddly, Little Richard, Jerry Lee Lewis, (I'll let you tell Jerry Lee he isn't black) Wilson Picket, Sam and Dave, Freddy King, Albert King, B.B. King, the mighty

> I assure you that my guitar does not gently weep. Its victims do.

Motown Funkbrothers, and of course his majesty, James Brown. Where on earth does an old guitarboy like me get all this energy, piss and vinegar, positive spirit, and attitude at the tender age of fifty-nine? I'll tell you where; write this down children (and all you old folk too)—DISCIPLINE. Good, old-fashioned, be the best that you can be, American Dream *discipline*. I've had fifty-nine years of being clean and sober. How cool, but more importantly, how simple is that? Totally. Can't get that smile off my face.

Enter the wonderful world of firearms-fun discipline. That's correct. My father, Godbless his U.S. Army Drill Sergeant soul, didn't only teach me gun safety and always-exciting marksmanship discipline—he *parented* it upon me. Of course, that used to be almost universally "Responsible Parenting 101." All you have to do is look around to see the slovenly, disheveled, fat, disconnected, rude, pierced, Ozzy-zombie-like youth so

"I AM THE NRA"

When I think of freedom
I got my Bill Of Rights
US Constitution is my guiding light
Our Founding Fathers, they were not confused
I always celebrate self-evident truths
I AM THE NRA I AM THE NRA
I am we the people
I don't need no OK
My pursuit of happiness will take me all the way
If you hate slavery as much as we all do
Come on join the fight, I'll tell you what we do
I AM THE NRA I AM THE NRA
If you hate tyrants and dictators and are ready to give freedom a whirl
Celebrate the NRA and the shot heard round the world
The shot heard round the world
I AM THE NRA I AM THE NRA

—Ted Nugent, 2008

prevalent today in order to witness the tragedy of abandoned discipline, and so often, horrifically, plain-and-lousy parenting. Such soulless conditions have permeated every nook and cranny of our great American society and it boggles the mind how careless so many Americans have become. It says a lot when a nation is constantly squallering and bellyaching about deserving "health care" when so many in that nation daily conduct themselves knowingly and intentionally in suicidal behavior which proves they clearly do not care about their health one bit. It's weird, Planet of the Apes behavior, the way I see it. Pray for America, she needs it.

But alas! Celebrate that absolute family quality of life that is indeed alive and well across the hinterland. Thank God that the good still out-weighs the bad and the ugly out there, literally, *out there.* As in the Great Outdoors. I am honored and privileged to proudly represent the most wonderful grass roots American family organizations to be found anywhere. And the upgrade of youthful discipline is looking better everyday. Those same powerful lessons in accountability that my mom and dad brought home to us kids can be found in organizations like the great Big Brothers Big Sisters, National Rifle Association, Texas Rifle and Pistol Association, the spectacular 4H programs, Texas Parks and Wildlife Youth Hunter program, the National Wild Turkey Federation, Safari Club International, Dallas and Houston Safari Clubs, National Shooting Sports Foundation, our Ted Nugent Kamp for Kids, and a plethora of youth oriented charities too numerous to list here. What all these volunteer-run operations have in common is their successful youth mentoring, firearms training, and shooting pro-grams. I cannot over-emphasize the irrefutable positives that occur when a kid is shown the basics of firearms discipline and the always intense fun therein.

A tsunami of evidence is pouring in nationwide; more and more kids across America are discovering and rejoicing in time-honored family outdoor shooting fun. The Olympic-class challenge of correct breath-ing, sight acquisition, and trigger control brings a Zen-like higher level of awareness to every participating youngster, all of whom naturally crave such individual excellence. Like the enormous "win-win" success-es of the National Archery in Schools programs, the shooting sports do indeed "cleanse the soul." Look what it did for this wild guitarboy from

Detroit. Jimi got high and Jimi is dead. I went shooting, and I'm still Ted. Go figure. I think I'll go clean my guitars and my guns, again.

Reach out to neighbor kids, your own children's friends, coworkers, and churchgoers. I assure you, the thrilling fun we experience at the range or casually plinking in the wild will increase tenfold when we bring along a new shooter. It is up to us to introduce new shooters properly to our love of the sport and help them gain understanding of introductory and safety procedures through experience. Recruiting new shooters is not only more fun, but knowing that we are driving the antigunners nuts is a wonderful bonus for simply doing the right thing. If we don't do it, who will? Giving these new shooters an NRA membership will put the icing on the cake. Happy, smiling kids with guns is the American way. Go for it. And I'll see ya at the range.

> ⭐
> **Happy, smiling kids with guns is the American way.**

Find dedicated and professional shooters who will steer you in the right direction in central Texas and the Waco area, at Keith's ACE Hardware stores, LoneStar Music and Archery, Praco Pawn Shop, Guns-R-Us, Brazos Feed & Supply, the Waco Gun Club at the Waco Airport, or deertexas.com. If you don't have the good fortune to live in Texas, go to tednugent.com to discover a long list of organizations dedicated to introducing America's youth to the discipline upgrade of the shooting sports. It's everywhere for everyone.

For more Nugent gun fun celebration, get a copy of *God, Guns, and Rock 'n' Roll* at tednugent.com or call 800-343-4868 for a Sunrize Safari.

ANOTHER GUN CELEBRATION

As always, with cover-ups running wild, denial nearly airtight, and unprofessional, deceitful, anti-American misrepresentation securely locked in place, the media is intently on course with its anti-U.S. Constitution, anti-freedom, and anti-individualism agenda. When it comes to guns and God, we can rarely expect to read anything even approaching how the vast majority of Americans feel, or what, in fact, we *know* in our hearts to be right. So the Yankee guitarplayer will cover central Texas for ya all. I know I stand with the best of the good folk, and I'm proud of it.

Jeanne Assam was one of approximately 7,000 worshippers at the New Hope Church in Colorado Springs in December 2007. She participated in a gathering of Christians praising God and dedicating themselves to a spiritual upgrade of being better Americans and human beings. It is the practice of churchgoers everywhere in this unique land where freedom of religion is considered a "self-evident truth" and individual right bestowed upon us by our Creator. A weekly thank you to Him seems to be in order by those good souls who still think clearly and pursue a good, positive way of life. It is all good.

But Jeanne, Godbless her righteous soul, was packing a handgun this fine church day. She had never fired one of her guns at anyone in the past, but as a thinking, caring American, she knew that rugged individualism and real world independence meant being prepared. And prepared she was when the loud, shocking concussions of rifle shots rang out in the entranceway of the

ROCK ON

I joyfully spend most of my American Dream days cleaning out the remnant trash from the deep, aggressive cleats of my Vibram soled, steel-toed work-boots following my hourly mashing of anti-gun and anti-hunt skulls underfoot. It is a delightful regimen. I then feed the liberal shrapnel goo to unsuspecting herbivores and swine for ultimate BBQ delight.

—Ted Nugent, somewhere in CA

church. Her natural instincts of good over evil kicked into gear, and like millions of concealed weapons carriers across America, the pistol in her belt gave her pragmatic confidence that she could neutralize an apparent evil force in the House of God.

Jeanne didn't run scared, scream, cower, or flee for her life. She knew that to do so was to give signals of helplessness and in fact, be helpless. Instead, she drew a gun and headed toward the approaching gunshots, just like I have encouraged in so many of my writings over the years. When a human being gives serious, genuine thought in preparing for and responding to danger instead of swallowing the incremental programming of sheepishness so thoroughly crammed down Americans' throats by a media infested with cowardly, individual rights-condemning liberals, natural instincts overcome fear in dictating the opposite response—and Jeanne was living proof.

And this dainty, svelte young woman couldn't possibly fit the profile so desperately dictated by anti-gun nuts, for she has no macho baggage and no intentionally misrepresented NRA imagery to overcome. She is a woman, a human being, with the natural right to defend herself and innocent lives from evil, and she did what her heart told her to do.

Further irritating the mainstream media's hatred of Christianity, she credits God as her guiding light, protecting her from the high-powered rifle, two handguns, and more than 1,000 rounds of ammo in the possession of the maniacal madman attacking her congregation. She courageously went toward the danger and shot the bum. Next.

We like it when maniacal madman hellbent on slaughtering innocents are shot dead instead. And we like brave people who know that innocent lives need to be protected by shooting madmen using guns on our persons. We know that gun-free zones are irresponsible, dangerous, anti-human, anti-security, and anti-American. We don't like politicians or people who pretend otherwise. We don't think a madman who opens fire in malls, cafeterias, churches, schools, or our neighborhoods has any rights whatsoever. We believe good should live and evil should be gotten rid of. And we know the difference between good and evil without some newspaper editor or bureaucrat telling us if we got it right or not. I wish there was a Jeanne Assam every one hundred feet in America so the bad guys would get the real message from America: "Don't tread on me!" Threaten innocent lives and we will shoot you dead.

I'm sending Jeanne Assam an expensive Christmas present and a life membership in the NRA.

GUN-FREE ZONE STRIKES AGAIN

Here we go again. Someone tell me why, with nearly 3,000 articles written worldwide within forty-eight hours following the tragic slaughter at the Omaha, Nebraska Westroads Mall, not a single one of them mentioned the most important fact of all. Thousands of "professional" writers converging on such an event, sharing their sleuthing in the world's most respected publications and electronic media, yet not a single one of them saw it meaningful in their "reporting" of the crime to mention all the "no guns allowed" signs throughout the mall? Got agenda? Sieg heil!

Even though Nebraska recently got a small piece of their Second Amendment back by finally allowing law-abiding citizens their "God given right" to keep and bear arms, it is truly anti-American and downright bizzarro that private property and business owners can deny (as in "infringe") this "inalienable" right bestowed upon free men by our Creator. This, of course, is the liberal dream known as "gun-free zones." As in Columbine, Virginia Tech, Luby's cafeteria in Killeen, Texas, and every other location where the wanton slaughter of unarmed, helpless victims is a virtual guarantee.

Except, of course, at the Salt Lake City mall last year where an armed, off-duty cop properly defied that mall's "gun-free" policy. Virtually indistinguishable (for all practical purposes) from an armed law-abiding

☆ ☆ ☆

CULT OF AGRICULTURE FERTILIZER

No one was foolish enough to debate Ryder truck regulations or ammonia nitrate restrictions or suggest there was a "cult of agriculture fertilizer" following the unabashed evil of Timothy McVeigh's heinous crime against America on that fateful day in Oklahoma City. No one faulted kitchen utensils or other hardware of choice after Jeffery Dhamer was caught drugging, mutilating, raping, murdering, and cannibalizing his victims. Nobody wanted "steak knife control" as they autopsied the dead nurses in Chicago as Richard Speck went on trial for mass murder. Evil is as evil does and laws disarming guaranteed victims makes evil people very, very happy. Shame on us.

Who has the audacity to demand unarmed helplessness? Who likes dead good guys? I'll tell you who, people who tromp on the Second Amendment, that's who. People who refuse to accept the self-evident truth that free people have the God-given right to keep and bear arms in order to defend themselves and their loved ones. These folks are so desperate in their drive to control others and so mindless in their denial that they might as well pretend that access to gas causes arson, Ryder trucks and fertilizer cause terrorism, water causes drownings, forks and spoons cause obesity, dialing 9-1-1 will somehow save your life, and that their greedy clamoring to "feel good" is more important than admitting that armed citizens are much better equipped to stop evil than unarmed, helpless ones.

citizen, he was able to thwart the mass shooting that would have unfolded were it not for a good guy with a gun. How dense must someone be to hide from this information? Denial runs deep in a growing population of "we the sheeple." For shame.

When did a nation of rugged individuals turn into helpless whiners, crying and running in fear from danger and evil? When did we abandon our natural instinct to counterpunch and attack evil, overpowering it and neutralizing it into submission? When were we forced to dial 9-1-1, losing and wasting precious, decisive time, instead of doing the right thing and stopping bad guys ourselves? When did we trade in independence for dependency? When did we decide that we can't handle tough situations ourselves, and we need to call big brother while we cower and hide like little, helpless children? Pathetic.

Every day in this country, according to the Department of Justice (and every study ever conducted), armed, law-abiding citizens stop dangerous, violent confrontations from escalating into death and tragedy, simply by having a gun handy to provide real "equality" on the mean streets of America. Dedicated cops across America will be the first ones to tell you that they not only can't possibly be there to protect us, but that they also have no legal requirement to do so. By the time the police show up, many innocents will likely have perished at the hands of evil while good people hang around, hoping and praying. Is it possible to continue to hide from the life and death truth that armed citizens save lives? If you have no soul, apparently so.

GUN-FREE ZONES ARE A MURDERER'S DREAM

Zero tolerance huh? Gun-free zones huh? Try this on for size; Columbine—gun-free zone. New York City pizza shop—gun-free zone. Pearl High School, Mississippi—gun-free zone. Luby's cafeteria— gun-free zone. Amish School in Pennsylvania—gun-free zone. Virginia Tech University—gun-free zone. Anybody see what the evil Sarah Brady and her denial-infested, gun-banning cult have created? I personally have zero tolerance for evil and denial. And America had better quickly

GET REAL

I would highly recommend that we finally learn from all these sense-less tragedies. Get real. Get rid of politicians who support gun-free slaughter zones. Get rid of gun-free zones. Get a gun, learn to use it, and do the right thing. Bad guys should be shot dead, not helpless Christmas shoppers.

wake up to the fact that the braindead celebration of unarmed helpless-ness will get you killed every time. I've about had enough of it.

Contrast the "gun-free zones" above with the Salt Lake City shopping mall rescue: an American citizen with a gun in his belt stopped a violent murderer from killing more innocent victims. Or what about the high school student in Springfield, Oregon who ran to his pickup truck, retrieved his .22 squirrel rifle, and halted a runaway murderer in his quest to turn his school into a Columbine tragedy? Just a few miles up the road from Virginia Tech, two college students used their legally owned firearms to stop a madman from slaughtering anybody and everybody he pleased—because these brave, average, armed citizens neutralized him pronto. My hero, Suzanne Gratia Hupp, was not allowed by Texas law to carry her handgun into Luby's Cafeteria that fateful day years ago, and due to bureaucrat, forced, unarmed helpless-ness, she could do nothing to stop satanic Hennard from slaughtering helpless innocents. Denial-ridden, "feel good" politics certainly has some responsibility in their deaths. Shame on them. Shame on America. Shame on the anti-gunners all.

Pray for the families of victims everywhere America. Study the methodology of evil. It has a profile, a system, and a preferred environ-ment—the one in which victims cannot fight back. Embrace the facts, demand upgrade, and be certain that your children's school has a better plan than Virginia Tech or Columbine. Eliminate the insanity of "gun-free zones" which will never, ever be gun-free zones. They will only be good guy gun-free zones, and that is a recipe for disaster written in blood on the alter of denial. I, for one, refuse to genuflect there.

CHAPTER FIFTEEN

WE KNOW

"And you can't stop me, you can't offend me
I ain't backing down
I'm here to stay
I won't go away."

★ ★ ★

"I Won't Go Away,"
Craveman, 2002

Much to the chagrin of my liberal neighbors in central Texas (who are obviously displaced and lost outside their preferred San Francisco and Bostonian habitat), the damn Yankee guitarboy from Detroit just keeps on raising Cain. Since coming home to The Lone Star State from my beloved home state of Michigan, with pure, unstoppable, logic-driven defiance coursing through my veins and slamming through my fingertips, I am compelled to exercise my glowing, "We the People" crowbar of truth in spite of the rhetorical anti-Texan, anti-American editorial policy running rampant across this otherwise Great Republic. I read it and hear it, but for the life of me cannot find any real Texans who agree with lefty *Waco Tribune* editor, John Young. Go figure. That I, a Texas transplant, better and more accurately represent the Great Texas Spirit than my editors is tragic. The good governor Rick Perry and I will continue to walk handgun-in-handgun down the streets of Austin unabated. I shall carryon. Remember the Alamo.

After recoiling in disbelief at the very un-Texas like drivel I read in every major newspaper in the state, I decided a simple letter to the editor wasn't quite "We the People" enough for me. I figured it was time to insert the pulse of the best, most productive, real American Texan's point of view into the hometown newspaper.

> **Step aside you pathetic, little squawkersheep: there's a new sheriff in town, and he ain't backing down one twit.**

I've been told that the hits on my columns are more than one thousand times that of the liberal writers. Duh.

Of course, the lunatic fringe got their diapers all in a tizzy, questioning just who I thought I was barging in here like this, daring to express myself and defy the entrenched liberals. Clearly, I am far beyond the thinking stage—as if I need to get anyone's authorization or to qualify my credentials in order to flex my First Amendment guaranteed God-given rights. Step aside you pathetic, little squawkersheep: there's a new sheriff in town, and he ain't backing down one twit. I'm from Detroit. We weren't the murder capitol of America because we are more violent. We are just better damn shots. Get over it.

With all due respect to the socialist fantasy of my editors and fellow writers, as I am the only author on the *Waco Trib* staff with two *New York Times* bestsellers and an annual readership that dwarfs my "professional" comrades, little ol' humble me shall carry on, thank you, with more confidence and supported authority than my journalistic brethren. Guitar players just wanna have fun.

So as I bring in national and global media to conduct interviews, representing the most positive and productive of Texas and America, I will continue to celebrate and promote, never defend, the self-evident truths that still inspire and guide the vast majority of good people everywhere. Get used to it.

THE LIST

If you turn it on, turn it off.
If you drop it, pick it up.
If you use it, put it back.
If you break it, fix it.
If you make a mess, clean it up.
If you use a cup, plate, or glass, wash it.
If you open it, close it,
If you don't know how, find out by asking.

—Boat rules from the galley of the
mighty 58' Eldorado Alaskan fishing trawler; part of The List.

There is a list on my wall. It has been there forever. It is the same list that is on your wall—or everybody's wall who has a heart, soul, brain, reasonable conscience, and who gives a good damn. It's there, it has

GOD BLESS AMERICA

We know that hunting, fishing, and trapping are perfect.

We know that venison is the ultimate freerange healthfood.

We know that it is renewable.

We know that animals have the right to garlic and butter.

We all loved Old Yeller but we know he had to go.

We know that our right to keep and bear arms is an individual, God-given right.

We know that "keep" means "it's mine, you can't have it," and that "bear" means "I've got it right here on me."

We know what "shall not be infringed" means.

We know what "don't tread on me" means, and we mean it.

We know all too well that "gun-free zones" are a guaranteed recipe for maximum innocent deaths.

We know that the current system of unfair over-taxation cripples entrepreneurs and small businesses while rewarding the most slovenly amongst us.

We know that upon the death of a loved family member, the government has no rational right to one red cent of our families' after-tax savings.

We know that the IRS is a joke.

We know that throwing more money at our failed education system will make it worse.

We know that blingbling and cell phones and beer do not make ends meet.

continued

We know that the current system of "testing" students is counterproductive to actually teaching them.

We know that violent criminals should never be let out of their cages.

We know that judges who let them out are as guilty for their next crimes as the criminals themselves.

We know that child predators should be put to death.

We know that the war on terror would be over if we fought the war to win and unleashed our magnificent military warriors to do their job.

We know that you cannot live the American Dream without speaking English. Properly.

We know that generations of welfare brats are slaves to this soulless policy.

We know that Reverend Wright is a racist.

We know that affirmative action is racist.

We know that as sick and twisted as the evil KKK is, they never killed as many blacks as blacks do, daily.

We know that it is loony and racist to think that the color of your skin determines what words you are allowed to use.

We know that though David Koresh was crazy, that the feds should have kept their noses out of the Branch Davidians.

We know that the U.S. government is criminal in using the military against its citizens.

We know that bureaucrats will ruin anything and everything they tamper with.

continued

We know that ethanol is a joke.

We know that bureaucrats have chosen our energy dependency.

We know that Willie Nelson is stoned.

We know that America is doomed if we don't secure our borders from illegal invaders.

We know that our borders could be secured overnight by simply allowing our heroes of law enforcement and the National Guard to perform their sworn-oath duties.

We know that Obama has made it clear he wants to change America for the worse.

We *don't* know what the hell John McCain wants to do.

We all know that O.J. is guilty.

We know that same-sex unions cannot be marriages.

We know how to end AIDS.

Godbless America and Godbless Texas. We know that Ted Nugent loves you.

always been there, and it is obvious and clear as hell to everybody I know, even though many Americans (I am sad to say) probably have to stop, think, and look real hard (not to find it necessarily) to admit that it's there. And for God's sake, America had better start reading it real soon and real hard.

On one side of this list are the good things to do in life; those self-evident, universal truths, attitudes, and guidelines for reasonable, decent conduct that benefits our own lives, the lives of our fellow man, and the good earth.

At the top of The Good List are the Ten Commandments, the Golden Rule, and a number of ridiculously logical truisms that many—maybe most—people still live by. More people today had better re-examine and return to these principles as quickly as humanly possible if this once great country is to glow like the shining City on the Hill that it is supposed to be. It is so simple, it's stupid.

That's right: The List kicks off with the Ten Commandments. Not the Ten Recommendations, not the Ten Possibilities, not the Ten Hunches, the Ten *Commandments,* dammit! And they are not the Ten "Catholic" Commandments or the Ten "Episcopal" Commandments, or the commandments of any specific religious denomination or cult. They are the sensible, quality of life guideposts for decency and positive human co-existence. Really. Do unto others, indeed.

And before the tsunami of hypocrisy grenades are hurled my way, let it be known how humbly I admit to my perfect, human fallibility. See me on bended knee, begging forgiveness? Get over it.

There was quite the extended era in my wildly adventurous, American Dream, inexhaustible quest for my own personal NorthWest passage, where I am certain that I did not literally reference the Ten Commandments for a good twenty-year period. Though, I am also rather certain I have consistently obeyed at least eight or nine of them even in the more trying years of my extremist rock 'n' roll explorations. I haven't killed anybody, yet, don't lie or steal, have always done my best to honor my mother and my father, have never coveted my neighbors' anything, wouldn't dare bring false witness, honor the Sabbath, (hell, I hunt or fish nearly every Sunday), and have been almost Mother Theresa-like in my best effort to be the best that I can be. I hurt no one, benefit all (as long as the soulless and terminally corrupt court system doesn't hinder me) and do so simply because I actually know that I should and make sure that I do. Choices meet effort. Excuse me whilst I buff my halo. Did I mention "get over it?"

HUMAN INTERACTION

I offer you a stellar example of a letter that places the proper perspective on what a gun means to a civilized society. Read this eloquent and profound letter and pay close attention to the last paragraph of the letter...

Human beings only have two ways to deal with one another: Reason and Force. If you want me to do something for you, you have a choice of either convincing me via argument, or forcing me to do your bidding under threat of force. Every human interaction falls into one of those two categories, without exception. Reason or force, that's it.

In a truly moral and civilized society, people exclusively interact through persuasion. Force has no place as a valid method of social interaction, and the only thing that removes force from the menu is the personal firearm, as paradoxical as it may sound to some.

When I carry a gun, you cannot deal with me by force. You have to use reason and try to persuade me, because I have a way to negate your threat or employment of force.

The gun is the only personal weapon that puts a 100-pound woman on equal footing with a 220-pound mugger, a 75-year-old retiree on equal footing with a 19-year-old gang banger, and a single guy on equal footing with a carload of drunk guys with baseball bats. The gun removes the disparity in physical strength, size, or numbers between a potential attacker and a defender.

There are plenty of people who consider the gun the source of bad force equations. These are the people who think that we'd be more civilized if all guns were removed from society, because a firearm makes

continued

it easier for a [armed] mugger to do his job. That, of course, is only true if the mugger's potential victims are mostly disarmed either by choice or by legislative fiat—it has no validity when most of a mugger's potential marks are armed.

People who argue for the banning of arms ask for automatic rule by the young, the strong, and the many, and that's the exact opposite of a civilized society. A mugger, even an armed one, can only make a successful living in a society where the state has granted him a force monopoly.

Then there's the argument that the gun makes confrontations lethal that otherwise would only result in injury. This argument is fallacious in several ways. Without guns involved, confrontations are won by the physically superior party inflicting overwhelming injury on the loser.

People who think that fists, bats, sticks, or stones don't constitute lethal force watch too much TV, where people take beatings and come out of it with a bloody lip at worst. The fact that the gun makes lethal force easier works solely in favor of the weaker defender, not the stronger attacker. If both are armed, the field is level.

The gun is the only weapon that's as lethal in the hands of an octogenarian as it is in the hands of a weight lifter. It simply wouldn't work as well as a force equalizer if it wasn't both lethal and easily employable.

When I carry a gun, I don't do so because I am looking for a fight, but because I'm looking to be left alone. The gun at my side means that I cannot be forced, only persuaded. I don't carry it because I'm afraid, but because it enables me to be unafraid. It doesn't limit the actions of those who would interact with me through reason, only the actions of

continued

those who would do so by force. It removes force from the equation...and that's why carrying a gun is a civilized act.

So the greatest civilization is one where all citizens are equally armed and can only be persuaded, never forced.

—By Marko Kloos

Also on The Good List you will find little ditties like: just be nice, polite, kind, thoughtful, generous, tolerant, funny, buoyant, helpful, clean, productive, considerate, positive, giving, and attentive. Love thy neighbor as thyself. Waste not, want not. Live within your means. Save money wherever you can. Work hard. Be the best that you can be. Take respectful care of your sacred temple. Keep it clean. Fuel it responsibly. Get enough sleep. Salute and reward the top dogs, but encourage and help the under-dogs too. The Good List is now almost uniquely American, as this glowing experiment in self-government is all about individuals striving to be an asset to the lives around them. This means that Americans have a duty to participate in the experiment by being activists with whistles firmly in mouth, ready to blow whenever suspicions arise about the performance and direction of our elected employees. Way too many Americans are more than content sitting on the sidelines as long as they have their six pack and a TV show to feed their state of disconnect. How convenient. How soulless. Stop, talk, listen, monitor, probe, guide, discipline, direct, and spend some quality time with the people in your life on a daily basis—especially your children.

The Bad Stuff list is also beyond self-evident. Don't poison yourself. Don't eat too much. Don't eat garbage. Don't litter. Don't drink and drive. Don't use tobacco. (You know that's on the list.) Don't make, sell, buy, or take drugs. Don't hurt anybody. Don't commit crimes. Don't hog the left lane. Use your turn signal. Don't tailgate. Don't put trash in the back of your pickup truck.

I am convinced that the abandonment of parenting can be most readily identified by dirty people who were allowed to be dirty kids, continue as dirty adults, and who let their kids be dirty. You stink. These are (more often than not) the same people who bloat into obesity from uncaring lifestyles and end up being in the liability column of their families, communities, and America as a direct result of their primate-like choices. Read the damn list and just do it.

That these violations run amok in America at this late date is abhorrent and unforgivable. The intentional disconnect by a growing segment of America is a deathwish curse of unimaginable proportions. These people know the outcome of their idiotic choices, but their actions are living proof that they simply don't give a damn. And that is the ball and chain hat they force on all of us that the liberal Democrats like Obama never, ever point out. Instead, they continue to squawk about how these people need another handout. The Democrats have created a Declaration of Dependence. Unbelievable.

Only the guilty need feel guilty of course, and I can hear the unclean skin curling as I write this. Tolerance has its limits when the irresponsible conduct of others begins to taint our personal space and alter our individual quality of life. We can tolerate dog lovers, but not when there are so many dogs that yowling and dogshit alters the neighbors' peace, quiet, and basic health concerns. We all know of the various outrageous examples of this and communities should be more swift and decisive in dealing with such disrespect-

> ☆
> **I can hear
> the unclean skin
> curling as
> I write this.**

ful, rude, irresponsible, royal pain-in-the-ass behavior. The logic police should take no crap—literally. And this just in—We the People are the logic police. Let me see some nightsticks out there, America.

ADVICE FOR YOUNG PEOPLE

Gather round boys and girls and listen good—real good. Pay attention. What I am about to tell you will help you immensely throughout the rest of your lives if you read, absorb, and commit to practicing and living your Uncle Ted's proven modus operandi for quality of life. It is highly unlikely that you would get this ironclad and loving advice in any classroom or from a textbook anymore, and sadly, some of you will not have received this advice from even your parents. Uncle Ted to the rescue. I'm an extremist. I give a damn.

Nobody owes you a thing. Nothing. Zilch. Zero. Nada. Everything you will get out of life will be based solely on what you put into it.

> ★
>
> **Uncle Ted to the rescue.**

Period. You will get no more than what you are willing to bust your ass to earn. As humorist Mark Twain said, "Don't go around saying the world owes you a living. The world owes you nothing. It was here first."

Get a job. If you work hard, real hard, at your favorite craft, you will ultimately succeed. A work ethic is the driving force to success and a rewarding life. If you are lazy, you will not succeed and can expect to be fired over and over again, aimlessly drifting from job to job, your soul as empty as your bank account. It does not matter how smart or gifted you are if you are lazy. You will not and cannot succeed without genuine heart and soul, ass-kicking effort. Right now is always the right time to be the best that you can be. There is a fire down below. Know it, love it, crave it, and pour gas on it. It is there and it is wonderful when you choose to let it roar.

Find your passion in life; your calling, something you crave—that special thing that makes you giddy. Set a goal and never, ever quit. When you get close to the brass ring, move it further away from your grasp. Always push yourself harder. Get up an hour earlier and stay up an hour later working like a human possessed on attaining your goals.

Walk through or over anyone who dares to tell you that you cannot do something. Avoid negative people and slobbering hippies like the plague. They never accomplish anything. Surround yourself with positive people who are better than you and will mentor, help, and guide you honestly.

The only free lunches are at the homeless shelter. If you want to dance, you have to pay the band. And you will get what you pay for.

Never miss an opportunity to say "thank you" to the men and women in our military and law enforcement. They are the defenders of freedom putting their lives on the line for you so that you have a chance to reach your American Dream. Thank them whenever and wherever you see them. They are the best America has to offer. Your American Dream has been fertilized with their blood and guts. Thank them by living it to your fullest. God bless the warriors all.

> ★
>
> **The only free lunches are at the homeless shelter.**

Don't wait for someone to kick you in the ass to motivate you. The best person for that job is you. Do it often. I prefer daily. No one is more critical of me and more demanding of me, than me.

You will be tested constantly. Life is going to knock you down over and over again. The only person who is ever defeated is the person who gets floored with one of life's massive suckerpunches and does not get back up. Be tough and tenacious. It feels good.

Sometimes you give the world the best you got, and you get kicked in the teeth. Give the world the best you got anyway.

Never do anything for money. Do what you thoroughly enjoy exceedingly well and money will come looking for you.

Be frugal. Live responsibly within your means. Buying blingbling is not making ends meet.

If you want to know how others perceive you, look around at who you associate with. In the end, all you have is your character and integrity. Do not ever compromise or sell them. No one trusts a liar—especially all other liars.

Do not complain. Any spineless whiner can do that. Instead, look for solutions to tough problems. This will earn you respect from your boss and get you promoted. Never let anything beat you. Work at it until you wrestle the problem to the ground and strangle the life out of it. Then move on to the next problem and strangle it, too.

Do not be afraid to take chances and blaze new trails. You cannot play the game of life by being content to sit on the bench. Get in the arena where the dust is swirling and blood, sweat, and tears pour forth. That is where the action is. Do not miss out. There will be a guy in the middle of the arena with the biggest smile who is swinging the largest crowbar. Do not be intimidated. It is just me, I am your friend, and I welcome you.

> **If you have not made a few well-deserving idiots boil over in anger by the time you are twenty-five, get busy!**

Engage life with unbridled passion. Never be afraid to let yourself go and exhibit unbridled raw emotion and enthusiasm. Emotions need exercise. March to the beat of making your own loud and obnoxious guitar-breeding noises no matter how many times they tell you to turn it down and stop the feedback. Following trends and peer pressure is for mindless sheep that are never happy.

Be intelligently and effectively defiant. Defiance is a uniquely American characteristic that courses through our veins. Defiance is the very spirit that gave birth to this country when our forefathers fought against overwhelming odds, signed the Declaration of Independence, and fired the "shot heard round the world." Lock and load. Really.

Remember Rosa Parks. Be prepared to defy stupidity wherever you find it. It is your duty and responsibility as an American to let your voice be heard. Stand up against idiotic, illogical laws and restrictions. Raise hell. Vote smart. Famous philosopher, legendary San Francisco police detective, and my hero Dirty Harry once said, "A good man has got to know his limitations." This is good advice. If you have not made a few well-deserving idiots boil over in anger by the time you are twenty-five, get busy!

We live in a target-rich environment of liberal denial. Drive idiots loony. It is much fun, quite easy, and is still legal in all fifty states. Stand up for what you believe in. Remain polite and courteous, but never back down. You have an obligation to leave America in better shape when you leave this country than when you arrived. Work to ensure that future generations of Americans have a better shot at the American Dream, more freedom, more liberty, and more pursuits of happiness than what you had. Upgrade constantly. That is the ultimate American Dream.

Volunteer. Choose truly needy people who can use a hand up, not a hand out. Stick with tried and true charitable organizations, who have a good reputation and minimal administrative costs. Find people in trouble through no fault of their own—like military heroes in veterans hospitals and children in intensive care units. Perform those small gestures of love and caring like pushing someone in a wheelchair out into a garden for some fresh air and thoughtful conversation. Bring a dog, as dogs have a way of taking away the pain and suffering, even for a little while. Take them fishing or hunting or anything outdoors that you can make happen for them.

"Good Friends and a Bottle of Wine"

I know that life has its moments, sometimes up and sometimes down.

Identify your opponents, and gather all your good friends around.

I got to have me some, good friends and a bottle of wine.

—Ted Nugent, *Weekend Warriors*, 1978

Cook up some fish or BBQ for them. Take them for a picnic by a river or lake. Help them identify wildlife with binoculars. Make them laugh, and tell and show them that you care. Your heart will glow with fulfillment when you give more than you receive.

Take care of your precious, sacred temple. Eat smart and stay clean. Do not smoke, use drugs, eat, or drink too much or chew on glass sandwiches. Partaking in these mindless misadventures will shorten your life. Do not go tap dancing in minefields. That is not a party.

Tough love is not the solution. Tougher love is. What America needs is tougher love. Coddling and excuse-making is for the weak and timid. We need people who are confident, rugged individuals. Tougher love will accomplish this every time.

Trust your gut feelings. They will not steer your wrong. Only trust people who have earned your trust. Trust but verify. Never trust the French.

Find a relaxing hobby to recharge your batteries that has nothing to do with your profession. I have found that peaceful time with family, friends, loved ones, and my dogs, or fishing, hunting, shooting, setting rocks on fire, giving birth to brass rainbows by shooting machineguns till their barrels burn up, and killing sacred protein with sharp sticks recharges my batteries beyond redline. I cleanse my soul as I cleanse the good mother earth by eating her surplus.

Take the time each day to show love and affection to your family and loved ones. The smallest gesture goes straight to the heart. Put in the extra effort to relax and shoot the shit with them. A good life is maximized when shared with the ones you love—most dynamically around a fire.

Don't keep discomforting thoughts bunched up inside. When you question something, express yourself immediately. Let 'er rip. Face the beast and shine the light on cockroaches every time. The only way to resolve conflicts is to tackle them right away without inhibitions. Don't worry about hurting feelings. Everyone benefits from open, honest discussions. There are no stupid questions.

Aim small, miss small. Have fun. Life is not a dress rehearsal. Live smart, live good. Rock hard.

CHAPTER SIXTEEN

IN CONCLUSION

"Something you do brings me back to life
It's so good to have a friend
You make me feel right at home."

★ ★ ★

"You Make Me Feel Right At Home,"
Ted Nugent, 1975

As Americans, we will always argue and debate political, cultural, and other ideological issues among ourselves, but at the end of the day we remain Americans. We may have differences of opinion on taxes, drilling for oil, health care, war, gun control, education, and many other issues, but watching Old Glory flutter in the breeze reminds us that we are all Americans united by a common love of freedom, liberty, and the pursuit of happiness. America still reverberates with the faint ringing of the liberty bell in our ears and the trace smell of gunpowder in our nostrils from the shot heard round the world at Concord Bridge. I like to think that through it all, we remain BloodBrothers of the Spirit.

You may or may not agree with my statements contained in this book. That's fine with me. I didn't write it to seek your approval. I wrote it because it is what I steadfastly believe. I always have and always will celebrate and promote—never defend—my beliefs, values, customs, and traditions. That's my right and obligation as a free man and I take that seriously. Always stand up for what you believe in.

Americans are united by our differences, not by what we agree on. This is what makes America unique and the last best place. Regardless of our differences, there is a lump in all of our throats when we slowly amble through Arlington National Cemetery and stare at the rows and rows of white tomb stones...watch the guards meticulously march in reverence at the Tomb of the Unknowns...stand in front of the eternal flame at President Kennedy's grave...stand in awe in front of the Lincoln Memorial as President Lincoln's eyes bore a hole in us, as if he's challenging us all to improve America...or when we see the soul-wrenching footage of jetliners plowing into those twin towers.

What good I may have done over the years is attributable to my mom and dad who set me on the right path so many years ago. I was blessed to have two amazing, loving, and understanding parents who encouraged, prodded, and did their best to put the initial wind in my youthful, wayward sails. My bad and ugly moments—of which there have been a few—are my sole responsibility. No one else's.

Which leads me to my final parting shots.

In the end, all politics remain local. By local I mean, the dinner table where families gather to pray, share meals and ideas, and to offer love and guidance to one another. Your dinner table tonight with your family is absolutely the most important place in America. Are there any dinner tables left out there?

Your family is more important and more powerful than our federal government. It is your family that makes the finely tuned engine of America hum. Without strong American families, the real fibers that hold Old Glory together become tattered and frayed. If we can agree on anything, it should be that family matters, and

> ★
> **Never miss an opportunity to say, "I love you."**

that everything good that happens in your personal or professional life is the result of your commitment to a loving, caring, and strong family.

Quality family time isn't when you are huddled around the television. Turn the television off and huddle around each other. Hug one another. Talk about your hopes, dreams, aspirations, problems, and events of the day. Tell each other you love one another every day. Never miss an opportunity to say, "I love you." Life is too short to miss those "I love you" opportunities.

If you want your son or daughter to be respectful, polite, courteous, and accountable, you have to set the right example. Make sure to set a good one.

If you want your kids to be smart, you have to take the time to check their homework, go to parent-teacher conferences, enroll your child in accelerated classes, and most importantly, challenge them to always pursue excellence. You must never accept mediocrity.

American children need to be healthy. The only way for that to occur is for you to feed them healthy, good food and to ensure they get a lot of exercise. Your child should be able to run faster than the wind.

I like cause and effect activities, such as planting trees with your children, taking care of pets, and doing routine chores. By doing these, they will see the benefits of their sweat equity. This is good. Your children will learn that all good things come from hard work and dedication.

Be involved in not only your child's life but in the lives of your child's friends. Get to know them, too. Guide and assist your children in making wise choices when selecting friends. Be attentive. Be involved.

Children crave discipline, order, and structure. Give it to them with lots of love, affection, and attention. They will love you for it.

If you want your children to be happy, laugh with them each day. Teach them that laughter is indeed the best of life's incredible, amazing, and healing powers.

Children make mistakes. They will disappoint and discourage you at times. That's part of being a parent. Ensure that they know that your love for them is unwavering and unshakeable. When they let you down the most are the times you need to love them even more.

As a parent you are more powerful than the president in what really matters most. The strength of your family is ultimately the very foundation of what makes America strong, vibrant, unique, and competitive. As a mom or dad, the very course our nation takes in the future will be set by you. Moms and dads are that important.

Lastly, each of us has a responsibility to leave this great country in better shape when we depart than when we arrived. That's the real American Dream; the shining city on the hill that President Reagan wrote of. It is the American Dream that our brave forefathers and parents embraced and sacrificed for so that you and I could enjoy a better life, more freedom, and more opportunity than they had.

I leave you with Dr. King's immortal words: "Free at last. Thank God Almighty, I'm free at last!"

I WILL

I will find goodness in life everyday and celebrate it with everything I've got.

I will share as many campfires with my family and friends as humanly possible.

I will look to those much wiser and greater than I am for inspiration.

I will not be a victim nor act like one. I will not abide by dumb laws. I will remain a defiant, free, independent American and will conduct myself according to logic and self-evident truth at all costs. I will remember Rosa Parks.

I will give respect to those who deserve it and none to those who do not. Respect is earned, never given.

I will wage my battles wherever I find them, including in the public arena. I never expect others to wield my crowbar for me. I will always help those who want to help themselves. I will not help those who only want to be helped.

I will do my best to expose the bad and the ugly and shine a light on the good.

I will set rocks on fire.

I will do the best I can with the talents, skills, and abilities God has blessed me with and constantly push myself to new heights. I will continue to believe God has blessed America. America sucks now but it sucks a whole lot less than every other place. America is the last best place. I will fight for her return.

I will never trust communists, socialists, bureaucrats, or elitists.

I will kill and eat more animals for animal rights activists.

I will not be tolerant of those who wish to diminish or harm my values. I will challenge them and grind them underfoot.

I will give more than I take.

I will love my family even more. I will not forget those who came before me nor neglect my obligation to those who will come after me. That is my responsibility as an American.

I will remember the Alamo.

I will make mistakes because I am trying but will do my best to not repeat my mistakes.

I will make decisions based upon my intellect and facts and never on emotion or supposition. I will laugh even more, especially at idiots. It is a target-rich environment.

I will hug my dogs everyday.

I will hunt more.

I will pray for good bombing weather over our enemies. I will never accept political correctness. I stand with common sense and the truth at all costs.

I will not worry about feelings; I will always speak honestly.

I will never surrender or retreat. Never. If a house gets in my way, I will burn it down.

I will attack and make love to my guitar like an animal.

I will always have the world's best band.

I will always turn to the face the howling storms like the buffalo.

I will pray daily for my U.S. Military BloodBrothers.

I will pray for my enemies.

I will always give the world the best I got, even when I get kicked in the teeth. I will give the best I got anyway.

THANKYOUS

★ ★ ★

My American Dream rocks! I thank and salute my wonderful family, Doug Banker, Linda Peterson, Jim & Penny Lawson, Paul Wilson, Dennis Arfa, Adam Kornfeld, Anneke Green, Harry Crocker, Al Regnery, Mick Brown, Greg Smith, Ted Emporellis, Mitch Schneider and the glowing tribe of humanity that so blesses me with such positive spirit each and every day. American BloodBrothers are alive and well and charging full speed ahead across America. Godbless you all.

A heart and soul American BloodBrother thank you and salute to Ward Parker and his Herculean effort assisting in this book. Without his unstoppable research and guidance, there is no way this written celebration of truth and logic and The American Way would have possible. I'm buying this man another gun.

And a sincere thank you to the world's greatest rockers for the best tour of my life in 2008, and all the great hunting families who have made my American hunting dream so perfect every year by joining me on my Sunrize Safaris. Godspeed BloodBrothers.

MORE TED

"Can't do this in France."

★ ★ ★

Ted Nugent

Celebrate the Spiritual Campfire!

Books

☆ *Blood Trails II*—Ted Nugent, Woods N' Water, Inc., and Bookspan, 2004

☆ *Married to a Rock Star*, Shemane Nugent, The Lyons Press, 2003

☆ *Kill It & Grill It*—Ted & Shemane Nugent, Regnery Publishing, Inc., 2002

☆ *God, Guns, & Rock 'N' Roll*—Ted Nugent, Regnery Publishing, Inc., 2000

☆ *Blood Trails*—Ted Nugent, Self-Published, 1991

☆ For the latest in official Nuge Merchandise, check out the Ted Nugent Store at **www.tednugent.com.**

Watch *Ted Nugent Spirit of the Wild* on the Outdoor Channel.

☆ Visit www.outdoorchannel.com for broadcast times in your area.

☆ To book Ted Nugent for a personal appearance, email Linda@tednugent.com

☆ To book a hunt with Ted, or our other professional guides, call Sunrize Safaris at 517-750-9060.

☆ Ted celebrated his 6000th show—with thousands of Detroit's finest—July 4, 2008 at DTE Energy Music Theatre.

☆ Ted is writing for over forty publications nationwide, including regular features in *Boar Hunter* magazine, *Bow & Arrow Hunting, Buckmasters, Deer & Deer Hunting, Iowa Sportsman, Journal of Texas Trophy Hunters, Midwest Outdoors, Insights, Petersen's Bowhunting,*

SCI magazine, Sportsman's Guide, TECH magazine, Texas Fish & Game, Waco Tribune-Herald, and *Human Events.*

⭐ Ted was named one of *Outdoor Life* magazine's **OL 25.** The December/January 2008 issue profiles the 25 leaders, innovators, conservationists, and unsung heroes who have had a major positive impact on the outdoor sports. Ted was honored in the Leaders Category, "who by their individual efforts and sheer strength of will have had the strongest impact on the hunting and fishing scene.

⭐ *TED NUGENT Spirit of the Wild* has been voted #1 Hunting Show on the Outdoor Channel four times...and counting! Ted and Shemane Nugent were additionally just named **Fan Favorite Show Hosts (2008).**

Awards

⭐ Ted is currently serving his fifth term on the NRA's Board of Directors.

⭐ Ted turned up the heat on hard rock—as only Ted can—along with Sebastian Bach, Jason Bonham, and more on VH1's *SUPERGROUP* (2006).

⭐ The Spirit of the Wild thrives in Lewiston, Idaho! Ted's cult classic, "I JUST WANNA GO HUNTING" was fall's most requested song at Z-Rock 96.5/KOZE FM (2006).

⭐ Ted Nugent performed for 55,000 Marines, sailors, & their families at Camp Pendleton's Rockin' the Corps on April 1, 2005, along with fellow musicians Destiny's Child, Godsmack, Kiss, and more.

⭐ Ted toured nationwide with Toby Keith in The Big Throwdown Tour, January-March 2005.

☆ The National Bowhunters Hall of Fame named Ted as their most recent inductee (2008). Ted is honored for two categories: Excellence in Bowhunting and Literary Excellence.

☆ Ted has been appointed ambassador for Big Brothers Big Sisters and the Pass It On! Outdoor Mentors Program (2006).

☆ MTV *Cribs* featuring the Nugent Ranch (2006).

☆ Ted's hunting anthem, "FRED BEAR" was voted 3rd Best All-time Rock Song in the state of Michigan (2006). ("Stairway to Heaven" and "Hotel California" placed 1st and 2nd respectively.)

☆ Ted received the James Fenimore Cooper Award in 2001 for his many accomplishments in the field of writing, and for his enormous contributions in the promotion of our American hunting and outdoor heritage.

☆ Ted Nugent was named Michigan Conservationist of the Year (1999).

☆ Ted Nugent has been profiled on both A & E's *Biography* (2001), and on VH1's *Behind the Music* (1998).

☆ Ted's hit reality show *Wanted Ted or Alive* was ranked the top-rated original series on OLN.

Nugent Discography

Sweden Rocks
2008

Love Grenade
2007

Take No Prisoners
2003

Urban Sounds 1990-1995
2003

Craveman
2002

The Ultimate Ted Nugent
2002

Noble Savage
2002

Full Bluntal Nugity
2001

Covered in Metal
2000

On the Edge/Over the Top
2000

Hunt Music
2000

Loaded For Bear:
The Best of Ted Nugent &
the Amboy Dukes
1999

Super Hits
1998

Live At Hammersmith '79
1997

Motor City Madness
[Sony Special Products]
1996

Spirit Of The Wild
1995

Out Of Control
1993

Don't Tread
1992

Damn Yankees
1990

Ted Nugent Hunt Music
1989

If You Can't Lick 'Em ... Lick 'Em
1988

Little Miss Dangerous
1986

Great Gonzos—
The Best of Ted Nugent
1986

Penetrator
1984

Nugent
1982

Intensities In Ten Cities
1981

Great Gonzos:
The Best Of Ted Nugent
1981

Scream Dream
1980

State Of Shock
1979

Double Live Gonzo!
1978

Weekend Warriors
1978

Cat Scratch Fever
1977

Ted Nugent & the Amboy Dukes
1976

Free For All
1976

Ted Nugent
1975

Tooth, Fang & Claw
1974

Call of the Wild
1973

Marriage on the Rocks
Rock Bottom
1971

Survival of the Fittest Live
1970

Migration
1969

Journey To The Center
Of The Mind
1968

The Amboy Dukes
1967

For more information on the truth I've laid out
in this Manifesto, check out these sources.

—TED

Foreword

Allen L. Roland, "Congressional Reform Act of 2010,"
http://allenlrolandsweblog.blogspot.com/2010/02/congressional-reform-act-of-2010-its.html

Dr. Adrian Rogers, "God's Way to Health, Wealth, and Wisdom," Love Worth Finding Ministries
http://www.lwf.org/site/PageServer?pagename=lis_quote

Two: Defy Gravity

Rodney Carrington and Toby Keith, *Beer for My Horses*," Directed by Michael Salomon, Los Angeles, CA: B4MH Productions, 2008.

Criss Angel, *Mindfreak.* Los Vegas, Nevada: Angel Productions Incorporated.

Wounded Warrior Project, Jacksonville, FL.
http://www.woundedwarriorproject.org/content/view/30/920/

U.S. Fish and Wildlife Service, "Interior Department Removes Northern Rocky Mountain Wolves from Endangered Species List," February 21, 2008.

All American Talent & Celebrity Network, "Celebrity Vegetarians and Vegans," http://www.allamericanspeakers.com/Celebrity_ Vegetarians.php Accessed August 13, 2008.

Rory Carroll, "Venezuela giving Danny Glover $18 m to direct film on epic slave revolt," *The Guardian*, May 21, 2007.

"Venezuela replaces opposition TV with state network," Reuters. May 28, 2007, http://www.reuters.com/article/topNews/idUSN2723008820070528

Three: If I Were President

Harry Julian Fink, R.M. Fink, John Milius, and Michael Cimino, *Magnum Force*, Directed by Ted Post, Burbank, CA: The Malpaso Company & Warner Bros. Pictures, 1973.

Four: Politics and Religion

Raymond Hernandez, "Short of Funds, G.O.P. Recruits the Rich to Run," *The New York Times,* November 26, 2007.

Albert Einstein, "Religion and Science," http://www.sacred texts.com/aor/einstein/einsci.htm

Ruth Gledhill and Phillip Webster, "Archbishop of Canterbury argues for Islamic law in Britain," *Times Online,* February 8, 2008, http://www.timesonline.co.uk/tol/comment/faith/article3328024.ece

Five: War Is the Answer

N.S. Gill, "Prepare for War – Latin Quote from Vegetius," About.com, http://ancienthistory.about.com/od/warfareconflictmor/f/PrepareforWar.htm.

Whitney, Mike, "Why America Needs To Be Defeated in Iraq," *Information Clearing House*, May 1, 2005.

Fred E. Foldvary, "The People's Republic of Berkeley," *The Progress Report,* 1998. http://www.progress.org/fold41.htm.

Code Pink: Women For Peace, "Current Campaigns: Berkeley Actions," http://www.codepink4peace.org/article.php?list= type&type=373

Staff Sgt. Kurt M. Sutton, "Chesty Puller: Everyone Needs a Hero," *Marine Magazine,* 1998.

Jimmy Carter Library and Museum. "The Hostage Crisis in Iran," February 9, 2006, http://www.jimmycarterlibrary.org/documents/hostages.phtml

Tony Long, "Nov. 15, 1864: Sherman's March to the Sea Changes Tactical Warfare," Wired.com, November 15, 2007, http://www.wired.com/science/discoveries/news/2007/11/dayintech_1115

A.C. Grayling, *Among The Dead Cities: The History and Moral Legacy of the WWII Bombing of Civilians in Germany and Japan,* New York: Walker & Company, 2007.

The History Place, "The Death of Hitler," website, http://www.historyplace.com/worldwar2/holocaust/h-death.htm Accessed August 12, 2008.

Martin Kelly, "Overview of World War II: The Origins of World War II," About.com. http://americanhistory.about.com/od/worldwarii/ a/wwiioverview.htm. Accessed August 12, 2008.

Eric Malnic, "Paul Tibbets, pilot who bombed Hiroshima, dies at 92," *Seattle Times*, November 2, 2007.

Richard Goldstein, "Charles Sweeney, 84, Pilot in Bombing of Nagasaki, Dies," *New York Times,* July 19, 2004.

Danny Kennedy, "Nuclear disease," *On Line Opinion*, August 14, 2006, http://www.onlineopinion.com.au/view.asp?article=4787&page=0

Jonathan Rauch. Firebombs Over Tokyo. *Atlantic Monthly*, July/August 2002.

Ben Hills, "Tokyo's hell on earth – the night a city died," Benhills.com. http://www.benhills.com/ articles/articles/ WAR09a.html. Accessed August 13, 2008. See also "The Incendiary Bombing Raids on Tokyo, 1945," EyeWitness to History, www.eyewitnesstohistory.com (2004).

Ronald Reagan, "First Inaugural Address," January 20, 1981.

Matthew Barakat, "25 Years Ago: Hostages in Iran," *CBS News*, November 4, 2004, http://www.cbsnews.com/stories/2004/11/04/world/main653636.shtml

"The U.S. Blames Iran for Training Iraqi Extremists Who Kill Americans," *U.S. News & World Report*, May 5, 2008.

"Iran speedboats 'threatened suicide attack on US' in Strait of Hormuz," *Times Online*, January 7, 2008, http://www.timesonlineco.uk/tol/news/world/middle_east/article3147217.ece?token =null&offset=0&page=1

Richard Beeston and James Bone, "Hostage fears over troops seized by Iran," *Times Online*, March 24, 2007, http://www.timesonline.co.uk/tol/news/world/middle_east/article1560788.ece

Yaakov and Herb Keinon, "Israel now fears Iran could have nuclear bomb by mid-2009," *San Francisco Sentinel.com*, May 6, 2008, http://www.sanfranciscosentinel. com/?p=12486

Associated Press, "Iranians say Israel spat is really about nukes," MSNBC, October 31, 2005 http://www.msnbc.msn.com/id/9823624/#storyContinued

Con Coughlin, "Only A Matter Of Time Before Terrorists use Weapons Of Mass Destruction," *The Daily Telegraph*, January 17, 2006.

General George S. Patton, "General George S. Patton, Jr. Quotations," The Estate of General George S. Patton Jr. c/o CMG Worldwide. http://www.generalpatton.com/quotes.html

Six: Tax Hell

"Institute for Policy Innovation: Current U.S. Tax System Violates Constitutional Principles; New Study Shows Liberty and Income Taxes Cannot Coexist," BNet, April 2, 2002, http://findarticles.com/p/articles/mi_m0EIN/is_2002_ April_2/ai_84337335

Rasmussen Reports, "62% of Voters Prefer Fewer Government Services with Lower Taxes," May 20, 2008.

Barack Obama, Issues. http://www.barackobama.com/issues/economy/

"Learn about Taxes: Colonial and Post-Revolutionary America," Taxgaga.com. 2000. http://www.taxgaga.com/pages/c-learnabouttaxes/taxes.html

Sheldon Richman, "Beware Income-Tax Casuistry, Part 2," *The Future of Freedom Foundation*, December 20, 2006.

Bryan Riley, Eric V. Schlecht, and Dr. John Berthoud, "Hidden Taxes: How Much Do You Really Pay?" *Institute for Policy Innovation*, Policy Report 160, July 2001.

Scott Hodge, quoted in "America Celebrates Tax Freedom Day," *The Tax Foundation*, 2008.

John Gallo, "We've won on Social Security – for now," *People's Weekly World*, October 20, 2005.

Ed Hall, "U.S. National Debt Clock," http://www.brillig.com/debt_clock/. Accessed August 11, 2008.

Scott A. Hodge, "Tax Reform: Flat Tax or FairTax?" Tax Foundation. 2007.

Seven: Uncle Sam Is a Pig

Martha Mendoza, "Review finds fiscal records of 2 federal agencies a mess," Associated Press, September 15, 2007.

President George W. Bush, "Remarks by the President on Corporate Responsibility," Regent Wall Street Hotel, New York, NY, July 9, 2002. See also "Remarks by the President at Malcolm Baldrige National Quality Award Ceremony," Washington Hilton Hotel, Washington, D.C., March 7, 2002.

Bill O'Reilly, "The O'Reilly Factor," Fox News Network, April 10, 2002.

Ronald D. Utt, "The Bridge to Nowhere: A National Embarrassment," The Heritage Foundation, October 20, 2005.

Taxpayers for Common Sense, "$315 Million Bridge to Nowhere," February 9, 2005. http://www.taxpayer.net/user_uploads/file/Transportation/gravinabridge.pdf

Kyle Hopkins, "Knik Arm bridge hits fork in the road," *Anchorage Daily News*, June 9, 2008.

Martin L. Gross, *The Government Racket: 2000 and Beyond* (NY: Harper Perennial, 2001).

"Missouri River Pedestrian Bridge to Link Trails," *Missouri River News*, April 2001.

Sharon Behn, "U.S. paid $42.4 million to Iraqis; Sum covers 'collateral' damage; number compensated unknown," *Washington Times*, February 27, 2008.

Citizens Against Government Waste, "Byrd Droppings: Words of Wisdom from the King of Pork."
http://www.cagw.org/site/PageServer?pagename=news_byrddroppings
Accessed August 9, 2008.

Amanda Sealy and Todd Schwarzschild, "Despite promises, few in House publicize earmarks," CNN.com, June 21, 2007.
http://www.cnn.com/2007/POLITICS/06/18/earmarks/index.html

Clinton, president of the United States, et al. v. City of New York et al., 524 U.S. 417 (1998).

"Obama's 'fact-finding' trip finds no facts," The Political Tracker, July 22, 2008.

James Turk, "World's Biggest Debtor Nation Posts $61.2B Trade Deficit for December 2006," The Daily Reckoning, February 14, 2007.

David Stout and Robert Pear, "Bush Seeks Budget of $3.1 Trillion," *New York Times*, February 4, 2008.

Edward Sylvester Ellis, The Life of Colonel David Crockett, Tennessee: University Press of the Pacific, 2004.

Second Emergency Supplemental Appropriations Act To Meet Immediate Needs Arising From The Consequences Of Hurricane Katrina, H.R.3673, Public Law 109-62, September 8, 2005, pg. 119, Stat. 1990.

Karen Sawislak, "Fire of 1871," The Electronic Encyclopedia of Chicago, Chicago Historical Society., 2005.
http://www.encyclopedia.chicagohistory.org/pages/1740.htm

USGS, "The Great 1906 San Francisco Earthquake," USGS,
http://earthquake.usgs.gov/regional/nca/1906/18april/index.php

John K. Nakata, Charles E. Meyer, Howard G. Wilshire, John C. Tinsley, William S. Updegrove, D.M. Peterson, Stephen D. Ellen, Ralph A. Haugerud, Robert J. McLaughlin, G. Reid Fisher, and Michael F. Diggles, "The October 17, 1989, Loma Prieta, California, Earthquake – Selected Photographs," USGS, 1999.

Eight: Get a Damn Job

John Lott, Jr., "Obama Comes Up Short in Approach to Poverty," FoxNews.com, July 21, 2008,
http://www.foxnews.com/story/0,2933,387262,00.html.

John F. Kennedy, Inaugural Address, January 20, 1961.

Jeff Tyler, "Toyota's number 1," American Public Media: Marketplace, April 24, 2007, http://marketplace.publicradio.org/display/web/ 2007/04/24/toyotas_number_1/.

Liz Pulliam Weston, "The truth about credit card debt," Msnmoney, April 2006. http://moneycentral.msn.com/content/Banking/creditcardsmarts/ P74808.asp.

Walt Kelly, We Have Met the Enemy and He Is Us, New York: Simon and Schuster, 1987.

Nick Taylor, "Works Progress Administration," *New York Times*, 2008.

Parth J. Shah and H.B. Soumya, "Who pays for welfare programmes?" Center for Civil Society, August 19, 2004.

Robert E. Rector, "How Poor Are America's Poor? Examining the 'Plague' of Poverty in America," The Heritage Foundation, August 27, 2007.

Thomas Sowell, "Who Really Cares? (Conservatives give more than Liberals)," *Free Republic*, November 28, 2006.

"Economic Report of the Holy See for 2000," http://www.zenit.org/ article-1900?l=english.

Laurie Goodstein, "Payout is Bittersweet for Victims of Abuse," *New York Times*, July 17, 2007.

Nine: Black Like Me

Martin Luther King, Jr., Strength To Love. New York: Harper & Row, 1963.

Martin Luther King, Jr., Mason Temple Memphis, TN, April 3, 1968.

David Josar, Paul Egan, and Christine MacDonald, "Detroit Mayor Kwame Kilpatrick shamed by text messages," *The Detroit News*, January 24, 2008.

President Ronald Reagan. First Inaugural Address, U.S. Capitol Building, January 21, 1981.

Darren "Dutch" Martin, "Single-parent "baggage," *Washington Times*, May 17, 2008.

Celeste Headlee, "Detroit Has Worst Graduation Rate," NPR, June 29, 2007.

Eric Schlosser, "The Prison Industrial Complex," *Atlantic Monthly*, December, 1998.

Jesse McKinnon, "The Black Populations: Census 2000," Report: C2KBR/01-5, August 2001.

Peter Kirsanow, "What's the Matter with Harlem?" National Review Online, January 17, 2007.

La Shawn Barber, "Why Courting the Black Vote Won't Work," *Washington Times*, January 9, 2004.

Charles Johnson, "Scratching By: How Government Creates Poverty as We Know It," Foundation For Economic Education, The Freeman: Ideas on Liberty. Vol. 57, No. 10, December 2007.

John R. Lott Jr., "Tough gun laws don't reduce crime," *The Australian*, October 23, 2002.

Peter Applebome, "Rise is Found in Hate Crimes Committed by Blacks," *New York Times*, December 13, 1993.

U.S. Department of Justice, Office of Justice Programs, Criminal Victimization in the United States, 2005 Statistical Tables., NCJ 215244. Washington, DC, December 2006.

Eve Troeh, "Hundreds Protest Violence, Policies in New Orleans," NPR, January 11, 2007. See also: Rex W. Huppke, "Hundreds gather at South Side gun violence protest," Chicago Tribune, July 13, 2008.

Rick Hampson, "Anti-snitch campaign riles police, prosecutors," *USA Today*, March 29, 2006.

Ayah Young, "Deadly Silence: Stop Snitching's Fatal Legacy," *Wire Tap Magazine*, March 28, 2008.

Anthony B. Bradley, "Does Black History Have a Future?" Acton Institute Commentary, February 22, 2006, http://www.acton.org/commentary/commentary_311.php.

Heather MacDonald, "Is the Criminal-Justice System Racist?" *City Journal*, Spring 2008.

Dave Workman, "Law-abiding citizens deserve the right to carry a gun," *Milwaukee Journal Sentinel*, October 26, 2003.

Robert J. Cottrol and Raymond T. Diamond, "'Never Intended to Be Applied to the White Population:' Firearms Regulation and Racial Disparity – The Redeemed South's Legacy to a National Jurisprudence," Chicago-Kent College of Law, Illinois Institute of Technology: Chicago, Illinois, 1995.

Lori Higgins, "State has lowest graduation rate for black males," The Free Press, July 26, 2008.

Anne Nelson, "Closing the Gap: Keeping Students in School," ASCD, No. 46. Summer 2006.

James J. Heckman and Paul A. LaFontaine, "The declining American high school graduation rate: Evidence, sources, and consequences," Vox, February 13, 2008.

"Gangs & Drugs," E.C. Police Department Gang and Drug Awareness, http://www.eastchicago.com/departments/police_department/gangs_drugs.html

"School or the Streets: Crime and California's Dropout Crisis," Fight Crime: Invest in Kids, California, http://www.fightcrime.org/ca/dropout/index.php

Walter Williams, "The Poverty in Black Education is Not Due to Racial Discrimination or Lack of Money in D.C.," Capitalism Magazine, July 5, 2006.

Maris Vinovskis, "Seeking an involved and informed citizenry," USA Today, September 2005.

Rebecca O'Neill, "Experiments in Living: The Fatherless Family," CIVITAS, November 2002.

Michael Tanner, Testimony Before the Senate Judiciary Committee, Subcommittee on Youth Violence, June 7, 1995.

Michael van der Galien, "Bill Cosby on Meet the Press," PoliGazette, December 11, 2007. See also: Bill Allen, "Obama talks tough on 'AWOL' fathers," Politico, June 15, 2008.

Isabel Vincent and Susan Edelman, "Rev. Al Soaks up Boycott Bucks," New York Post, June 15, 2008.

"Holding a Four-Year College Degree Brings Blacks Close to Economic Parity with Whites," The Journal of Blacks in Higher Education, 2005.

John Perazzo, "How the Left Trashes Black Conservatives," FrontPage Magazine, July 10, 2002.

Larry Elder, "Revenge of the "Uncle Toms," FrontPage Magazine, January 8, 2001.

Armstrong Williams, "Learning through images," Townhall.com, November 10, 2003. http://townhall.com/columnists/ArmstrongWilliams/2003/11/10/learning_through_images.

Clarence Thomas, My Grandfather's Son, New York: Harper Collins Publishers, 2007.

Editorial, "Campaign News," The National Journal, June 5, 2008

Paul Steinhauser, "Poll: Obama makes big gains among black voters," CNN, January 19, 2008.

Mark Leibovich, "The Senator's Humble Beginning," Washington Post, February 24, 2005.

Brian Friel, Richard E. Cohen, and Kirk Victor, "Obama: most liberal senator in 2007," *The National Journal*, January 31, 2008.

John P. Cleary, "Five questions for Obama," Star-Gazette, June 28, 2008.

Lawrence Kudlow, "Obama's Big-Government Vision," *New York Sun*, February 15, 2008.

Star Parker, "Is Obama really the man blacks need?" Townhall.com, May 12, 2008.

Barack Obama, "Healthcare," http://www.barackobama.com/issues/healthcare/.

"Obama calls for talks with Iran over Iraq," Breitbart.com, 2008.

Tami Luhby, "Uncle Sam can fund retirement – Obama," CNNMoney.com, June 16, 2008.

"Barack Obama on Gun Control," Campaign website, On the Issues, http://www.ontheissues.org/2008/barack_obama_gun_control.htm.

Martin Luther King Jr., "I Have a Dream," 1963.

Ronald Reagan, "Farewell Address to the Nation," Oval Office of the White House, January 11, 1989

Ten: Immigration

Theodore Roosevelt, Letter to Richard Hurd. Library of Congress, Manuscript Division. 1919.

Robert Rodat, "The Patriot," Directed by Roland Emmerich. Culver City, CA: Columbia Pictures Corporation, 2000.

Randall Wallace, "Braveheart," Directed by Mel Gibson. Santa Monica, CA: Icon Productions, 1995.

Howard Parker Moore. A Life of General John Stark of New Hampshire. Howard Parker Moore author and publisher, 1949.

CDR Michel T. Poirier, "A Brief History of the U.S. Navy Jack," Undersea Warfare. Quoted in http://www.navyjack.info/history.html Accessed August 12, 2008.

Pat Buchanan, *State of Emergency*, New York: Thomas Dunne Books, 2006.

Rep. Tom Tancredo, "A Day Without an Illegal Immigrant," National Review Online, May 1, 2006, http://article.nationalreview.com/?q=NTBlOTVlNDFkNTYwOTg4YWYxMTh kZmE2MWZhMmVjMWM=.

Mike Nizza, "Estimate for Deporting Illegal Immigrants: $94 Billion," The Lede, September 13, 2007, http://thelede.blogs.nytimes.com/2007/09/13/estimate-for-deporting-illegal-immigrants-94-billion/

The American Resistance, "How many illegal aliens are in the U.S.?" http://www.theamericanresistance.com/ref/illegal_alien_numbers.html. Accessed August 12, 2008.

Amanda B. Carpenter, " 'Sanctuary Cities' Embrace Illegal Immigrants," Human Events, May 4, 2008.

"Is Illegal Immigration Grounds for State of Emergency?" Fox News, October 18, 2005, http://www.foxnews.com/story/0,2933,172531,00.html

Jon Dougherty, Illegals: *The Imminent Threat Posed by Our Unsecured U.S.-Mexican Border*, Tennessee: Thomas Nelson, 2004.

Jim Kouri, "Illegal Aliens Linked to Rise in Crime Statistics, *Sierra Times*, June 23, 2006.

Robert B. Gunnison, "Anti-Immigrant Law Left with Little to Enforce," *San Francisco Chronicle*, July 29, 1999.

Center for Immigration Studies, "The High Cost of Cheap Labor: Illegal Immigration and the Federal Budget. 2004. http://www.cis.org/articles/2004/fiscalexec.html

Mark Minton, "Aliens' Kids Born In U.S. Add To Debate," *Arkansas-Democrat Gazette*, Inc., October 10, 2005.

The American Resistance, "Anchor Babies," Issue sheet. http://www.theamerican resistance.com/issues/anchor_babies.html. Accessed August 12, 2008.

Sean Holstege, "National Guard wrapping up its US – Mexican Border duty," azcentral.com, June 12, 2008. http://www.azcentral.com/news/articles/2008/06/12/20080612jumpstart0612.html

The White House, "Fact Sheet: Operation Jump Start: Acting Now to Secure the Border." http://www.whitehouse.gov/news/releases/2006/08/20060803-7.html

Ray Walser, "Mexico, Drug Cartels, and the Merida Initiative: A Fight We Cannot Afford to Lose," The Heritage Foundation, July 23, 2008, http://www.heritage.org/Research/LatinAmerica/bg2163.cfm

Jerome R. Cosi, "'Where's the fence?' activist asks Congress," WorldNetDaily, December 12, 2007. http://www.worldnetdaily.com/news/article.asp?ARTICLE_ID=59159.

Nelson Lichtenstein, "A Failure That Changed the World," *New York Times*, April 3, 1988.

Walter Goodman, "Television Review; An Old-Style Mayor's Struggle in a City of the '60s," *New York Times*, January 22, 1996,

Larry Elder, "Minutemen: Don't call us vigilantes. WorldNetDaily, April 14, 2005, http://www.worldnetdaily.com/news/article.asp?ARTICLE_ID=43794

Dave Michaels, "Administration increases penalties for knowingly hiring illegal immigrants," The *Dallas Morning News*, February 22, 2008.

John Dillin, "How Eisenhower solved illegal border crossings from mexico," *The Christian Science Monitor*, July 6, 2006, http://www.csmonitor.com/2006/0706/p09s01-coop.html

Joseph M. Arpaio, "Sheriff." Bio. http://www.mcso.org/index.php?a=GetModule&mn=Sheriff_Bio Accessed August 12, 2008.

Joanne C. Twaddle, "Arpaio shares his thoughts on immigration," *Daily Courier*, January 14, 2008.

Eleven: Health Care: Not a Handout

Extract from Barack Obama, Speech in Iowa City, May 27, 2007, http://www.barackobama.com/issues/

"Blame Game Intensifies," CBS News, September 6, 2005. http://www.cbsnews.com/stories/2005/09/06/earlyshow/main816647.shtml

National Coalition on Health Care, "Health Insurance Costs," 2008. http://www.nchc.org/facts/cost.shtml

"Medicare, Medicaid, and Controlling Healthcare Costs," Facing up to the Nation's Finances. http://www.publicagenda.org/facingup/pdfs/CD_MedicareMedicaidHealthCareChoicework.pdf

Joseph A. Califano, "1960s – Decade," *Washington Monthly*, October 1999.

Robert Samuelson, "Medicare: The Monster at Our Door," Real Clear Politics, September 13, 2006. http://www.realclearpolitics.com/articles/2006/09/we_must_overhaul_medicare.html

Stanley Hupfeld, "Politicians fiddle while Medicare burns," Journal Record (Oklahoma City), May 26, 1999. See also "Medicare's Financial Condition: Beyond Actuarial Balance," Issue Brief, American Academy of Actuaries.

Jonathan Gruber, Ph.D, "The Role of Consumer Copayments for Healthcare: Lessons for the RAND Health Insurance Experiment and Beyond," The Henry J. Kaiser Family Foundation, October 2006. http://www.kff.org/insurance/upload/7566.pdf

National Coalition on Healthcare, "The Impact of Rising Health Costs on the Economy: Effects on Business Operations," 2008. http://www.nchc.org/facts/Economy/effects_on_business_ operations.pdf

George B. Mosley III, JD, MBA, "The U.S. Healthcare Non-System, 1908-2008," Virtual Mentor, May 2008. http://virtualmentor.ama-assn.org/2008/05/mhst1-0805.html

"U.D. Health Care: World's Most Expensive," News VOA.com, February 28, 2006. http://www.voanews.com/english/archive/2006-02/2006-02-28-voa59.cfm?CFID= 22581151&CFTOKEN=11803963

Conti, Craig, Elek, and Steven, "Investing in health care. (Personal Finance)," Healthcare Financial Management, September 1, 2002, http://www.allbusiness.com/personal-finance/274277-1.html

Amanda Gardner, "U.S. Health-Care Costs to Top $4 Trillion by 2016," Washington Post, February 21, 2007.

Michael Moore, Sicko. Directed by Michael Moore. Dog Eat Dog. 2007.

Atul Gawande, "Piecework; Medicine's money problem," The New Yorker, April 4, 2005.

"1 in 5 Health Care Dollars Used for Insurance Paperwork," PNHP, November 11, 2005. http://www.pnhp.org/news/2005/november/1_in_5_health_care_d.php

Conrad F. Meier, "'Snake Oil' Cures in Health Care Policy Blunderland," Medical Sentinel, May/June 1999. http://www.jpands.org/hacienda/article17.html

Lawrence W. Reed, "Pre-Existing Condition Mandate is Unhealthy Policy," Mackinac Center, November 4, 1996. http://www.mackinac.org/article.aspx?ID=44 See also: Victoria Craig Bunce and JP Wieske, "Health Insurance Mandates in the States 2008," The Council for Affordable Health Insurance, 2008, http://www.cahi.org/cahi_contents/resources/pdf/HealthInsuranceMandates2008.pdf

Glen Whitman, "Bad Medicine for Healthcare," Newsweek, October 15, 2007.http://www.businessweek.com/magazine/content/07_42/b4054081.htm

Elizabeth Solomont, "'Worst of Both Worlds' Hits Insurance," New York Sun, July 3, 2007.

"Medical Malpractice," Insurance Information Institute, March 2008. http://www.iii.org/media/hottopics/insurance/medicalmal/ See also Phyllis Schlafly, "Problems With John Edwards," Eagle Forum, July 21, 2004. http://www.eagleforum.org/column/2004/july04/04-07-21.html.

Michael Fumento, "John Edwards vs. Babies and Moms," Michael Fumento, March 21, 2007. http://www.fumento.com/fumento/ edwards2007.html or Selwyn Duke, "Little boy sue: legalized theft and John Edwards," American Thinker, August 26, 2004. http://www.americanthinker.com/2004/08/little_boy_sue_legalized_theft.html

Marc Morano, "Did 'Junk Science' Make John Edwards Rich?" *Free Republic*, January 20, 2004.

"'Junk Science' propelled Edwards' career?" WorldNetDaily, July 7, 2004. http://www.wnd.com/news/article.asp?ARTICLE_ID=39310.

Adam Hanft, "John Edwards, Malpractice, Cancer and an Existential Moment," The Huffington Post, March 26, 2007, http://www.huffingtonpost.com/adam-hanft/john-edwards-malpractice_b_44269.html

Wendy Davis, "Edwards's career tied to jury awards debate," *Boston Globe*, September 15, 2003.

Tanya Albert, "Physicians win award cap as Texas passes tort reform," Amednews.com, June 23, 2003. http://www.ama-assn.org/amednews/2003/06/23/gvsa0623.htm

"Obama Offers Plan for Universal Health Care," Fox News, May 29, 2007. http://www.foxnews.com/story/0,2933,275998,00.html

Perry Bacon Jr., "McCain's Health Care Proposal," *Washington Post*, October 10, 2007.

EBRI Research Analysts, "Immigrants Comprise Larger Share of U.S. Uninsured, Study Says," EBRI News, August 5, 2008, http://www.ebri.org/pdf/PR_809_05Aug08.pdf

Richard Wolf, "Rising health care costs put focus on illegal immigrants," *USA Today*, January 21, 2008. http://www.usatoday.com/news/washington/2008-01-21-immigrant-healthcare_N.htm

Jon E. Dougherty, "Taxpayers foot bill for aliens' care," WorldNetDaily, April 1, 2004. http://www.worldnetdaily.com/news/article.asp?ARTICLE_ID=37834

"Illegal aliens threaten U.S. medical system," WorldNetDaily, March 13, 2005. http://www.worldnetdaily.com/news/article.asp? ARTICLE_ID=43275.

Daniel J. Popeo, "Commentary: Illegal immigrants are bankrupting our hospitals," Examiner.com, July 29, 2008. http://www.examiner.com/a1510775~Illegal_immigrants_are_bankrupting_our_hospitals.html.

"Health Care," The American Resistance.
http://www.theamericanresistance.com/issues/health_care.html.

"Politics," CNN.com, May 10, 2005.
http://www.cnn.com/2005/POLITICS/05/10/heallth.illegal.ap/.

National Coalition on Healthcare, "Health Insurance Coverage," 2008.
http://www.nchc.org/facts/coverage.shtml

Julia A. Seymour, "Health Care Lie: '47 Million Uninsured Americans,' "
Business & Media Institute, July 18, 2007.
http://www.businessandmedia.org/articles/2007/20070718153509.aspx.

"Prevention: Aiming towards Better Health," Statistics.
http://preventdisease.com/prevention/prevention.html Accessed August 8,
2008.

"Obesity by the Numbers," ObesityinAmerica.org.
http://www.obesityinamerica.org/bythenumbers.html Accessed August 14,
2008.

Mary Carter, "Heart disease still the most likely reason you'll die," CNN.com,
November 1, 2006. http://www.cnn.com/2006/HEALTH/
10/30/heart.overview/index.html

Eric Schlosser and Richard Linklater, Fast Food Nation. Directed by Richard
Linklater. BBC Films, 2006.

Maggie Fox, "U.S. smoking rate stalled at 21 percent, CDC says," Reuters,
November 8, 2007. http://www.reuters.com/article/domesticNews/
idUSN0823760820071108?feedType=RSS&feedName=domesticNews&rpc=22
&sp=true

Health and Human Services, Administration for Children and Families.
"Daniel C. Schneider, Biography." http://www.acf.hhs.gov/
orgs/bios/schneider.htm

"HHS Launches Childhood Overweight and Obesity Prevention Initiative,"
U.S. Department of Health and Human Services, November 27, 2007.
http://www.hhs.gov/news/press/2007pres/11/
pr20071127a.html

Kaiser Family Foundation, "Media Multi-tasking" Changing the amount and
Nature of Young People's Media Use," press release. March 9, 2005.

Centers for Disease Control, "Childhood Obesity," 2007.
http://www.cdc.gov/HealthyYouth/obesity/index.htm

Bryan Walsh, "Child Obesity Rate Levels Off," Time, May 27, 2008.

Peter T. Kilborn, "No Work for a Bicycle Thief: Children Pedal Around Less," *New York Times*, June 7, 1999.

Centers for Disease Control, "Physical Activity Levels Among Children Aged 9–13—United States, 2002," August 22, 2003.

TM Dokheel, "An epidemic of childhood diabetes in the United States?" Diabetes Care, 1993.
http://care.diabetesjournals.org/cgi/content/abstract/16/12/1606

Richard H. Carmona, prepared remarks for "The Obesity Crisis in America," United States Department of Health & Human Services, July 16, 2003.
http://www.surgeongeneral.gov/news/testimony/obesity07162003.htm

Twelve: High (On Energy)

National Resources Defense Council, "Safe, Strong, and Secure: Reducing America's Oil Dependence," Issues.
http://www.nrdc.org/air/transportation/aoilpolicy2.asp

Marcus Hooper, "Farmers fight plans for new oil refinery," CNN.com, July 16, 2008.

Frank Hornig, "Prefab Reactors and Longer Life-Spans," Speigel Online International, July 11, 2008. http://www.spiegel.de/international/world/0,1518,565397,00.html

John McCain, quoted in Mark Matthews, "Fact Check: McCain, Obama policies," abc7news.com, June 25, 2008. http://abclocal.go.com/kgo/story?section=news/politics&id=6225264.

Jonah Goldberg, "That '70s Show," National Review Online, June 20, 2008.

Raymond J. Learsy, "Obama Pledges Imposing 'Oil Windfall Profits Tax' – Right Message, Wrong Language," The Huffington Post, June 12, 2008.

Jack Torry, "Congress must act on drilling ban," *Columbus Dispatch*, July 18, 2008.

Richard Simon and James Gerstenzang, "Bush lifts ban on offshore drilling," *Los Angeles Times*, July 15, 2008.

Associated Press, "Petroleum Joyride Almost Over?" Wired, May 29, 2005.
http://www.wired.com/techbiz/media/news/2005/05/67679

Daniel Workman, "Countries Dependent on Oil Imports," Suite101.com. Copyright Daniel Workman. May 4, 2008. http://import-export.suite101.com/article.cfm/countries_dependent_on_oil_imports

Congressman J. Randy Forbes, "Point of View," Capitol Monitor, May 2, 2005, http://www.house.gov/forbes/newsroom/enewsletter/2005/05022005.htm

Charles Pope, "Senate OKs oil drilling in Alaska's ANWR," Seattle Post, March 17, 2005.

Erika Bolstad, "Senate rejects ANWR drilling," Anchorage Daily News, May 13, 2008.

Energy Information Administration. International Energy Outlook 2008. Report #:DOE/EIA-0484(2008). http://www.eia.doe.gov/oiaf/ieo/highlights.html

Greg Gunner Guenthner, "Coal: It's Filthy, It Pollutes, the US Depends on It," Whiskey and Gunpowder, July 11, 2008. http://www.contrarianprofits.com/articles/coal-its-filthy-it-pollutes-but-the-us-depends-on-it/3695

Clean Air Task Force, "Cradle to Grave: the Environmental Impacts from Coal," June, 2001. http://www.catf.us/publications/reports/Cradle_to_Grave.pdf

U.S. Department of the Interior, U.S. Geological Survey. "Hydroelectric power use," 1995. http://ga.water.usgs.gov/edu/wuhy.html

U.S. Congress. Senate. 110th Cong., 1st sess., Roll Call vote 425. December 13, 2007.

Pam Belluck, "Plan for Wind Farm Off Massachusetts Clears State Hurdle," New York Times, March 31, 2007.

Energy Information Administration, "Renewable Energy." Table: 10.1. 2007. http://www.eia.doe.gov/emeu/mer/renew.html

Ed Hiserodt, "Solar Power: Not the Brightest Idea," The New American, September 17, 2007.

Bill Tomson, "Focus: US Ethanol Demand Outgrows Need For Tax Subsidy," June 30, 2008. Dow Jones Newswires.

John R. Lott, Jr., "Ethanol Mandates Cause Rising Food Prices," FoxNews.com, April 28, 2008. http://www.foxnews.com/story/0,2933,352968,00.html

Jeff Goodell, "The Ethanol Scam: One of America's Biggest Political Boondoggles," Rolling Stone, August 9, 2007.

Science Daily, "Study: Ethanol Production Consumes Six Units of Energy to Produce Just One." April 1, 2005. http://www.sciencedaily.com/releases/2005/03/050329132436.htm.

Sarah Smith, "Magellan, Buckeye consider pipeline," Ethanol Producer Magazine, web exclusive: February 28, 2008. http://www.ethanol-producer.com/article.jsp?article_id=3764

NPR. "Study Says Ethanol Pollution Could Rival Gas,"Day to Day, July 29, 2008. http://www.npr.org/templates/story/story.php?storyId=9647424.

Jim Mann, "Grizzly Man," The Daily Inter Lake, April 1, 2005

President George W. Bush, "President Discusses Advanced Energy Initiative in Milwaukee," Milwaukee, Wisconsin, February 20, 2006.

Energy Information Administration, "U.S. Nuclear Reactors," December 31, 2007. http://www.eia.doe.gov/cneaf/nuclear/page/nuc_reactors/reactsum.html

Energy Information Administration, "States with commercial Nuclear Industries." http://www.eia.doe.gov/cneaf/nuclear/page/at_a_glance/reactors/states.html

Catherine Dominguez, "Nuke plant's good track record paying solid dividends for CPS," San Antonio Business Journal. March 7, 2008.

Patrick Moore, "Going Nuclear," *Washington Post*, August 16, 2006.

James Bridges, Mike Gray, & T.S. Cook, The China Syndrome. Directed by James Bridges. Culver City, CA: I.P.C. Films.

United States Nuclear Regulatory Commission. "Fact Sheet on the Three Mile Island Accident," February 20, 2007.

President Jimmy Carter, "Statement from Former U.S. President Jimmy Carter on Effort ot Reclassify Nuclear Waster. June 14, 2004.

Jack Spencer, "Recycling Nuclear Fuel: The French Do It, Why Can't Oui?" FoxNews.com, December 27, 2007.

"The Chernobyl accident: What happened," BBC News, June 5, 2000.

International Atomic Energy Agency, World Health Organization, United Nations Development Programme. "Chernobyl: the True Scale of the Accident: 20 Years Later a UN Report Provides Definitive Answers and Ways To Repair Lives." September 5, 2005.

Ali Akbar Dareini, "Ahmadinehad says Israel doomed," Breitbart.com, 2008. http://www.breitbart.com/article.php?id=D90LI2I00&show_article=1

Science Daily, "Carbon Dioxide Emissions From Power Plants Rated Worldwide," November 15, 2007.

Thirteen: Global "Warming"

Leonard Doob, *Public Opinion and Propaganda*, New York: Henry Holt, 1948.

Martin Durkin, *The Great Global Warming Swindle,* (London, UK: WAGtv, 2007).

Lloyd Alter, "Americans Care More About Gay Marriage Than Global Warming," August 29, 2007. Treehugger.com/files/2007/08/americans_care.php

The National Academies, "New Evidence Helps Reconcile Global Warming Discrepancies; Confirms That Earth's Surface Temperature Is Rising," news release, January 12, 2000. See also William Stevens, "Global Warming: The Contrarian View," *New York Times*, February 29, 2000.

"Gore, U.N. climate panel win Nobel Peace Prize," October 12, 2007. Msnbc.msn.com/id/21262661/

"Michael Moore Wins Palme d'Or," FoxNews.com, May 23, 2004. http://www.foxnews.com/story/0,2933,120671,00.html

Rock and Roll Hall of Fame Musuem, "Patti Smith," Induction Year: 2007.

Greg B. Smith and Larry McShane, "Subpoenas for Al Sharpton's aides," *NY Daily News*, December 13, 2007.

"Past Climate Change," Environmental Protection Agency, March 24, 2008. http://www.epa.gov/climatechange/science/pastcc.html.

Nigel Calder, "An experiment that hints we are wrong on climate change," *Times Online*, February 11, 2007. http://www.timesonline.co.uk/tol/news/uk/article1363818.ece see also Sophie Borland, "Global warming 'is good and is not our fault,' " *Telegraph*, September 17, 2007.

Adam Rink, "Global Warming Man Made or Natural Cycle?," Nolanchart.com, June12, 2008. http://www.nolanchart.com/article4029.html

Tennessee Center for Policy Research, "Al Gore's Personal Electricity Consumption Up 10% Despite "Energy-Efficient" Renovations: Energy guzzled by Al Gore's home in past year could power 232 U.S. homes for a month," news release, June 17, 2008.

Tennessee Center for Policy Research, "Al Gore's Personal Energy Use Is His Own "Inconvenient Truth': Gore's home uses more than 20 times the national average," news release, February 26, 2007.

Science Project, "Carbone Dioxide and Man." Undated. url: http://www.scienceproject.com/projects/intro/primary/PX053.asp

Encyclopedia Britannica Online, s.v "Photosynthesis," http://www.britannica.com/EBchecked/topic/458172/photosynthesis#tab=active~checked%2Citems~checked&title=photosynthesis%20—%20Britannica%20Online%20Encyclopedia Accessed August 4, 2008.

"Global Warming is Caused by Natural Geologic Trends," WiseTo Social Issues. http://socialissues.wiseto.com/Articles/FO3020630210/ Accessed August 4, 2008.

The Global Warming Truth, "Carbon Dioxide," undated. http://theglobalwarmingtruth.com/Carbon_Dioxide.html

National Oceanic and Atmospheric Administration, "Greenhouse Gases: Frequently Asked Questions," December 1, 2005. http://lwf.ncdc.noaa.gov/oa/climate/gases.html#wv

Richard Black, "Next decade 'may see no warming,'" BBC News, May 1, 2008. http://news.bbc.co.uk/2/hi/science/nature/7376301.stm

Erika Bolstad, "Is China drilling oil off the Florida coast?," *Anchorage Daily News*, June 12, 2008. See also: China, Cuba reported in Gulf oil partnership: U.S. firms stand by, prohibited from bidding on contracts; lawmakers propose opening up U.S. coast for drilling," Cnnmoney.com, May 9, 2006.

Monte Hieb, "Global Warming: A Chilling Perspective," October 5, 2007. http://www.geocraft.com/WVFossils/ice_ages.html

Kent Jeffreys, Why Worry About Global Warming, NCPA Policy Report No. 96, National Center for Policy Analysis: Dallas, TX, February, 1991.

ScienceDaily, "Atmospheric Carbon Dioxide Greater 1.4 Billion Years Ago," September 19, 2003.

"Antarctic's ice 'melting faster': A team of UK researcher claims to have new evidence that global warming is melting the ice in Antarctica faster than had previously been thought," BBCNews, February 2, 2005.

John Nielsen, "White House Lists Polar Bears as 'Threatened.'" NPR, May 14, 2008.

Robin McKie, "The heat is on . . . and it's getting hotter still: Temperatures over the past decade are the highest for 2,000 years, scientists say," *Guardian*, July 13, 2003.

Jeff Jacoby, "B-r-r-r! Where did global warming go?" *Boston Globe*, January 6, 2008. http://www.boston.com/bostonglobe/editorial_opinion/oped/articles/2008/01/06/br_r_r_where_did_global_warming_go/

Alexi Mostrous, "Floods, hurricanes, blizzards— and there is more to come," *Times*, March 11, 2008.

Nigel Calder, "An experiment that hints we are wrong on climate change," *Times Online*, February 11, 2007. http://www.timesonline.co.uk/tol/news/uk/article1363818.ece

Evelyne Ogutu and Mathias Ringa, "Mt. Kenya is Losing Crucial Ice Mass, Says NGO Official," East African Standard, Ocotber 12, 2006.

Fred Langan and Tom Leonard, "Polar bears 'thriving as the Arctic warms up,'" Telegraph, March 9, 2007.

Sarah Lewis, "Whatever happened to our ice age?"Argus, April 21, 2008.

Paul R. Ehrlich, The Population Bomb, New York: Ballantine Books, 1968.

Ben Lieberman, "Ozone: The Hole Truth," The Heritage Foundation, September 14, 2007.

Gregory McNamee, "Attack of the Killer Bees," Tuscan Weekly, December 19, 1996.

Sarah Hagedorn and David Havlick, "The Northern Spotted Owl," Forest History Society, November 1, 2004.

Michael Kranish, "McCain vows to fight global warming," Boston.com, January 7, 2008.

Joseph Coleman, "Study: $45 Trillion Investment Needed to Fight Global Warming," The Huffington Post, June 6, 2008,

Andrea Thompson, "'Green' Light Bulbs Pack Toxin Ingredient," Live Science, July 9, 2007.

Noel Sheppard, "Al Gore and 'An Inconvenient Truth' Win Oscar for Best Documentary," NewsBusters, February 26, 2007.

J. Scott Armstrong, "How I Became a Skeptic about Global Warming Forecasts," The Global Warming Challenge, April 15, 2008

U.S. Senate Committee on Environment & Public Works, "U.S. Senate Report: Over 400 Prominent Scientists Disputed Man-Made Global Warming Claims in 2007: Senate Report Debunks 'Consensus,'"December 20, 2007.

Marc Sheppard, "The IPCC Should Leave Science to Scientists," American Thinker, February 8, 2007.

National Center For Policy Analysis, "Climate Science: Climate Change and Its Impacts," undated. http://www.ncpa.org/pub/st/st285/st285b.html

Craig Wilson, "You don't need a weatherman to tell you it's raining," USA Today, August 17, 2004.

Dustin Till, "One Step Forward, Two Steps Back," Marten Law Group, July 9, 2008.

"USW, Sierra Club Urge Senate Fixes in Climate Security Act," Reuters, June 5, 2008.

"Worldwide Energy Demand Will Rise 51 Percent by 2030, Energy Department Report Says," FoxNews.com, June 25, 2008. http://foxnews.com/story/o,2933,271286,oo.html

Fourteen: God, Guns, and Rock 'n' Roll Revisited

District of Columbia et al v. Heller, Supreme Court of the United States, No. 07-290, decided June 26, 2008.

John R. Lott. Straight Shooting: Firearms, Economics, and Public Policy. New York: Merrill Press, Inc, 2006.

Bill Mears, "Child rapists can't be executed, Supreme Court rules," CNN.com, June 25, 2008. http://www.cnn.com/2008/CRIME/06/25/scotus.child.rape/

Benedict D. LaRosa, "Can Gun Control Reduce Crime? Part 1," The Future of Freedom Foundation, October 2002.

National Archery in the Schools Program, "National Archery in the Schools Program Foundation Chooses Research Firm." October 22, 2007.

"Security Guard: 'God Guided Me and Protected Me,' " *Denver News*, December 10, 2007.

"Hero Praises God for Steady Hand," ABC News, December 11, 2007.

"Off-duty Cop Saved Lives in Mall," CBS News, February 13, 2007.

Raymond McCaffrey, Paul Duggan, and Debbi Wilgoren, "Five Killed a Pa. Amish School," *Washington Post*, October 3, 2006.

"Off-duty Cop Saved Lives in Mall," CBS News, February 13, 2007.

Quotes from Dr. Suzanne Gratia Hupp. http://www.hkweaponsystems.com/cgi-bin/quote.pl?suzanne_gratia Accessed August 15, 2008.

Fifteen: We Know

Evan Esar. 20,000 Quips & Quotes. New York: Barnes & Noble, 1995.

Harry Julian Fink, R.M. Fink, John Milius, and Michael Cimino, "Magnum Force," Directed by Ted Post. Burbank, CA: The Malpaso Company & Warner Bros. Pictures, 1973.

Marko Kloos, "Why the gun is civilization," blog, The Munchkin Wrangler, March 23, 2008; available at: http://munchkinwrangler.blogspot.com/2007/03/why-gun-is-civilization.html.

Sixteen: What Is Most Important

President Ronald Reagan, Farewell Address to the Nation, Oval Office, January 11, 1989.

Dr. Martin Luther King, Jr., Lincoln Memorial, August 28, 1963.

I Won't Go Away

I wasn't afraid of your lightning baby,
Your thunder was a part of me,
I'd dance with the devil at midnight maybe.
Your threat is a catastrophe.
And you can't stop me,
You can't offend me,
I aint backing down.
I won't go away,
I'm here to stay.
I won't go away.
I'm like a grizzly bear on a rampage,
A firestorm in your face.
Time to assess the damage baby,
I will not git outta this race.
I absolutely love your attitude.
You & me we should go wild in the night.
I won't go away.
I'm here to stay.
I won't go away.

Craveman, 2002

ABOUT THE AUTHOR

✦ ✦ ✦

Author photo: Brigham Mayfield

With over 35 million albums sold and more media face-time than most active politicians, Ted Nugent has earned his status as an American icon.

Renowned for modeling the high-octane civic activism he unabashedly encourages, he is a respected guest of top-rated, high-profile network, cable, news, sports, political commentary, and rock programs on television and radio. *Ted Nugent Spirit of the Wild* television show continues to be Outdoor Channel's #1 Hunting Show year after year and Ted and Shemane are Fan Favorite Hosts.

A recipient of numerous commendations from law enforcement agencies nationwide, Ted has been lauded for his Ted Nugent Kamp for Kids and Freedom's Angels, work as a national spokesman for D.A.R.E., and as Ambassador for Big Brothers Big Sisters and the Pass It On-Mentors Program.

As America's top proponent of the Second Amendment, Ted has served on the Board of Directors of the NRA since 1995.

Ted Nugent continues to fight for personal freedoms on the lecture circuit. He is an award-winning writer for more than forty publications, and author of the *New York Times* bestseller *God, Guns, and Rock 'n' Roll*, as well as *Kill It and Grill It*, *BloodTrails II*, and now, *Ted, White, and Blue: The Nugent Manifesto*.

In 2008, he celebrated the most successful tour of his 50-year career with Operation Rolling Thunder, setting attendance records in America and Europe and performing his 6,000th concert.

Ted Nugent's unbridled musical fury throttles on.